The Oldest Vocation

In this late fifteenth-century wood carving, St. Anne holds the Virgin
Mary on her knee, while Mary—herself a childlike figure—holds the
Christ Child. From the Münster Landesmuseum für Kunst and
Kulturgeschichte. Photo courtesy of Marburg /Art Resource

The Oldest Vocation

Christian Motherhood in the Middle Ages

Clarissa W. Atkinson

Cornell University Press

ITHACA AND LONDON

First published 1991 by Cornell University Press.

International Standard Book Number 0-8011-2071-7
Library of Congress Catalog Card Number 91-16078
Printed in the United States of America
*Librarians: Library of Congress cataloging information
apperars on the last page of the book.*

For Holley, Meg, and Matthew

Contents

[vii]

Preface

Writing of her experience of motherhood "in the family-centered, consumer-oriented, Freudian-American world of the 1950's"—and of her own wrenching ambivalence—Adrienne Rich said: "I did not understand that this circle, this magnetic field in which we lived was not a natural phenomenon" (*Of Woman Born*, pp. 4–5). Rich made a vital contribution to the recognition of the historicity of motherhood, the ancient vocation that is also an institution. My work was inspired in part by that recognition, which challenges both scholars and activists and continues to produce questions and demand answers. As an institution, how is motherhood constructed? How are its ideologies developed and proclaimed? How have "good" and "bad" motherhood been defined and evaluated—by whom, and in what contexts? How is the work of mothers related to the political and economic institutions of a society? How are the language and imagery of motherhood related to other cultural symbol systems, particularly those of religion? With these and other questions in mind, I set out to extend the exploration of the history of motherhood into medieval Europe, where its roots are inextricably entangled with the history of Christianity.

A complicated project such as this touches several centuries and geographic areas and makes use of many kinds of materials: its scope is much too large to be confined to any "field." I have accumulated many debts and depended very much on the learning and insights of others. Apart from works cited in the notes and bibliography, I have gained greatly from discussions with colleagues and friends. Constance Buchanan read every chapter, sometimes more than once, and suggested the title. I very much appreciate the excellent advice of Bernadette Brooten and Margaret Miles, the patience and good humor of my friends at Cornell University Press, and the persistence of Holley Atkinson in transatlantic negotiation. Rosemary Hale and Claire Sahlin generously shared their own researches into the lives and works of medieval holy women. I am especially grateful for the care, attention, and affection with which Kay Shanahan and Margie Thornton worked on the manuscript.

My dear friend and colleague, the late Nancy Jay, made wise and helpful comments on several drafts; her enthusiasm always inspired further effort. Her students and friends miss her very much.

I have the advantage of an interested and loving family. My sisters, Elizabeth Hogeland and Eleanor Shakin, are long-time boosters of me and my projects. The three people to whom the book is dedicated are responsible for my intense, sustained passion for the subject. Whatever may be said about the historical construction of motherhood, it has embodied rewards.

CLARISSA W. ATKINSON

Cambridge, Massachusetts

Abbreviations

AS	*Acta sanctorum*	SUSF	*Samlingar utgivna*
CSEL	*Corpus scriptorum*		*av svenska*
	ecclesiasticorum		*fornskriftsällskapet*
	latinorum	WA	*D. Martin Luthers*
LW	*Luther's Works*		*Werke*
PL	*Patrologiae cursus*	WA Br	*D. Martin Luthers*
	completus: Series		*Werke: Briefwechsel*
	latina	WA TR	*D. Martin Luthers*
SRM	*Scriptores rerum*		*Werke: Tischreden*
	merovingicarum		
SRP	*Scriptores rerum*		
	prussicarum		

The Oldest Vocation

CHAPTER ONE

Christian Motherhood: "Who Is My Mother?"

According to a very old story, a woman pope ruled the Church of Rome for a few years in the middle of the ninth century. Her name was Joan, and as a young woman she lived in England, where she fell in love with a traveling student who was a monk. (Before there were universities, most students were monks, and the intellectually curious among them moved from library to library and from teacher to teacher, in search of books and instruction.) Monks were not allowed to marry, but Joan was brave as well as beautiful and brilliant, and she joined her lover in his studies and travels, wearing male clerical clothing for safety and concealment. The two wandered through Europe, acquiring vast learning, until the man died and Joan was left alone. She continued to study and to dress like a monk: Boccaccio, who told the story in the fourteenth century, said that she refused "to attach herself to anyone else or acknowledge that she was a woman."[1] Eventually she found her way to Rome, where her outstanding virtue and learning were rewarded with election to the papal throne.

Joan reigned as pope for a time, with nobody the wiser. Boccaccio remarked: "This woman was not afraid to mount the Fisherman's throne, to deal with all the sacred mysteries and proffer them to

---

1. Giovanni Boccaccio, *Concerning Famous Women*, trans. Guido A. Guarino (New Brunswick, N.J.: Rutgers University Press, 1963), p. 231.

others, something which the Christian religion does not allow to any woman." Such audacity was soon punished. Boccaccio says that the devil tormented her with lust and "the Pope happened to become pregnant. Oh, what a shameful crime!"[2] Joan's celebrated wisdom did not help her to appreciate the implications of her condition, or even to recognize the beginning of labor. During a solemn procession through the streets of Rome, the pope gave birth and died in shameful agony.[3]

In the salacious iconography that surrounds this story, Joan frequently is depicted lying in the street in a crowd of horrified onlookers, a triple crown on her head and an infant emerging from beneath the papal robes. Lawrence Durrell, working with a modern Greek version of the legend, captured the chaotic, sacrilegious atmosphere of visual representations of Joan's travail:

> Great was the consternation when a premature infant was produced from among the voluminous folds of the papal vestments. The attending archdeacons recoiled in horror while the great circle of worshippers pressed in even closer, screaming and crossing themselves. Women climbed on the backs of their menfolks for a better view, while those already mounted on horses and mules stood in the saddle until the deacons were forced to use their standards and crucifixes as clubs to hew a passage through the mob.[4]

The uses to which the story has been put are no more edifying than its iconography. It gave Boccaccio an opportunity to castigate

2. Ibid., p. 232.

3. In most versions of the tale, she died in the street; in Boccaccio's story, the cardinals put Joan in prison, "where this wretched woman died in the midst of her laments." On the implications of the story for his own time, Boccaccio noted that "when the Pope goes on a procession with the clergy and the people. . .when they reach the place where Joan gave birth, the Pope turns away and takes different streets because of his hatred for that place" (ibid., p. 233). Constance Jordan points out that Boccaccio's Joan is virtuous as long as she stays in the private sphere, "monstrous" in the public: "As an event, her motherhood figures her grotesqueness"; see "Boccaccio's In-Famous Women: Gender and Civic Virtue in the *De mulieribus claris*," in *Ambiguous Realities: Women in the Middle Ages and Renaissance*, ed. Carole Levin and Jeanie Watson (Detroit, Mich.: Wayne State University Press, 1987), p. 33.

4. *Pope Joan: A Romantic Biography by Emmanuel Royidis*, trans. Lawrence Durrell (London: André Deutsch, 1960), pp. 154–155.

bold women, but it has also been used to discredit the clergy, to make fun of pious hypocrites, and to denounce the papacy and the entire Roman Catholic Church.

The legend of Pope Joan begins with a love affair and ends with an out-of-wedlock birth, but it is not about love or sex, and Joan was not punished for sexual immorality. Boccaccio's comments and Durrell's description of the birth scene make it clear that the story is about disorder, and about the filth and chaos that ensue when objects and persons and events are out of place—a woman on the throne of Peter, a child in the belly of a pope, a birth in a public procession.[5] The woman whose learning and virtue carried her to the heights was destroyed by motherhood. Joan was not betrayed by a lover or discovered by an enemy; she was brought down by her own body, which was inherently and catastrophically unfit for ecclesiastical dignity. The literary and artistic images that surround the birth of her child display a range of responses from hysterical laughter to horrified disgust. The notion of a female pope was scandalous; of a pregnant pope, ludicrous; of a pope giving birth, disastrous.

The earliest written sources for the legend of Joan come from the eleventh century, although its elaboration is the work of the Renaissance.[6] The story is set in the ninth century, partly because of obscurities in the historical record but also because that era was consigned to the Dark Ages by Renaissance thinkers. To such critics, who assumed dismal scandals to be the norm in early medieval church and society, it seemed a plausible period for a female pope: the ninth century deserved nothing better.[7]

Whatever the likelihood of a woman pope in any century, the legend of Joan is a fine starting point for an investigation of certain

5. In *Purity and Danger: An Analysis of Concepts of Pollution and Taboo* (New York: Praeger, 1966), p. 2, Mary Douglas argues that "dirt is essentially disorder."

6. For a thorough and original examination of the legend and its history, see Cesare D'Onofrio, *La Papessa Giovanna: Roma e papato tre storia e leggenda* (Rome: Romana Societa Editrice, 1979).

7. The tenth century would have been even more suitable. During the so-called "pornocracy" of that era, powerful women—mothers and lovers of popes—controlled political and ecclesiastical affairs in Rome. Contemporary chroniclers

interactions of the history of motherhood with the history of Christianity in the medieval West. In the eleventh and twelfth centuries, when the story was taking shape, devotion to the mother of Christ was blossoming in new artistic, liturgical, and theological expressions. At first sight, the legend of Joan and the cult of Mary have no common characteristics except that each sheds light on the imagination of medieval Christians, who produced images of "mother" and notions of motherhood that ranged from tender and sacred to vulgar and blasphemous. The boundaries of this work are drawn wide enough to include both of these expressions, and many others, within the general topic of the construction of motherhood in medieval Europe.

In the chapters that follow, which are separated chronologically but linked by common themes and questions, medieval motherhood is approached as a social-historical institution with attendant ideologies—systems of ideas that shape consciousness and validate social and religious systems.[8] Medieval motherhood was constructed by persons whose primary ideology was Christianity: Christian stories and moral teaching shaped their imaginative boundaries, their sense of self and world, and their social, legal, and domestic arrangements. This was the case even for those who were illiterate and relatively "unchurched," and to an extent also for those who were not Christians at all: Jewish communities within Europe, Muslims on the borders, and pagans in the remote interior countryside. Jews were profoundly affected by the dominant institutions and prevailing ideologies; Muslims came into commercial and intellectual and belligerent contact with Christians; and country people were gradually driven and persuaded into the fold by warriors, monks, and missionaries. From the vantage point of late twentieth-century pluralism, it is difficult to appreciate all the ways in which a religious system may dominate the public and private experience of persons within its sphere, unless we remember that "Christianity" included a

---

and later historians have ascribed the troubles of the tenth century to "overmighty" women.

8. I use the complicated term "ideology" without a pejorative implication in the Marxist sense of false consciousness.

near-monopoly of cultural expression, of education, and (at least indirectly) of political power.

In order to investigate medieval motherhood, then, we must look closely at Christianity in western Europe in the Middle Ages, a complex religious and cultural system with a unique set of stories, beliefs, and institutions inherited from the Mediterranean Christianity of the first centuries C.E. The interpretations of stories, formulations of beliefs, and institutions established in the first four hundred years were the building blocks of medieval Christianity, although every aspect was transformed in the new society of medieval Europe. Social historians frequently treat religious ideologies and institutions as epiphenomena, but Christianity was central to the formation of the social, political, intellectual, and psychological structures of the West, and medieval religious imagery and assumptions have not disappeared from our secular and pluralistic society. Modern people understand the legend of Pope Joan differently from those who encountered Boccaccio's version in the fourteenth century, but one need not be a medieval Christian to feel the story's power or appreciate its significance.

All religious systems develop norms for behavior and relationships, including family relationships, with explicit and implicit ideas and prescriptions concerning sexuality and parenthood, mothers and children. Interactions between the history of Christianity and the history of motherhood have been intense and complicated, perhaps in part because Christianity is a religion of embodiment—of Incarnation—whose god entered history as a human being, ate and drank with men and women on earth, was born and died like them. Physicality or embodiment—birth and death—lay at the heart of the faith of those who accepted the bodily resurrection of Jesus Christ. And physicality necessarily lies at the heart of constructions of motherhood in any society. Our wishes, fears, and fantasies about embodiment are inextricably linked to our experience of mothers and notions of maternity.

The history of motherhood also requires careful examination of the status and image of women in particular cultures. Although not all women are mothers, all mothers are women: gender arrangements play a crucial role in organizing the institution of motherhood and shaping its ideologies. Images of women in the Scriptures, the roles available to them in churches and communities, and the pronouncements on sex and gender of preachers and theologians had critical impact on the construction of medieval motherhood. The relationship of women to Christianity has never been simple, and it certainly was not simple in medieval times. The messages were loud and numerous, but not consistent. On the one hand, a woman might "be saved through bearing children, if she continues in faith and love and holiness, with modesty" (1 Tim. 2:15); on the other, women were constantly reminded that death came into the world with Eve, "the mother of all living" (Gen. 3:20). Like modern stories, medieval stories are strikingly ambivalent about women's "nature," and about motherhood. Twelfth-century tales of the Virgin's miracles present a mother who is powerful and good, dignified and merciful, while the legend of Pope Joan insists on the gross incompatibility of pregnancy and birth with beauty and holiness.

In any culture, the construction of motherhood carries the mixed messages of the experience of that culture with life and death, sex and gender. Such experience is not universal: the specific psychohistorical circumstances of each generation shape social arrangements and individual consciousness. Motherhood varies not only among families and individuals but according to time, place, race, class, and culture. Like the Christian church or the United States of America, it is a historical phenomenon subject to development and change.

Until quite recently, however, motherhood had no history; it was too thoroughly identified with the private sphere and with the "changeless" biological aspects of the human condition. Women's lives were organized and their capacities defined by their status as mothers, potential mothers, and non-mothers, but motherhood itself was not perceived as an institution shaped by culture and subject to history. Styles of child rearing and other elements of family life in nonindustrial societies outside the West were more accessible to cultural analysis, thanks to the anthropologists, but even there, historical development was ignored or lost in the ethnographic present. Furthermore, most anthropologists regarded fatherhood as a social construction, motherhood as "natural" (or biological). Not even practitioners of the new social history of the twentieth century thought to study motherhood as a specific institution related to the image and status of women and to the political, social, and religious variables of historical change.

Inspired by new questions about women and families, thinkers in the late twentieth century have begun to discover a variety of approaches to the vast, buried history of motherhood and its ramifications in society and culture.[9] Searching for the roots and sources of our own family systems and ideologies, historians turned first to the recent past, and studies based on evidence from modern Europe and the United States have begun to appear in substantial numbers. Work in the field of family history has broadened the scope of women's history and vice versa; the interaction is extremely productive. We also enjoy the fruits of the brilliant school of the history of *mentalités*, whose works reflect appreciation of the historical aspects of such "timeless" phenomena as childhood, sexuality, and even death itself. In the meantime, scholars in the natural sciences and humanities are working with mothering and motherhood as critical principles in many fields; their work nourishes and is supported by historical studies.[10]

This book extends the historical study of motherhood into medieval Europe and examines its interactions with medieval Christianity. In the remainder of this introductory chapter, I look briefly

9. Adrienne Rich, *Of Woman Born: Motherhood as Experience and Institution* (New York: Norton, 1976), recognized motherhood as a sociocultural institution. Moreover, by exposing the social and emotional circumstances of her own motherhood, Rich made us sharply aware of the historical determinants of "private" experience. Among the early influential works on motherhood shaped by feminist theory in the social sciences are Nancy Chodorow, *The Reproduction of Mothering: Psychoanalysis and the Sociology of Gender* (Berkeley: University of California Press, 1978); and Mary O'Brien, *The Politics of Reproduction* (Boston: Routledge & Kegan Paul, 1981). Chodorow works from the perspective of psychology; O'Brien from that of political science.

10. See, among many more, Jessica Benjamin, *The Bonds of Love* (New York: Pantheon Books, 1988); Evelyn Fox Keller, *Reflections on Gender and Science* (New Haven, Conn.: Yale University Press, 1985); Shirley Garner, Claire Kahane, and Madelon Sprengnether, *The (M)other Tongue* (Ithaca: Cornell University Press, 1985); Susan Moller Okin, *Justice, Gender, and the Family* (New York: Basic Books, 1989); Sara Ruddick, *Maternal Thinking: Toward a Politics of Peace* (Bos-

at certain aspects of the legacy of early Christianity and at their implications for the construction of medieval motherhood. In some respects—for example, its subversion of the patriarchal household—Christianity was extraordinary among the religious systems of the ancient Near East. Furthermore, the experience of persecution and martyrdom in the early centuries shaped Christian communities in ways that affected the development of distinctive ideologies of motherhood and family life.

Chapter 2 addresses some of the physiological assumptions underlying learned and popular notions about mothers and motherhood in the Middle Ages. Ideas about women's bodies and reproduction, inherited from Greek science and learned through the practice of midwifery, were essential in the construction of beliefs about what mothers were. The third chapter focuses on the development of "spiritual motherhood" as a concept emerging out of monastic ideologies of the early Middle Ages and a reality in the lives of certain unusual women. Chapter 4 approaches medieval motherhood from a theological perspective: the cult of the Virgin and the Church's teachings about the mother of Christ are examined in relation to twelfth-century religion and romance. In the fifth chapter the religious and domestic experience of the female saints of the later Middle Ages, many of whom were wives and mothers, are studied against the background of social and religious change in that era. Chapter 6 carries the discussion up to the early modern era and the religious reformations of the sixteenth century, when family and household became centers of energy and organization in religion and society. The book is summarized and concluded in Chapter 7.

This work belongs to the history of ideas more than to social history, but wherever possible I have attempted to consider experience as well as ideology, and to look not only at what was preached about motherhood by "experts" but at the lives of women and children. When most of the written evidence pertains to the ideas of learned men or the experience of a few extraordinary women,

ton: Beacon Press, 1989); Joyce Trebilcot, ed., *Mothering: Essays in Feminist Theory* (Totowa, N.J.: Rowman & Allanheld, 1984).

the challenge always is to discover the relevance of teaching and preaching in people's lives.

A revolution in domestic values and family ideology accompanied Christian missionaries through the Mediterranean world in the first centuries of the Christian era. Jesus and his disciples were Palestinian Jews from a traditional rural society of villages based on patriarchal households linked by ties of kinship. Palestine itself was a small, politically weak nation on the fringes of the Roman Empire, which was engaged at that period in rapid and distant expansion. Among the great variety of sexual, social, and domestic arrangements and ideologies within the empire, the most influential for western Christianity, besides those of the Jews, were those of Rome itself—an urban patriarchy resting, at least in theory, on the unlimited authority of fathers within the family and the state. Some early Christians, following the teaching and example of Jesus, overturned traditional beliefs and practices concerning sex, gender, and authority. Self-selected communities in a hostile or indifferent world, they departed from both Jewish and Roman precedents to form new kinds of "families" whose ethics and attitudes left significant traces in medieval Christianity.

The social arrangements of first-century Jews were shaped by their history as a pastoral people and guided by their Scriptures, especially by the laws of Moses and commentaries on the law by learned teachers. The Hebrew Scriptures affirmed the positive use of sexuality, marriage, and the reproductive powers, assuming their value not only to individuals and families but to the community and the people of God.[11] From the first command to Adam and Eve, "Be fruitful and multiply" (Gen. 1:28), repeated to Noah after the Flood, the Scriptures are filled with injunctions to procreation. Sexual differentiation and reproduction were understood to be intrinsic to Creation, not (as some Christians believed) second-

11. For the purpose of this work I treat the Hebrew Bible as if it were one text, which of course it is not. Distinctions of date, genre, authorship, etc., are not essential to this discussion of the influence of the general tone of the Scriptures on Jewish attitudes toward family at the time of Jesus.

best accommodations to the Fall. God was credited with direct responsibility for the conception and birth of children; announcing the birth of Cain, Eve said, "I have gotten a man with the help of the Lord" (Gen. 4:1).

For the Jews, children were a blessing and barrenness a divine curse or punishment. The birth of Isaac to a woman who was ninety years old required God's intervention in God's own process, for "it had ceased to be with Sarah after the manner of women" (Gen. 18:11). The cycle of ovulation and menstruation, with the recurrent possibility of conception, was limited to women of childbearing age, and that cycle, like the cycles of the tides and the seasons, was understood to be expressly arranged for God's people. The reproductive miracle of Sarah was so basic and so crucial that it was used to effect God's choice of Israel. (Later, the birth of Isaac became a model for other miraculous births to aged or barren parents. In medieval hagiography an infant so conceived was a divine agent, and miraculous conception and birth were marks of a saint.) God's favor was also expressed through the number and sex of one's offspring and posterity. Abraham was given not only a son in his old age but the promise of innumerable descendants: " 'Look toward heaven, and number the stars, if you are able to number them.' Then he said to him, 'So shall your descendants be' " (Gen. 15:5).

The sacred writings of the Jews reflect the material value of children in a society in which sons and daughters, especially sons, were an important form of wealth. Prosperity was measured by the increase of family and servants and flocks and herds; sterility, sickness, and death among people or animals brought material and emotional disaster and showed divine displeasure. The physical well-being of a family and the happiness of its members depended on the practical skills and moral characteristics of the parents. A good wife was, above everything, the careful and energetic mistress of a household—and neither her household nor her work was set apart in a "private" sphere. Before the Industrial Revolution, production and reproduction were not separated; both men and women worked at home. The good wife of Proverbs bought a field, planted a vineyard, and sold her goods at the market. The role of the biblical housewife was much larger than that of her modern sisters. When her children "rise up and call her blessed" (Prov. 31:28), it is not for sentimental reasons but because she provides for everyone under her roof. Typical responses to conception and birth and healthy children included the kind of satisfaction expressed by a farmer with a fine crop as well as the devout gratitude of a believer who receives a token of divine favor.

The Hebrew Scriptures emphasize the social dimensions of holiness, describing virtue and morality in terms of their contribution to the welfare of the Jewish people. Appropriate expressions of sexuality served the community, and the value and importance of marital sex was recognized beyond its function in procreation. Sexual expression was acceptable within marriage even when women were pregnant or nursing, while sexual activity outside of marriage was discouraged even for men, with strict sanctions against male homosexuality.[12] Young women married shortly after puberty, and there was no interest in virginity as a permanent status for adults. Ascetic, celibate groups did exist within Judaism during the period preceding the life of Jesus, but under ordinary circumstances it was the religious obligation of every man to marry and raise a family in a devout and responsible manner. The only satisfactory social role for a woman was that of wife-mother-housewife; a childless woman was regarded as unhappy and unfortunate.

The "Jesus movement"[13] was soon carried out of its traditional Jewish context into the diverse, heterogeneous Greco-Roman cities around the Mediterranean, where its missionaries encountered people with all kinds of religious affiliations, domestic customs, and sexual practices and ideologies. In the development of Christian ideas and practices concerning families, the most significant converts were the Romans themselves. Roman men tended to assume, as instructed by their Greek mentors, that

12. Vern. L. Bullough suggests that such sanctions may have grown more strict during the Hellenistic period, when Jews reacted against the customs of Gentiles; see his *Sexual Variance in Society and History* (New York: Wiley, 1976), pp. 85–86.

13. See the discussion in Elisabeth Schüssler Fiorenza, *In Memory of Her: A Feminist Theological Reconstruction of Christian Origins* (New York: Crossroad, 1983), chap. 4.

women were inferior to men, vulnerable to endless infirmities connected with childbearing, and temperamentally incapable of the *gravitas* required by Roman ideals of character. There was a gap between the mythology and the realities of life under the empire, however, and Roman women were not in fact confined to the segregated and submissive status of their Athenian counterparts. During the early Christian period upper-class Roman women achieved a substantial degree of autonomy and access to property and sociability, at least in relation to other women of classical antiquity. Some women and men chose to marry late or not at all and to prevent or postpone childbearing; abortion was available, along with a variety of contraceptive devices and prescriptions.[14] In the first century C.E., faced with a declining population inadequate to the military and administrative requirements of the empire, Augustus enacted legislation designed to reward marriage and fertility. Under the new laws autonomy was one reward of motherhood: free women with three children and freedwomen with four were released from the tutelage of male relatives and guardians. In Roman as in Jewish society, no class of persons was expected to remain celibate indefinitely, and all men and women were encouraged to marry and raise children to serve the community.[15]

In relation to matrimony and motherhood, as in other matters, the Romans were caught between the realities of imperial society and a shared, idealized "memory" of the Golden Age of the Roman Republic. The image of the republican family—noble husbands and faithful wives, careful parents and obedient children—survived into the late empire. For matrons, the mythical model (from the second century B.C.E.) was Cornelia, daughter of the great general Scipio Africanus and mother of the Gracchi. Cornelia was widowed with twelve children, of whom three survived to adulthood, and she refused to remarry even when Ptolemy asked her to be his queen. Plutarch wrote that Cornelia raised her two

14. See John T. Noonan, Jr., *Contraception: A History of Its Treatment by the Catholic Theologians and Canonists* (Cambridge, Mass: Harvard University Press, 1966), chap. 1.
15. The Vestal Virgins were few in number (only six at one time), and each served for a term of thirty years, after which she was free to marry.

sons "with such scrupulous care that, although confessedly no other Romans were so well-endowed by nature, they were thought to owe their virtues more to education than to nature."[16] She was admired for her continued chastity, her discretion, and her willingness to accept her sons' deaths in the service of the state. This aristocratic woman, venerated by Plutarch and by her contemporaries for her lineage as well as her behavior, was a much more prominent person than the woman of Proverbs. Nonetheless, both of these exemplary figures received extravagant praise for the "feminine" virtues of devotion to family and household—virtues that also served the community. Their stories reveal the interlocking systems of patriarchal society, the private/public service of women to the family and the state.

Within the far-flung empire of the first centuries of the Christian era were people and groups whose sexual and familial codes and practices were very different from those of the Jews and also from those represented by the myths and realities of imperial Rome. Long before the arrival of the Christian missions, Greek philosophical schools included powerful strains of sexual asceticism and other-worldliness. Eventually, through Neoplatonism, these became major elements in patristic Christianity (see Chapter 3). Philosophers and their disciples, perceiving irreconcilable conflict or incompatibility between soul and body or between philosophy and "family" (defined to include property, obligations to kin, and other attachments), tended to reject sexual activity and domestic life in favor of contemplation and the possibility of union with the divine.

Even among such moderate groups as the Stoics, whose influence on Christianity was substantial over time, there was an attitude of cautious reserve toward human affections, both sexual and parental. Stoics recognized the necessity of sexual expression for procreation but disapproved of passion; a primary virtue was *apatheia*—an exemplary indifference to loss and pain achieved through the surrender of harmful possessiveness. Plutarch praised Cornelia, the model of Roman maternity, who was "most admira-

---

16. "Tiberius Gracchus" 1, in *Plutarch's Lives*, vol. 10, ed. Bernadotte Perrin (Cambridge, Mass.: Harvard University Press, 1959), p. 147.

ble when she spoke of her sons without grief or tears, and narrated their achievements and their fate to all enquirers as if she were speaking of men of the early days of Rome." But Plutarch also reveals that not everyone was sufficiently influenced by Stoic ideals to be impressed by Cornelia's reserve. He said it made some people "think that old age or the greatness of her sorrows had impaired her mind and made her insensible to her misfortunes."[17]

The philosophical schools constituted a significant presence among learned people in the cities but did not define normative family structure or attitudes toward sex, gender, and parenthood. Notwithstanding the great variety of family feeling and ideology and expression, the distinct and dominant pattern in the Mediterranean world was that of the patriarchal family. Most adults married, and except in highly unusual circumstances, motherhood was the primary social and religious duty of women.

Unlike Jewish kings, rabbis, and householders and responsible Roman citizens, Jesus was not married, and he called his disciples—women as well as men—away from their families. His following was based not on blood but on discipleship, and he proclaimed the constituency of his "family" in a saying reported in all three synoptic Gospels:

> And his mother and his brothers came; and standing outside they sent to him and called him. And a crowd was sitting about him; and they said to him, "Your mother and your brothers are outside, asking for you." And he replied, "Who are my mother and my brothers?" And looking around on those who sat about him, he said, "Here are my mother and my brothers! Whoever does the will of God is my brother, and sister, and mother." (Mark 3:31–35).

The absence of any mention of a father is significant. In the new family there was one Father in heaven, but no one on earth with the dominion (power over others) of traditional patriarchs.[18] The passage has been discussed at length by scholars and by apologists who resist or insist upon a perceived rejection of the Virgin Mary.

17. "Caius Gracchus" 19, in ibid., p. 241.
18. See the discussion in Schüssler Fiorenza, In Memory of Her, pp. 146–147.

It seems clear, however, that this is a comment on the membership of the new family and not on the biological family of Jesus, except that he used his own relatives to make the point that the criteria for "family" were new in the New Age. Again, when a woman said to Jesus, "Blessed is the womb that bore you, and the breasts that you sucked," he answered, "Blessed rather are those who hear the word of God and keep it!" (Luke 11:27–28). Elisabeth Schüssler Fiorenza interprets this text to mean that "faithful discipleship, not biological motherhood, is the eschatological calling of women."[19] I believe that her interpretation is correct, and I understand this reversal to be a significant contribution to the history of motherhood.

In its first centuries, the Jesus movement appealed strongly to the dispossessed—to the poor, to slaves, to social outcasts. It appealed to women among these and other groups, doubtless in part because of their subordination in traditional patriarchal societies but also because Jesus accepted women as companions and disciples. He ate and drank with women, talked and listened to them, and even touched and healed a woman who was ritually unclean, having "had a flow of blood for twelve years" (Mark 5:25). According to the Gospels, Jesus encouraged women to step outside of their assigned roles. He refused to insist that Mary leave his teaching in order to join her sister in the kitchen, where Martha, like the good wife of Proverbs, was "distracted with much serving" and "anxious and troubled about many things" (Luke 10:40–41).[20] Because the roles of housewife and mother were identified, the opportunity for women to choose a "good portion" that was not housewifery suggested that under certain circumstances, motherhood also might be a lesser good.

Members of the Jesus movement left home, abandoned physical security and conventional sources of emotional security, and were adopted into a new family with no stable home in this world. After Pentecost the missionaries carried their new relationships around the Roman world. In confident expectation of the immi-

19. Ibid., p. 16.
20. According to Schüssler Fiorenza (ibid., p. 330), the intention was "to portray the true disciple Mary of Bethany as counterpart to the unfaithful disciple Judas Iscariot."

nent arrival of the Kingdom but in existing circumstances of isolation and danger, they depended on the warmth and acceptance of
brothers and sisters in the faith. Like other adherents of cults and
new religions, they willingly left behind the disappointments and
limitations of biological families and conventional relationships.
Among the attributes of *communitas*, as defined and applied by
Victor Turner, is the "suspension of kinship rights and obligations
(all are siblings or comrades of one another regardless of previous
secular ties)." This description suits some early Christians very
well, as does Turner's use of the term "liminality," which refers
to a marginal condition of passage from one state to another.
Liminality is usually associated with sexual continence—essential, according to Turner, when kinship ties are suspended and
there is a high degree of egalitarianism in gender relations.[21]

Although most of the first disciples were married, the radical
nature of the eschatological "family" produced an ethic of continence among Christian converts. It may have been practiced most
extensively among women, but it is best known from the writings
of St. Paul, who said, "To the unmarried and the widows I say that
it is well for them to remain single as I do" (1 Cor. 7:8). In his own
time Paul's example was as important as his words, which were
intended to help Christians live and work effectively in the short
time remaining. Marriage was no sin, Paul believed, "yet those
who marry will have worldly troubles, and I would spare you
that. . . . the appointed time has grown very short" (1 Cor. 7:28–
29). Recently it has been suggested that the "widows" of New
Testament texts were groups of celibate women, some of whom
were never married. Their calling was to prayer, chastity, and
ministry, and they received support from the community.[22] The
Apocryphal Acts of the Apostles include stories celebrating the
miraculous adventures of charismatic apostles, including the heroic virgin Thecla.[23] In some of these Acts, biological parenthood

21. Victor Turner, *The Ritual Process* (Chicago: Aldine, 1969), pp. 111, 104.
22. In *The Revolt of the Widows: The Social World of the Apocryphal Acts*
(Carbondale: Southern Illinois University Press, 1980), esp. pp. 70–109, Stevan L.
Davies argues that the Apocryphal Acts were generated for (and perhaps by) the
widows.
23. For the story of Thecla and the "battle" between the legends and the Pastoral
Epistles, see Dennis R. MacDonald, *The Legend and the Apostle: The Battle for
Paul in Story and Canon* (Philadelphia: Westminster Press, 1983).

is either ignored or discussed in terms unlike anything in the Hebrew Bible, in Roman biography, or in the Gospels. In one extreme example, the author counters the argument that procreation justifies sexual intercourse:

> But if you get many children, then for their sakes you become robbers and avaricious. . . . For the majority of children become unprofitable, possessed by demons . . . they become either lunatic or half-withered [consumptive] or crippled or deaf or dumb or paralytic or stupid. Even if they are healthy, again will they be unserviceable, performing useless and abominable deeds; for they are caught either in adultery or murder or in theft or in unchastity, and by all these you will be afflicted.[24]

With the triumph of the "orthodox" canon, these writings were consigned to the marginal status of "heterodox" texts. As we shall see, however, some of their themes, including the pain and futility of biological parenthood, lived on in the history of Christianity.

The requirements of discipleship, including vulnerability to persecution and the surrender of family ties, caused consternation among outsiders, and particularly among the relatives of converts. Some Christians were reputed to be unfilial troublemakers. To the disciple who asked, "Lord, let me first go and bury my father," Jesus said, "Follow me, and leave the dead to bury their own dead" (Matt. 8:21–22). Such an exclusive commitment, characteristic of radical sects, rarely survives when a movement grows and begins to appeal to established social groups. After a time, not all of those who were attracted to aspects of the Christian movement were able or willing to follow homeless, charismatic preachers into social oblivion. From very early days there were wide differences of opinion within the movement about the need for "structure" and the varieties of leadership.[25] At the beginning of the second century, Ignatius of Antioch instructed Christians to "regard the

24. *Acts of Thomas* 1.12, in *New Testament Apocrypha*, vol. 1, ed. Wilhelm Schneemelcher (Philadelphia: Westminster Press, 1983), p. 449.

25. See "The Didache," 15.1, in *The Apostolic Fathers*, vol. 1, ed. Kirsopp Lake (Cambridge, Mass.: Harvard University Press, 1945), p. 331, which described the different roles of "prophets and teachers" and "bishops and deacons," and instructed believers to treat both groups with respect.

bishop as the Lord himself."[26] Bishops soon became teachers, rulers, and "fathers"; Ignatius told the Magnesians, whose bishop was a young man, "to render him all respect according to the power of God the Father."[27] The patriarchal authority of men was easily conflated with the authority of God and restored to the "households" of the new churches.

With the emergence of ecclesiastical hierarchy in Christian communities came new writings, of unknown authorship but ascribed to Paul in order to borrow his prestige.[28] In the second century, the letters to the Colossians and Ephesians and the Pastoral Epistles were enlisted in the struggle against Christian radicalism. These texts are marked by concern for the reputation of Christians in the world, by attention to the structures and leadership of the developing churches, and by a determined campaign against the threat of egalitarianism in gender and class relations. Composed late in the first and early in the second century, these writings ignored the break with the biological family proclaimed in some sayings of Jesus and promoted by certain other Christian texts and practices. They incorporated ancient household codes reflecting patriarchal values shared by Jews and Gentiles, assuming that household and state were established on the "natural" (biological) inferiority of women and identifying the relationship of husband and wife with that of parent and child, or master and slave.[29] In the first letter to Timothy—despite Jesus' attitude toward Mary of Bethany—women are directed toward traditional roles. The order of widows was restricted to women at least sixty years old who had been married to one husband, raised children, and served the community. Groups of celibate women of various ages were discouraged from living together; young women were urged to "marry, bear children, rule their households, and give the enemy no occasion to revile us" (1 Tim. 5:14). By the beginning of the second century, powerful voices within the Christian move-

26. Ignatius of Antioch, "Letter to the Ephesians," 6.1, in *The Apostolic Fathers*, p. 181.

27. Ignatius, "Letter to the Magnesians," 3.1, in *The Apostolic Fathers*, p. 199.

28. For questions concerning Pauline authorship, see Helmut Koester, *Introduction to the New Testament*, vol. 2 (Philadelphia: Fortress Press, 1982), pp. 261–308.

29. See the discussion of the household codes in Schüssler Fiorenza, *In Memory of Her*, pp. 251–270.

ment were working to restore women to the patriarchal household and the patriarchal household to the center of Christian society.

The Pastoral Epistles won places in the scriptural canon while more radical writings were excluded, but only after an extended period of conflict and struggle, much of which has been hidden from Christian historiography.[30] The eschatological vision of the new family did not capture the institutions and ideologies of Christianity, but neither did it completely disappear: it is preserved in the Gospels, in certain Pauline passages, and in a variety of other writings. Some of these, such as the Apocryphal Acts, have been dismissed as heterodox or trivial, but others, such as the Acts of the Martyrs, have always held a central place in doctrine and devotion. During the long period of persecution preceding the establishment of Christianity in the fourth century, martyrdom and persecution undercut the values of the dominant culture, breaking traditional bonds and forging new ones. Faced with violent, immediate death, the martyrs recreated the family of discipleship modeled by the men and women who followed Jesus to his crucifixion. In many respects they shared the voice and vision of the disciples as well as their experience of *communitas*. Their mutual love and support withstood terror, and even death itself, as attested in the Acts that preserved their memory and immortalized their experience.

Most of the Acts of the Martyrs were written in the third century, at the same time that the Pastoral Epistles were accepted into the canon. These Acts present very different models of family and of gender relations; they demonstrate the martyrs' renunciation of traditional concerns and reversal of ordinary priorities. Perpetua, a young North African matron waiting for death in the arena, was plagued by her father's arguments and tormented by his tears. He kept begging her to recant, saying: "Have pity on my grey head—have pity on me your father. . . . Think of your brothers, think of your mother and your aunt, think of your child, who will not be able to live once you are gone."[31]

Perpetua grieved for her father—"I felt sorry for his pathetic old

30. Ibid., pp. 245–250.
31. "The Martyrdom of Saints Perpetua and Felicitas," in *Acts of the Christian Martyrs*, ed. Herbert Musurillo (Oxford: Clarendon Press, 1972), 5, p. 113.

age"—but neither pity nor reverence for the *paterfamilias* tempted her to recant. She was much more troubled about her infant son, and her father played on her fears by threatening the child's welfare and depriving her of his presence. God intervened to frustrate the father's intentions and relieve the young mother of pain, responsibility, and anxiety:

> But my baby had got used to being nursed at the breast and to staying with me in prison. So I sent the deacon Pomponius straight away to my father to ask for the baby. But father refused to give him over. But as God willed, the baby had no further desire for the breast, nor did I suffer any inflammation; and so I was relieved of any anxiety for my child and of any discomfort in my breasts.[32]

The memory of Perpetua as a heroic representative of Christian motherhood was not lost on later Christians. St. Augustine, preaching on her passion in the fifth century, emphasized that she was not only a woman but "a mother likewise, that unto the frailty of that sex might be added a more importunate love."[33] With divine favor clearly expressed in the down-to-earth business of weaning an infant, no questions were raised about motherhood as an obstacle to religious leadership, and no Christian commentator expressed the view that Perpetua should have stayed at home with her child. Her "good portion" was not in the household; maternal responsibility and "importunate love" were superseded by the new birth into Christ.

The story of Felicitas, Perpetua's companion and serving maid, also exhibits the place of motherhood in the *communitas* of martyrs. Felicitas was eight months pregnant and fearful that she would be left behind when the others were given to the beasts, for Roman law prohibited the execution of pregnant women. She did not want to die alone or with ordinary criminals, and the other Christians were worried also;

---

32. Ibid., 6, p. 115.
33. Augustine, *The Passion of Perpetua and Felicity: The Sermons of S. Augustine upon the Feast of Sts. Perpetua and Felicity*, trans. W. H. Shewring (London: Sheed & Ward, 1931), p. 35.

for they were afraid that they would have to leave behind so fine a companion to travel alone on the same road to hope. And so, two days before the contest, they poured forth a prayer to the Lord in one torrent of common grief. And immediately after their prayer the birth pains came upon her. She suffered a good deal in her labor, because of the natural difficulty of an eight months' delivery.[34]

God intervened again, bringing premature labor and delivery; Felicitas gave birth to a healthy infant, "and one of the sisters brought her up as her own daughter." The delivery enhanced Felicitas's glory, for she was "glad that she had safely given birth so that now she could fight the beasts, going from one blood bath to another, from the midwife to the gladiator, ready to wash after childbirth in a second baptism."[35]

The recent motherhood of both women was obvious when they were stripped in the arena: "Even the crowd was horrified when they saw that one was a delicate young girl and the other was a woman fresh from childbirth with the milk still dripping from her breasts."[36] The youth, sex, and maternity of Perpetua and Felicitas won them sympathy from the hostile crowd, the special love of their companions, and divine assistance in the physical processes of birth and lactation. They were neither protected from horrible deaths nor disqualified for heroism or holiness. Childbirth was recognized as a tough physical challenge, comparable to the contest in the arena; motherhood made the struggle more difficult and the sacrifice more valuable. Childbirth in prison, and the physical evidence of recent labor and delivery, were occasions of admiration and respect—not, as in the story of Pope Joan, of caricature and cruelty.

For these early Christians, then, motherhood was not especially relevant to holiness. Although it did not necessarily bring women closer to God, it did not block their access to the sacred. Responding to the faith of the woman with the flow of blood, Jesus healed

34. "Martyrdom of Saints Perpetua and Felicitas," 15, p. 123. An eighth-month delivery was believed to be especially dangerous and difficult—according to the Hippocratic tradition, more dangerous than a seventh-month delivery.

35. Ibid., p. 125; 18, p. 127.

36. Ibid., 20, p. 129.

her of her illness, and God facilitated the martyrdom of Perpetua and Felicitas despite their physiological condition. The biological demands of motherhood, accepted in the ancient world as marks and determinants of female incapacity, were not allowed to stand in the way of the martyrs' witness. Motherhood was not in itself redemptive, but neither did it preclude participation in the most sacred vocation. Under extraordinary circumstances a woman might belong to an eschatological family whose requirements preempted those of the biological family. The institutions and ideologies of Christian motherhood had deep roots in Jewish and Roman and other ancient sources, but medieval Europeans inherited a construction more complex than any of its multiple components.

Physiological Motherhood: The Wandering Womb

The construction of motherhood, as institution and ideologies, is based in part upon physiological assumptions about what mothers are. Such assumptions are themselves historical constructions varying widely over time, among cultures, and even within cultures: there can be significant differences between male and female or learned and popular descriptions of female anatomy and the reproductive processes. Physiological assumptions are building blocks in belief systems that define the moral, social, and emotional characteristics of motherhood. What is known and believed about conception, pregnancy, birth, and lactation not only describes what mothers are but colors expectations of what they should be, shaping our judgments of "good" and "bad," "natural" and "unnatural." The facts of life, like other scientific data, are not discovered and interpreted in an ideological vacuum. They may be presented as accounts of objective reality, but scientists, like other people, see what they are looking for and what they are able to see, given their perspectives, contexts, and socialization.[1] Profound and powerful presuppositions about gender, sexuality, and parenthood color observations of maternity in its physiologi-

1. On scientific "objectivity," see esp. Keller, *Reflections;* and G. E. R. Lloyd, *Science, Folklore, and Ideology* (Cambridge: Cambridge University Press, 1983), pt. 2.

cal as well as its psychological and social aspects. I am describing a circular phenomenon: beliefs shape or even dictate perceptions, and the perceived "facts" in turn shape ideologies.

In the late twentieth century, for example, we *know* that each biological parent contributes half of the chromosomes that determine the genetic constitution of a child, and we believe that children belong to two families. On the other hand, certain ancient Greek thinkers and their medieval disciples *knew* that an embryo received its "form" from the male parent—and in fifth-century Athens a father had the power of life and death over "his" child. Today we *know* that mother's milk supplies valuable antibodies to the newborn infant, and we believe that nursing encourages maternal bonding and contributes to the infant's psychic health. Fifteenth-century Italians *knew* that moral, intellectual, and physical characteristics were transmitted in milk, making the choice of a wet nurse a crucial responsibility for middle-class parents. The legal, emotional, and theological ramifications of physiological systems are important aspects of the history of motherhood.

As we confront the implications of late twentieth-century science, it is obvious that ethics and social theory have not kept pace with reproductive technology. Who *is* a mother: the donor of an ovum, the woman who carries a fetus to term, or the person who raises a son or daughter to maturity?[2] With the new possibility and reality of so-called "surrogate" motherhood, ancient distinctions between biological and adoptive parents are no longer adequate or clear. Rapid developments in physiological "facts" are experienced as threats to psychic and social stability; new technology forces us to abandon outworn assumptions and to recognize the power of our belief systems. The relationship of physiology to social and domestic ideology has never been so apparent, or so complicated.

In the chapters that follow, I examine certain intersections of the history of Christianity and the history of motherhood in medieval Europe and, in this chapter, some of the physiological notions

2. Twentieth-century feminists have raised the question of men's ability to "mother" and its implications: see Chodorow, *Reproduction of Mothering*; and Dorothy Dinnerstein, *The Mermaid and the Minotaur* (New York: Harper & Row, 1976).

prevalent in that time and place. I do not suggest that motherhood or reproductive physiology was a primary focus of Christian thought and activity. The Church Fathers did not design a program for Christian mothers or write handbooks of obstetrics, gynecology, or infant care. (They had a great deal to say about sexuality and parenthood from moral and theological perspectives, but that is not the subject of this chapter.) However, the absence of a Christian biology does not imply an absence of biological assumptions. To take one well-known instance, at the end of the sixth century C.E., Pope Gregory the Great wrote to the Roman missionaries in England in response to their anxious questions about baptism, marriage, and the pollution of sacred space. Gregory's moral and ecclesiastical judgments were rooted in a set of inherited beliefs and assumptions—among them, the association of menstruation with disease and discomfort, and the notion that women should not be sexually active while they were nursing babies.[3] The pope was concerned primarily with the conversion of new Christians and secondarily with church order and domestic morality, but he approached these concerns with a distinct set of ideas about "nature."

Early and medieval Christians, along with their Muslim neighbors, were heirs of classical Greek science, although their inheritance was modified, diluted, and in some cases transformed over time. The works of Aristotle were translated into Latin and introduced to the learned elite of western Europe in the twelfth and thirteenth centuries, but the nuances of classical biology were not understood or appreciated until the sixteenth century at the earliest. Incompatible theories survived side by side, and the interest and erudition necessary to recognize inconsistencies, much less to resolve them, were not available. Medieval Europeans inherited a complex and diverse set of ideas that included widely different interpretations of basic processes: the opposing Aristotelian and Galenic descriptions of conception are perhaps the best-known but by no means the only example. Varied and conflicting views survived in different medieval texts and schools, and even

---

3. *Bede: A History of the English Church and People*, ed. Leo Sherley-Price (London: Penguin Books, 1970), 1.27, pp. 76–81.

within single texts. There was no systematic reproductive biology, not even among learned people.

The more difficult questions about the physiological beliefs of medieval people do not ask *what* the assumptions were but *whose* they were. Mothers did not read Aristotle or Soranus, nor did the women who delivered babies and provided most of the available gynecological care.[4] Our sources for the history of ideas about reproductive physiology, like those for most of the history of ideas, have traditionally been confined to the writings of learned men and a few unusual women. Much has been done in recent years to expand the sources and enrich our appreciation of the world of medieval people, but we cannot discover directly what most women believed about the physical meanings of motherhood. The writings of the learned tell us little about the experience of mothers, and until recently, few women wrote books at all, much less books on biological theory or obstetrics—although there are a few interesting exceptions, as we shall see.

Mothers did not write about motherhood, but their lives and experience were profoundly affected by the work of those who did. Certainly Aristotle's definition of women as defective men, which was argued in terms of biological "facts," cast a long shadow. Greek gynecological texts, cited and copied and rewritten for many centuries, influenced the care given to women. Still, most midwives learned their trade from their own mothers, or from teachers who did not read. A few women were trained by doctors who knew the Greek and medieval texts, but not the vast majority of those who delivered their own daughters' or their neighbors' babies. Ironically, the closer we are to the texts, the farther from most women's experience. Nonetheless, these writings do provide clues, in some cases our only clues, to a world of thought and opinion about the physiology of motherhood. We have to extrapolate from scattered and diverse sources and to expect the picture to be indistinct. The aim of this chapter is to gather together some of the major themes that appear and reappear in certain significant

4. In "Women's Medical Practice and Health Care in Medieval Europe," *Signs* 14 (1989), 434–473, Monica Green calls for a more careful account of women as healers and patients; the assumption that medieval women's health care was entirely women's responsibility may be oversimplified.

ancient and medieval sources. Without attempting to impose system where there was none, it sketches some persistent notions about women's bodies and about conception, pregnancy, birth, and lactation.

However mothers may be characterized, they are always female parents—that is, they are women, and scientific and other knowledge about women pertains also to mothers. As a matter of fact, women are frequently perceived as mothers or potential mothers even if they have no children, and medical writings especially tend to focus on their reproductive organs and capacities. In the Hippocratic writings, women appeared most often in gynecological contexts; in discussions of injuries to the head or the feet, references were generally limited to male patients. The shadowy figure of Hippocrates retained immense prestige during the Middle Ages, although the treatises known by his name were actually produced by many authors between the late fifth and early fourth centuries B.C.E. Certain fundamental and long-lived ideas about women can be found in these Hippocratic works—for example, the assumption that the womb is directly connected to other bodily systems. One of the Hippocratic "aphorisms" recommends a test for sterility that depends on such a connection, and variations are found in many medieval works: "If a woman does not conceive and you wish to know if she will conceive, cover her round with wraps and burn perfumes underneath. If the smell seems to pass through the body to the mouth and nostrils, be assured that the woman is not barren through her own physical fault."[5]

We tend to assume that medieval ideas about the nature of women were based either on religious doctrine or on social theory and practice. Certainly medieval thinkers did justify denunciations of women by castigating Eve's sin; and they did look around, see women subordinate everywhere, and conclude that female subordination must be "natural." They were informed of female weakness and inferiority, however, not only by theologians and

5. Hippocrates, "Aphorisms" 5.59 in *Hippocrates*, vol. 4, trans. W. H. S. Jones (Cambridge, Mass.: Harvard University Press, 1967), p. 175.

philosophers but by biologists who discussed women's nature in physiological language.[6] In the classical scientific legacy, women appeared as human creatures with wombs, defined by their likeness and unlikeness to men. Sexual difference was perceived and described from the male point of view.

In the *Timaeus*, the only Platonic work available in Latin in the medieval West, Plato included the creation of women, along with heterosexual passion and sexual difference itself, among the consequences of wrong-doing:

> All those creatures generated as men who proved themselves cowardly and spent their lives in wrong-doing were transformed at their second incarnation, into women. And it was for this reason that the gods at that time contrived the love of sexual intercourse by constructing an animate creature of one kind in us men, and of another kind in women.

Plato explained that semen is spinal "marrow" provided with an outlet through the penis:

> The marrow, inasmuch as it is animate and has been granted an outlet, has endowed the part where its outlet lies with a love for generating by implanting therein a lively desire for emission. Wherefore in men the nature of the genital organs is disobedient and self-willed, like a creature that is deaf to reason, and it attempts to dominate all because of its frenzied lusts.

He imagined that the womb must be similarly self-willed and difficult, as anxious to bear children as the penis to beget them:

> Whenever the matrix or womb . . .—which is an indwelling creature desirous of child-bearing,—remains without fruit long beyond the due season, it is vexed and takes it ill; and by straying all ways through the body and blocking up the passages of the breath and preventing respiration it casts the body into the uttermost distress,

6. This point was made by Vern L. Bullough in "Medieval Medical and Scientific Views of Women," *Viator* 4 (1973), 485–501.

and causes, moreover, all kinds of maladies; until the desire and love of the two sexes unite them.[7]

The sense of a rebellious, quasi-autonomous power in the flesh, so striking in the writings of male Christians, apparently touched a common or even a universal aspect of male experience. In his letter to the Romans (7:23), St. Paul wrote, "I see in my members another law at war with the law of my mind and making me captive to the law of sin which dwells in my members." The traditional response to anxiety about loss of control is to attach such fears to women, blame women for arousing rebellion, and assume that the womb is as troublesome as the penis. The habit of analyzing female physiology from a male perspective was well established in the Greek texts.

In the entire legacy of the classical world, no scientific writings approached in influence the works of Aristotle, who was venerated as "The Teacher" and "The Philosopher" by medieval scholars. Between the twelfth and sixteenth centuries, but indirectly much longer, Aristotle's assumptions, vocabulary, categories, and modes of thought dominated learned discourse, especially in the logical and scientific fields. His views about women and sexual difference shaped not only medical knowledge but Christian teaching about human minds and bodies. Aristotle's biological theories were not universally accepted in his own time, and the disagreements are instructive, but his ideas about men and women survived in fields far from biology. They did not stand alone but endured as intrinsic elements in a towering system of philosophy and natural history.

On the physiological differences of the sexes, Aristotle wrote: "The male is that which has the power to generate in another . . . while the female is that which can generate in itself." *In* itself, not *of* itself, for the female is "that out of which the generated offspring, which is present in the generator, comes into being."[8] Males and females have different functions, therefore different

7. Plato, *The Timaeus*, in *Plato*, vol. 7, trans. R. C. Bury (Cambridge, Mass.: Harvard University Press, 1961), pp. 249, 251.
8. Aristotle, *The Generation of Animals* 1.2, trans. A. L. Peck (Cambridge, Mass.: Harvard University Press, 1979), p. 13.

parts, and these differences are of the essence. Aristotle asserted that castration is more than the loss of an organ, for it changes the entire nature of a castrated male; this convinced him that "it is not merely in respect of some casual part or some casual faculty that an animal is male or female. It is clear, then, that 'the male' and 'the female' are a principle."[9] Males can be made effeminate by castration, but females can never be made masculine, for femaleness is identified with a deficiency—the inability to generate. Aristotle elaborated on this theme in many ways—for example, "A boy actually resembles a woman in physique, and a woman is as it were an infertile male."[10] In this world view, sexual difference is central to all of nature, and to human nature most of all.

For Plato, on the other hand, women were somewhat like men, with different but analogous organs. In the *Timaeus*, despite its assumption that cowardly men were transformed into women and its alarming account of the behavior of the womb, it is evident that men and women, with all their differences, are more alike in their humanity than different in their sex. This conviction stands at the heart of the famous passage in the *Republic* concerning the education of guardians:

> If it appears that the male and the female sex have distinct qualifica-
> tions for any arts or pursuits, we shall affirm that they ought to be
> assigned respectively to each. But if it appears that they differ only
> in just this respect that the female bears and the male begets, we
> shall say that no proof has yet been produced that the woman differs
> from the man for our purposes, but we shall continue to think that
> our guardians and their wives ought to follow the same pursuits.[11]

9. Ibid., p. 15. The notion of sex as a "principle" remains central in Roman Catholic teaching: see, e.g., "The Ordination of Women," Declaration of the Sacred Congregation for the Doctrine of the Faith, October 15, 1976, esp. p. 119.

10. Aristotle, *Generation of Animals* 1.20, p. 103. Among many commentators on the centrality of sexual difference in the Aristotelian tradition, see Maryanne Cline Horowitz, "Aristotle and Women," *Journal of the History of Biology* 9 (1976), 183–213.

11. *The Republic* 5.5, in *Plato*, vol. 5, trans. Paul Shorey (Cambridge, Mass.: Harvard University Press, 1982), p. 445.

Such reasoning was impossible for Aristotle, for whom the difference between conceiving and begetting was of monumental importance. For him, there was one normative human being, the adult male, and women were inherently (that is, biologically) inferior. Aristotle's biological views, like Plato's, were carried into political theory. His ideal state was based on the family, in which men "naturally" rule: "The male is by nature superior and the female inferior, the male ruler and the female subject. And the same must also necessarily apply in the case of mankind as a whole." Men and women shared almost nothing, not even virtues, and here again Aristotle diverged from Plato: "The temperance of a woman and that of a man are not the same, nor their courage and justice, as Socrates thought, but the one is the courage of command, and the other that of subordination, and the case is similar with the other virtues."[12] The education of women ought to be completely unlike the education of men because their destiny was different, and the goal was not to overcome but to recognize and affirm the essential (biological) division.

Soranus of Ephesus, who studied medicine in Alexandria and practiced in Rome in the second century C.E., wrote a treatise on gynecology that was translated into Latin in the fifth century and circulated in several versions in medieval Europe. Soranus belonged to a sect that comprehended human physiology in terms of relationships between dry or constricted and fluid or relaxed states; medical practice consisted mainly of maintaining an appropriate balance. His sect did not believe in theoretical anatomy or physiology, and the practical tone of Soranus's writings is appealing to a modern ear. He disagreed with those who ascribed too much independence to the uterus: "Although the uterus is not an animal (as it appeared to some people), it is, nevertheless, similar in certain respects, having a sense of touch, so that it is contracted by cooling agents but relaxed by loosening ones." Soranus disapproved of many contemporary therapies—foul-smelling fumigations, or blowing air into the vagina with a blacksmith's bellows,

12. Aristotle, *The Politics* 1.2, 1.5, trans. H. Rackham (Cambridge, Mass.: Harvard University Press, 1959), pp. 21, 63.

or banging metal plates near the patient to frighten the uterus into its proper place: "The uterus," he said, "does not issue forth like a wild animal from the lair, delighted by fragrant odors and fleeing bad odors."[13]

Galen of Pergamos, a near-contemporary of Soranus, was more directly influential in medieval Europe, and he too disagreed with Plato on the "wandering womb." (The Platonic imagery and the skeptics' responses reappeared in the nineteenth century in arguments over hysteria and women's "nature.") Galen identified himself with Hippocrates and with the tradition of humoral medicine that predated the Hippocratic writings. Humoral theories divide the material world into four elements—fire, air, earth, and water—and four opposing conditions of heat, cold, dryness, and moisture. These conditions are associated with bodily "humors"—blood, yellow bile or choler, black bile, and phlegm—and these in turn with temperamental states or moods: sanguine, choleric, melancholy, and phlegmatic. For centuries, adjustment of the humors was the primary task of medical theory and practice.

Heat, cold, dryness, and moisture were not balanced opposites or equivalents, for it was generally assumed that hot and dry were preferable to cold and wet. Men were believed to be hotter and drier than women, and according to Aristotle and his followers, lack of heat accounted for the basic female deficiency—the inability to generate.[14] In the early Middle Ages, through Latin translations and compilations, these ancient Greek ideas about the humors and their association to notions of male superiority became established assumptions, at least among learned men.

The book of the legendary Trotula of Salerno, however, opens with a statement of sexual difference based on humoral theory but in spirit unlike the writings of the classical theorists. Expressing appreciation of God's chosen method of perpetuating the human species, Trotula said: "He made the nature of the male hot and

13. Soranus of Ephesus, *Soranus' Gynecology*, ed. Oswei Temkin (Baltimore, Md.: Johns Hopkins University Press, 1956), pp. 9, 153.

14. Rose E. Frisch has demonstrated that in fact men are not drier than women but wetter: the ratio of total body water to body weight is higher in males. See her "What's Below the Surface?" *New England Journal of Medicine* 305 (1981), 1019–1020.

dry and that of the female cold and wet so that the excess of each other's embrace might be restrained by the mutual opposition of contrary qualities. The man's constitution being hot and dry might assuage the woman's coldness and wetness and on the contrary her nature being cold and wet might soothe his hot and dry embrace."[15] Trotula is not generally accepted as a historical figure, at least not (as legend claims) as a medical practitioner and professor at the medical school of Salerno in the eleventh century.[16] Whoever the authors of the various versions of Trotula's *Diseases of Women*, the treatises survived in many manuscripts and in printed editions of the sixteenth century. The originality of "Trotula" rests less on diagnoses and prescriptions than on insight into the situation of women. The treatises emphasize women's weakness and express sympathy for their difficulties with male doctors:

> Since then women are by nature weaker than men it is reasonable that sicknesses more often abound in them especially around the organs involved in the work of nature. Since these organs happen to be in a retired location, women on account of modesty and the fragility and delicacy of the state of these parts dare not reveal the difficulties of their sicknesses to a male doctor. Wherefore I, pitying their misfortunes and at the instigation of a certain matron, began to study carefully the sicknesses which most frequently trouble the female sex.[17]

Hildegard of Bingen, undeniably a woman and the author of her own writings, was not primarily a medical practitioner but a

15. Trotula of Salerno, *The Diseases of Women by Trotula of Salerno*, trans. Elizabeth Mason-Hohl (New York: Ward Ritchie Press, 1940), p. 1.

16. See Edward F. Tuttle, "The *Trotula* and Old Dame Trot: A Note on the Lady of Salerno," *Bulletin of the History of Medicine* 50 (1976), 61–72. Tuttle believes that the figure of Trotula emerges from "the accretion of credulous citation upon risky assumption" (p. 61), assumes that the author of *The Diseases of Women* was male, and says that Trotula, if she existed at all, was an illiterate midwife. He rests his case on the "bawdy association" (p. 71) of the verb "trot." John F. Benton also dismisses Trotula, at least as a respected authority; see his "Trotula, Women's Problems, and the Professionalization of Medicine in the Middle Ages," *Bulletin of the History of Medicine* 59 (1985), 30–53.

17. Trotula, *Diseases of Women*, pp. 1–2.

mystic, a theologian, and an abbess. She was a significant figure in the twelfth-century Church; her writings extend over so many fields that Peter Dronke compares her to Avicenna in the range of her interests: "cosmology, ethics, medicine and mystical poetry."[18] She wrote on trees, plants, and precious stones as well as human bodies; most of her reflections on physiology are gathered in the treatise *Causae et curae*. Hildegard perceived the entire natural world, including human bodies, as elements of God's great design. Her writings were products of her visions and her insight into natural processes is inseparable from her perception of supernatural activity. Yet she learned physiology also from study and experience—from attention to her own body and her own frequent and serious illnesses, and from those of other nuns and of the people who came to the convent for care. Medieval convents were also hospitals.

Hildegard's vision of the material world is stated primarily in a context of divine creation and activity but also in terms of earth, air, fire, and water. She understood human bodies in relation to the book of Genesis, to the Hippocratic-Galenic tradition, and to the physical universe: she wrote at length on the influence of the waxing and waning of the moon on bodily fluids and processes. Men and women were differentiated first by the material from which they were created—Adam from the earth, Eve from Adam's flesh. Men were strong, solid, and earthy; women were weak, light, and airy. Hildegard wove together scriptural and humoral theories and interpretations. Contrary to most medieval thinkers, she believed that women were less carnal and lustful than men and based her belief on physiology. She understood sexual passion as originating in a kind of windstorm in the brain that travels through the body. Because the fire of passion cannot burn itself out in the narrow confinement of the male groin, men are likely

18. Peter Dronke, *Women Writers of the Middle Ages* (Cambridge: Cambridge University Press, 1984), p. 144. See also Barbara Newman, *Sister of Wisdom: St. Hildegard's Theology of the Feminine* (Berkeley: University of California Press, 1987), esp. chap. 4. In her brilliant study of the entire range of Hildegard's works, Newman examines the *Causae et curae* in a larger context that reveals the saint's ambivalence about the goodness of sexuality, along with a pervasive "tension between ascetic renunciation and frank appreciation of created goods" (p. 122). My treatment of Hildegard in this chapter is based on the *Causae et curae* alone.

to be carried away by fierce, almost irresistible forces of delight; female lust is more easily restrained because the storm can expand in the open spaces of the uterus. Women feel passion less violently than men but more frequently, on account of their moisture.[19] Hildegard appreciated sexuality as a difficult but essential aspect of the human condition—contaminated by sin, certainly, but part of the continuing creation of the world and the people of God.

In the thirteenth century, Christian as well as Jewish and Muslim philosophers and theologians faced the challenge of integrating and interpreting the newly translated Aristotelian corpus in the light of revealed religion. Among the influential Christian synthesizers was Albert the Great, a provincial of the Dominican order, a teacher of Thomas Aquinas, and a commentator on all the books of Aristotle. In his commentary on *The Generation of Animals*, Albert took up matters of sex and sexual difference along with many other questions about living beings. Asking whether females were "necessary," he concluded, with Aristotle, that although the intention of nature in any individual act of generation was to reproduce a male, a defect in the material of the embryo or the heat of generation might produce a female. This result must be counted a failure in itself, yet it served the purposes of nature, for "the species of animals cannot be conserved without the generation of individual creatures, for which females are required as well as males."[20]

Like Aristotle, Albert was thoroughly convinced of male superiority. Heat and dryness, such excellent qualities, ought to assure men's greater longevity—but here he faced a difficulty. Aristotle had said that men lived longer than women, as was appropriate, and yet when Albert looked around at his own world, he saw that women seemed to outlive men. He solved the problem with a nature/accident hypothesis: by nature, men lived longer; but by

---

19. Hildegard of Bingen, *Hildegardis causae et curae*, ed. Paulus Kaiser (Leipzig: Teubner, 1903), esp. bk. 2, pp. 69, 76–103. I am indebted to Kelly del Tredici for assistance with the translation of this text. See also Bernhard W. Scholz, "Hildegard von Bingen on the Nature of Woman," *American Benedictine Review* 31 (1980), 361–383.

20. Albert the Great, "Quaestiones super de animalibus" 15.2, in *Alberti Magni Opera Omnia*, vol. 12, ed. Bernhardus Geyer (Aschendorff: Monasterii Westfalorum, 1955), p. 260.

accident or circumstance, women frequently outlived them. Women did not work so hard, were not so debilitated by sexual intercourse, and were purged of unhealthy impurities by menstruation. As David Herlihy pointed out, Albert's confusion was understandable: men *had* outnumbered women in Aristotle's time, but the demographic ratio was reversed by the thirteenth century.[21]

Albert's discussion of the question "whether men are more inclined to morality than women" is an extreme example of the use of "scientific" rationalization to justify prejudice. The topic provoked a strident digression in the midst of a volume of reflection on the nature of plants, animals, and human beings. In customary scholastic style the discussion opens with a statement of the arguments to be opposed: women are more teachable than men, so it should be easier to train them to morality. Furthermore, they are more prudent, and prudence is a necessary virtue. On the other hand, everyone knows that women are deceitful, immodest, and weak—devils in human form. This is so, Albert explained, because women are moist, and their moisture makes them slippery, inconstant, and forever seeking novelty; when they are with one man, they wish they were with another. As failed men, their nature is defective and deprived: they can accomplish nothing on their own except through deception. "If I may speak briefly," Albert said, "a woman ought to be avoided like a poisonous serpent or horned devil; if I were to say everything I know about women, the whole world would be astonished."[22] After this outburst, he returned to his "logical" arguments. It is true, he believed, that in some respects women are more teachable than men but only because they can be moved through their feelings: their cold constitutions resist intelligent argument. Women are not really more prudent than men, but only more shrewd in the evil-doing with which they compensate for their deficiencies. Lacking true intellectual power, which consists in the knowledge of good and evil, women must depend on the sensitive appetites or feelings, which

21. Ibid., 15.8, p. 264. See David Herlihy, "Life Expectancies for Women in Medieval Society," in *The Role of Women in the Middle Ages*, ed. Rosemarie Thee Morewedge (Albany: State University of New York Press, 1975), p. 11.

22. Albert, "Quaestiones" 15.11, p. 266.

tend toward evil unless regulated by reason. The senses incline women toward evil, men toward good.

Thomas Aquinas asked the same question from a theological perspective. Why was Eve—an inferior being, foreknown by God to be an occasion of sin for Adam—included in the original creation? Thomas repeated the explanation that women are defective as individuals but necessary to the species in the work of procreation. Eve was created to help Adam in that work; for any other, a male helper would have been preferable. Women's subjection to men, which is implied by their inferiority in "the power of rational discernment," is not like the subjection of slaves, arranged for the benefit of the ruler and appropriate only in a fallen world. Women's subjection is inherent in their defective nature. It is "domestic or civil, in which the ruler manages his subjects for *their* advantage," and it supplies the human race with "the benefit of order."[23] Thomas stated his views without vitriolic commentary, but his opinions were no different from those of his masters. Thomist philosophy, which predominated in Roman Catholic teaching by the sixteenth century, carried a profound distrust of women and of "feeling" (meaning, according to the scholastics, the opposite of "reason"). The work of thirteenth-century Dominican philosophers paved the way for later witch-hunters, including the Dominican authors of the *Malleus maleficarum* at the end of the fifteenth century (see Chapter 6).

The scientific legacy of Aristotle was not confined to Dominican scholarship but received in many places, including the encyclopedias—compendiums of knowledge popular among learned people in the later Middle Ages. A thirteenth-century Franciscan known as "Bartholomew the Englishman" produced an encyclopedia, *On the Properties of Things*, designed to address every topic that might puzzle students of Scripture. Making copious use of Aristotle, Bartholomew wrote on everything from stones to human beings and plants to planets, and his work was copied and translated into several languages: John Trevisa produced an English version late in the fourteenth century. On sexual difference

23. St. Thomas Aquinas, *Summa theologiae* Ia.92.1, vol. 13, ed. Edmund Hill (London: Blackfriars, 1964), p. 39.

Bartholomew generally stayed with the Aristotelian point of view, ascribing men's superior qualities to their greater heat, although he quoted St. Paul and St. Augustine to back up his arguments. His comparison of male and female qualities is comprehensive without being vicious: "Men are more hot and dry than women, more strong and mighty, more bold and hardy, more wise and witty, more steadfast and stable, and they love women dearly."[24]

The reiteration of Aristotle's notions by learned philosophers and scholars would be more disturbing if these men had been directly involved in the care of female patients. Fortunately, most of the medical (as opposed to biological and philosophical) writings of the later Middle Ages exhibit a different spirit. These works provide herbal and other remedies for diseases and injuries, incorporating ancient practices and subordinating theory to diagnosis and therapy. One such text, a fifteenth-century English manuscript (Sloane 2463 from the British Museum) has been published under the title of *Medieval Woman's Guide to Health*.[25] The editor, Beryl Rowland, believes that the scribe and possibly the author were men.

Male or female, the author begins, like Trotula, with an expression of sympathy and concern; women suffer more than men realize, and they are embarrassed and abused by male doctors. The author's stated intention is "to help their secret maladies so that one woman may aid another in her illness and not divulge her secrets to such discourteous men." Adjustment of the humors was the essential treatment, but humoral theory does not in this

24. Bartholomaeus Anglicus, *On the Properties of Things: John Trevisa's Translation of Bartholomaeus Anglicus De proprietatibus rerum* 6.12, vol. 1, ed. M. C. Seymour (Oxford, Clarendon Press, 1975), p. 307. Most of Bartholomew's medical knowledge came from Greek sources by way of Constantine the African, an eleventh-century monk of Monte Cassino who translated Arabic works into Latin.

25. *Medieval Woman's Guide to Health: The First English Gynecological Handbook*, ed. Beryl Rowland (Kent, Ohio: Kent State University Press, 1981). Rowland's introduction includes discussion of the history of women healers in medieval Europe, of the "Trotula" question, and of the "birth figures" or drawings of infants *in utero* from Sloane 2463. Monica Green ("Women's Medical Practice," p. 463) pointed out that Rowland used only one manuscript of this text and that a second has now been transcribed; she called for a critical edition of this important work.

text carry implications of moral or intellectual inadequacy. It does suggest courses of treatment, and the writer was interested in the relationship of the humors to sexual and emotional as well as physiological states—for example: "The signs of phlegm [in the uterus] are these: women feel much humidity and have no desire to consort with men."[26] The author observed the close connection between physical condition and sexuality and expended little energy on moral commentary. Some of the remedies seem reasonable, others lethal, but women's "nature" is not disparaged or their behavior harshly judged.

The author did distinguish among groups of women, suggesting, for example, "a good syrup that is very effective in bringing out corrupt blood from the uterus, and it is for ladies, nuns, and other women who are delicate." Many texts make distinctions between women who do physical work and those who do not; class as well as gender is a significant variable in medical history. The *Woman's Guide* proposes different treatments for rich and poor women in the unhappy predicament of carrying a dead fetus: "When she comes from the bath, if she is a rich woman, give her 1 ounce of the juice of the balsam tree in warm wine; if she is a poor woman, boil roots of costmary and artemisia in wine, add to it 2 ounces of bull's gall, and let her drink the mixture when she comes from the bath."[27] In this passage the distinction is explicitly financial and based on the cost of the ingredients, but elsewhere there is an additional assumption that women who work hard are stronger than upper-class women, whose habits are presumed to be sedentary.

Apart from pregnancy and birth, the aspect of female physiology that distinguished it most vividly from male experience was menstruation, that ubiquitous sign of women's fallen nature. Since relatively few medieval women lived past fifty, an adult woman—except when she was pregnant or nursing—was commonly a menstruating woman.[28] Male fear and anxiety about the meaning of

26. *Woman's Guide*, pp. 59, 65.
27. Ibid., pp. 71, 137.
28. In "The Age of Menarche in Medieval Europe" and "The Age of Menopause in Medieval Europe," *Human Biology* 45 (1973), 363–369, 605–612, Darrel W.

menstruation and the polluting qualities of menstrual blood are typical of many societies, including those of medieval Europe, where Christians adopted certain passages from the Hebrew Bible that identified menstruating women as unclean.[29] Along with painful childbirth and domestic subordination, menstruation was understood as women's punishment for Eve's sin—an evil, painful, and troublesome condition directly related to female sexuality and to fertility. The story of Jesus' acceptance and healing of the bleeding woman was very important in Christian teaching but could not by itself reverse prevailing fears and stereotypes.[30]

Popular culture and learned texts alike tended to repeat old stories. Menstrual blood had magical powers; it was believed to be an essential ingredient in witches' potions. In his widely circulated *Natural History*, the second-century Roman writer Pliny reported that the glance of a menstruating woman discolors a mirror and causes wine to sour, buds to drop, and dogs to go mad.[31] Men of science repeated these tales with "rational" explanations: Albert the Great said that the humors abounding in the eye of a menstruating woman discolor the air next to her eye, and the stain is carried along through the air to the air next to the mirror.[32] The shame and danger ascribed to menstruating women and their blood have a long history. Propounded and justified by men, internalized by women, they survive in the silence and embarrassment surrounding women's "curse."

Biologists, ancient and medieval, had much to say about the purpose and nature of menstrual blood. Aristotle believed that

Amundsen and Carol Jean Diers suggest thirteen or fourteen as the age of menarche—an improbably early age—and pay no attention to class, although class-based differences in diet must have been significant variables. Hildegard (*Causae et curae*, p. 106) believed that birth defects increased in mothers under twenty and over eighty (!)—a medieval version of the "biological clock."

29. Cf. Leviticus 15. The first half of the chapter is devoted to male pollution; the second half, to female—but the first half is traditionally ignored.

30. Gregory the Great referred to this story in his advice to Augustine of Canterbury, distinguishing between the strict menstrual taboos of the Hebrews and the accepting attitude exemplified by Jesus; see Bede, *History*, 1.27, p. 78.

31. *Pliny: Natural History*, vol. 8, trans. W.H.S. Jones (Cambridge, Mass.: Harvard University Press, 1963), bk. 28, chap. 23, pp. 55–63.

32. Albert, "Quaestiones" 5.11–14, p. 160.

the "menstruum," which became the matter of the embryo, was analogous to semen. Both substances originated in blood, but women lacked the heat necessary to "concoct" semen out of blood; hence the menstruum, being incomplete, was less perfect than semen. Women, after all, were defined by this incompleteness—a female was female "on account of inability of a sort, viz., it lacks the power to concoct semen out of the final state of the nourishment . . . because of the coldness of its nature. Thus, just as a lack of concoction produces in the bowels diarrhoea, so in the blood-vessels it produces discharges of blood of various sorts, and especially the menstrual discharge." Menstrual blood was not only analogous to semen; in a manner of speaking it *was* semen, "not indeed semen in a pure condition, but needing still to be acted upon." The menstruum was the matter on which the form acted: "Compare the coagulation of milk. Here, the milk is the body, and the fig-juice or the rennet contains the principle which causes it to set."[33]

Aristotle and his followers believed that when conception was not accomplished, the potential matter of the embryo became superfluous and was discharged in menstruation. Albert the Great thought that this accounted for the growth of the breasts at puberty, when "the superfluities of all the humors . . . gather in the womb and are sent toward the breasts." He observed that during pregnancy, when women do not menstruate, their breasts grow larger. Female animals do not menstruate because they are not troubled with superfluities (and perhaps, although he does not say so, because they do not inherit Eve's sin). They are less moist than women; they eat less, lead more active lives, and convert what food remains into horns and hoofs and hair. Women's experience differs in different climates: in hot countries, their moisture is consumed by the heat, and they menstruate less copiously and frequently than women in temperate places. Poor women and those who work hard may not menstruate at all, since they use up their food and produce no excess to be carried away. Albert added that "viragoes," by which he meant manlike women, do

33. Aristotle, *Generation of Animals* 1.20, pp. 103, 109.

not menstruate because their superfluities are consumed by their heat.[34] Apparently he assumed that most women in temperate places led inactive lives and had enough to eat. His tone suggests that female discomforts can be blamed on overeating and inactivity.

Gynecological texts exhibit a more positive attitude toward menstruation than do those of biological theorists. Soranus said that "those women have menstruated in right measure who after the excretion are healthy, breathe freely, are not perturbed, and whose strength is not impaired." He too believed that menstruation was nature's way of disposing of impurities, a kind of alternative to perspiration: "Men rid themselves of surplus matter through athletics whereas women accumulate it in considerable quantity because of the domestic and sedentary life they lead."[35] Concerned with the upper-class women of his own practice, he took no account of women who worked hard all the time, like the omnipresent female slaves of Roman society.

The perceived relationship of menstruation to activity recurs frequently in medical texts. For women whose superfluities were consumed by activity, such as "women engaged in singing contests," said Soranus, it was natural *not* to menstruate, as it was for children, pregnant women, and older women.[36] Trotula thought that women, lacking heat, could not "use up the moistures which daily collect in them" and that "Nature herself, on account of this deficiency of heat, has assigned for them a certain specific purgation namely the menses, commonly called flowers."[37] Medical writers appreciated the purgative function of menstruation; Albert believed it was one of the "accidents" that allowed women to outlive men.

Some texts display an enthusiasm for menstruation that goes beyond recognition of its purgative function, perhaps because bleeding itself, natural or induced, was thought to bring about a

---

34. Albert, "Quaestiones" 4.6, 9.5, pp. 150, 205. This last belief may account for the attention paid to Joan of Arc's failure to menstruate, a matter of great significance to her judges.

35. Soranus, *Gynecology*, pp. 18, 23.

36. Ibid., p. 19.

37. Trotula, *Diseases of Women*, p. 2.

healthy adjustment of the humors. The Hippocratic writings said that "when menstruation is suppressed, a flow of blood from the nose is a good sign."[38] Hildegard thought that the volume of blood in all human beings increased and diminished with the lunar cycle and that women suffered less when their periods synchronized with the moon. Most women ceased to menstruate after the fiftieth year, she observed, but those who continued were so healthy and strong that they might keep menstruating until they were seventy—at which time, and not before, they developed the wrinkles and sagging skin of old age.[39] Similarly, the author of the *Woman's Guide* saw delayed menopause as a sign of good health and prosperity: "Some women have purgations for a longer time because they are of a high complexion and are nourished with hot food and drink and live in much ease. And they have this purgation once every month unless they are pregnant or are of a dry complexion and work hard." Frequent menstruation was another mark of health and well-being: women "who are of a high complexion and are prosperous and live in comfort have this purgation more than once a month."[40]

Failure to menstruate was taken very seriously in medical writings. Trotula said: "Sometimes the periods fail because of excessive grief or anger or excitement or fear. If they have ceased for a long time there is a suspicion of serious future illness."[41] A variety of causes was suggested in the *Woman's Guide*: "the heat or the cold of the uterus or the heat or cold of the humors that are enclosed inside the uterus, or excessive dryness of their complexion, or being awake too much, thinking too much, being too angry or too sad, or eating too little."[42] These writers devoted much attention to the causes and cures of amenorrhea, which they regarded as a significant problem. An exception was Albert the Great (not primarily a medical writer, of course), who commented that he had known many chaste virgins, emaciated by fasting and wakefulness, who did not menstruate for long periods of time but

38. Hippocrates, "Aphorisms" 5.33, p. 167.
39. Hildegard, *Causae et curae*, p. 78.
40. *Woman's Guide*, pp. 59, 61.
41. Trotula, *Diseases of Women*, p. 3.
42. *Woman's Guide*, p. 61.

came to no harm. His remark ran counter to his own view of the beneficent effects of regular menstruation, as well as to those of other authorities on female physiology.[43]

Such widespread enthusiasm for the health-giving aspects of menstruation and the accompanying prescriptions for the maintenance of menstrual regularity raise questions in relation to the history of women and Christianity. Many medieval female saints were renowned for extreme asceticism. According to their biographers and to the legends that collected around them, these women ate very little or almost nothing, slept and rested as little as possible, and sought out psychic and physical suffering in penance for their own sins and the sins of the world and in imitation of the suffering of Christ and the sorrows of Mary.[44] Their habits and behavior were not simply bizarre or exceptional; they also ran directly counter to rules of health that were recognized in their own culture. Medieval medical writers reiterated that menstruation depended on good food, with as much meat as possible, on plenty of rest and sleep, and on the avoidance of excessive anger and sadness and worry. Holiness, as it was defined for women, prescribed ways of living that were understood specifically to suppress menstruation and, therefore, reproduction.

Recent research has uncovered relationships between nutritional status and reproductive health, between height-to-weight and muscle-to-fat ratios and menstruation in modern women. Rose Frisch demonstrated that the "onset and maintenance of

43. Albert the Great, *De animalibus libri XXVI, nach der Colner Urschrift,* vol. 1 (Munster, 1916), p. 682. Caroline Bynum noted this comment in "Fast, Feast, and Flesh: The Religious Significance of Food to Medieval Women," *Representations* 11 (1985), 11.

44. Among recent analyses of medieval holy women and their ascetic practices, see Rudolph M. Bell, *Holy Anorexia* (Chicago: University of Chicago Press, 1985); Caroline W. Bynum, *Holy Feast and Holy Fast: The Religious Significance of Food to Medieval Women* (Berkeley: University of California Press, 1987); Richard Kieckhefer, *Unquiet Souls: Fourteenth-Century Saints and Their Religious Milieu* (Chicago: University of Chicago Press, 1984). Bell attends to gender but ignores the amenorrhea of anorexia: Kieckhefer emphasizes mental and emotional suffering in the asceticism of the late medieval saints. On the historical development of anorexia nervosa down to modern times, see Joan Jacobs Brumberg, *Fasting Girls: The Emergence of Anorexia Nervosa as a Modern Disease* (Cambridge, Mass.: Harvard University Press, 1988).

regular menstrual function in the human female are each dependent on the maintenance of a minimum weight for height."[45]
Amenorrhea can be produced by malnutrition, by hard athletic
training, or by anxiety or depression or grief, and it is a significant
feature of the anorexia nervosa of modern times. Frisch says that
a "loss of body weight of 10 to 15 per cent below the normal
weight for height, which represents a loss of about one-third of
body fat, results in amenorrhea."[46] The height-to-weight and muscle-to-fat ratios required for medieval women were not necessarily
the same as those for modern women, but there is always a relationship between body fat and menstruation. In order to ovulate
and menstruate, to conceive and carry a pregnancy to a successful
delivery, women in any culture require a certain minimum of food
and rest.

The instructions of the *Woman's Guide* for the care of women
who fail to menstruate are typical of medieval medical advice on
this subject: "But if this illness is a result of anger or sorrow, cause
her to be cheerful, give her refreshing food and drink, and get her
used to bathing herself sometimes. And if it is the result of much
fasting or overwakefulness, see that she eats good food and drink
which will give her good blood, and get her to enjoy herself and
be happy and give up gloomy thoughts."[47] That would have been
hateful advice to Catherine of Siena, or to any medieval Christian
woman with aspirations to exceptional holiness. The saints were
actively engaged in seeking God. They experienced their physical
needs and appetites as obstacles to be overcome, and they expected—indeed, welcomed—physical and emotional suffering.
Their goals and concerns were spiritual, not physiological, but
their approaches to those goals incapacitated them for motherhood. Medieval medical writings reveal that the relationship between ways of living and reproductive health, and the physiological implications of female asceticism, were appreciated in the

45. Rose E. Frisch, "Food Intake, Fatness, and Reproductive Ability," in *Anorexia Nervosa*, ed. R. A. Vigersky (New York: Raven Press, 1977), p. 149.

46. Rose E. Frisch, "Population, Nutrition, and Fecundity," in *Malthus Past
and Present*, ed. J. Dupâquier, A. Fauve-Chamoux, and E. Grebenik (London:
Academic Press, 1983), pp. 396–397.

47. *Woman's Guide*, p. 71.

culture surrounding the saints and those who loved and supported them.

For most of the medieval centuries, saints were seldom mothers, or mothers saints (unless they were mothers *of* saints), for excellent physiological reasons. Hagiographers emphasized the saints' avoidance of sexual intercourse by persistence in virginity, or by continence if they were married, but paid little attention to other significant aspects of their rejection of sexuality and motherhood. Adolescent girls in modern times, obsessed with the thinness celebrated in their culture, become amenorrheic and infertile as a side effect of anorexia nervosa. In the Middle Ages, women obsessed with the holiness celebrated in their culture became amenorrheic and infertile as a side effect of what Rudolph Bell calls "holy anorexia"[48]—the starvation associated with extreme asceticism. In both instances, active sexuality and motherhood are circumvented in favor of other values, values reinforced by social and cultural norms but accompanied by physical suffering that may end in death. Medical texts, unlike the *vitae* and legends of the saints, reveal that medieval people were not blind to the reproductive implications of the ways in which women ate or did not eat, cared for or abused their bodies.

In terms of physiological theory, as opposed to medical practice, the most interesting and crucial questions for ancient and medieval thinkers were related to conception. How do human beings come into existence? What does each parent contribute to the generation of the child? What determines the sex of the offspring? Theories of conception supply hints about the values and family patterns of a society. For the Greeks, whose ideas were so influential in the medieval West, the male parent was the significant figure. Convinced that men were the stronger, dominant, and more perfect sex, Greek biologists developed theories compatible with their convictions.

Before the fourth century B.C.E., some thinkers held to the ancient "seed and soil" formulation voiced by Apollo in Aeschylus's *Eumenides*. Defending Orestes against a charge of matricide, he

48. See n. 44 above.

says: "It is not the mother who begets the one called her child; she but nourishes the seed sown in her. The begettor is the man who fecondates her; she a stranger safeguards a foreign sprout, when the gods do not injure it."[49] The seed-and-soil image persisted. It appeared even in medieval texts whose authors knew that a man did not plant a tiny, complete human being in a woman's womb, and it reappeared in an extreme form in the "preformationist" biological theories of the seventeenth and eighteenth centuries.

According to the Hippocratic treatise "The Seed," however, both parents produce sperm. The mother as well as the father "releases something from her body, sometimes into the womb, which then becomes moist, and sometimes externally as well, and the womb is open wider than normal." The male sperm generally is expelled after intercourse, but when conception occurs, "the moisture causes the womb's orifice to contract. Then both what is provided by the man and what is provided by the woman is mixed together." Both parents are actively involved in conception; the child is made from a mixture of male and female seed. Both mother and father produce both strong and weak sperm, and male children are produced by strong sperm from one of the parents: "The male being stronger than the female must of course originate from a stronger sperm." In each characteristic of the offspring, including its sex, the seed of either parent may prevail, so that girls can resemble their fathers and boys their mothers. Most birth defects result from an injury to the fetus, and "deformed" parents generally have healthy children: injury and disease, not the "components" of a child, produce deformities.[50]

A different picture emerges in Aristotelian biology. Here the mother contributes only the matter of the embryo, which is informed—given shape, soul, spirit, meaning—by the father's

---

49. Quoted in Anthony Preus, "Galen's Criticism of Aristotle's Conception Theory," *Journal of the History of Biology* 10 (1977), 67. Historians of science frequently cite this passage to illustrate the "progress" made by Aristotle: e.g., Joseph Needham, *A History of Embryology* (New York: Abelard-Schuman, 1959), chap. 1.

50. "The Seed" 4–6, in *Hippocratic Writings*, ed. G. E. R. Lloyd (London: Penguin Books, 1978), pp. 319–320.

sperm. Sperm, "concocted" out of blood by male heat, in turn "concocts" the menstruum into human life. The menstruum, of course, lacks the heat necessary to concoct itself, and this lack defines the female, who is "as it were a deformed male."[51] Aristotle's theory of conception was much more complex than the older seed-and-soil notion, but he retained its powerful imagery. Recommending physical exercise for pregnant women, he said: "As regards the mind, however, on the contrary it suits them to pass the time more indolently ... for children before birth are evidently affected by the mother just as growing plants are by the earth."[52]

Aristotle believed that when semen is as hot as it should be, and under the right conditions, it overcomes the weakness of the menstruum to produce a male child: "If [the male semen] gains the mastery, it brings [the material] over to itself; but if it gets mastered, it changes over either into its opposite or else into extinction. And the opposite of the male is the female, which is female in virtue of its inability to effect concoction, and of the coldness of its bloodlike nourishment." The conditions are correct if, for example, the parents are the right age and the wind in the right quarter: a south wind, with its humidity, creates too much moisture for successful concoction.[53]

Aristotle disagreed with those who thought that male-producing semen was stored in the right testicle and that males were conceived and carried on the right side of the uterus: such notions could be disproved by the dissection of pregnant mammals. He knew that many kinds of imperfections were responsible for the birth of females, even "hard, cold water in some cases causes barrenness, in others the birth of females." Perfect (normative) human beings were male, but the entire process was represented as a power struggle, and the conditions for achieving perfection were complex: "Any one who does not take after his parents is really in a way a monstrosity, since in these cases Nature has in

51. Aristotle, *Generation of Animals* 2.3, p. 175. This notorious phrase is usually given in Latin as *mas occasionatus*. A. L. Peck, the translator, suggests (p. 174 n.10) that it might be rendered in English as "imperfectly developed," "malformed," "mutilated," or "congenitally disabled."
52. Aristotle, *Politics* 7.14, p. 623.
53. Aristotle, *Generation of Animals* 4.1–2, pp. 395, 397.

a way strayed from the generic type. The first beginning of this deviation is when a female is formed instead of a male, though this indeed is a necessity required by Nature, since the race of creatures which are separated into male and female has got to be kept in being."[54]

Galen attempted to synthesize Aristotelian biology with Hippocratic and earlier theories. He appreciated the active role of both parents, but he never questioned male superiority or female weakness and deformity, and he fell into the common assumption that there must be a purpose for a "mutilation" involving half the human race. Nonetheless, Galen quoted the Hippocratic treatise "On the Nature of the Child" to argue that women do produce seed and that the menstrual fluid is not the matter of the embryo. He knew that conception required the mixing of two seeds, and he insisted—opposing Aristotle—that the male seed contributed its own matter to the embryo, and that the female seed provided not only matter, but "a source of movement" as well. Unlike the earlier Hippocratic writers or Aristotle, Galen was aware of the discovery of the ovaries by Herophilus in about 300 B.C.E., although like other ancient writers, he saw ovaries from the male perspective as "female testicles." Galen was extremely influential in the earlier Middle Ages; Trotula quoted him more than any other authority.[55]

Aristotle provided the biological foundation for the identification of matter with the female and of form (or energy, or spirit) with the male, and that association remained powerful and consistent in the history of Christian thought. There were competing biologies, however, and in the early Middle Ages the notion of "two seeds" generally prevailed over strict Aristotelian theories of conception.

Hildegard of Bingen, who was always original, constructed a theory of conception out of her reading of Genesis, the Hippocratic-Galenic tradition, and a visionary theological imagination. Her description of the process of conception was unique in its female

54. Ibid., p. 401
55. For discussion of Galen's views on conception, see Lloyd, *Science, Folklore and Ideology*, pp. 109–111; Preus, "Galen's Criticism"; and Michael Boylan, "The

perspective and emphasis on female activity. Hildegard believed that the woman's heat, aroused by sexual passion, attracts and holds the male seed, which mixes with her own seed and blood. When conception occurs, the woman's members contract to hold the seed "as if in a strong man's fist." The mother's blood mixes with the semen and makes it flesh, surrounding it with a little nest or cocoon. It grows, held and warmed by the mother, until it becomes human on receiving from God the breath of life. Meanwhile, in the passion of intercourse, the woman's seed and sweat have entered into the man, and the two become one flesh in him as they were in Adam, and as they are in the child conceived.[56] Men and women are truly partners in the work of reproduction. Women are weaker than men, properly subordinate in a social context, but their weakness and lightness are functions of woman's creation out of Adam's flesh and the work of carrying and giving birth to children; there is no association of male with spirit and female with flesh. In Hildegard's writings, men and women are mingled in passion, and flesh and spirit are not divided. Her biological views were quite compatible with her moral and theological convictions.

With the reception of Aristotle's writings in the twelfth and thirteenth centuries and the rise of universities and scholastic philosophy, learned men produced a Christian reinterpretation of Aristotelian biology. For Albert the Great, man's part was to provide the seed; woman's, to condense and "ferment" the seed and to keep the fetus in her womb.[57] Thomas Aquinas, addressing the question "whether woman ought to have been produced in the original production," offered theological arguments for women's existence. He repeated Aristotle: barring accidents, "the active

---

Galenic and Hippocratic Challenge to Aristotle's Conception Theory," *Journal of the History of Biology* 17 (1984), 83–112.

56. Hildegard, *Causae et curae*, pp. 104, 67–68. See Joan Cadden, "It Takes All Kinds: Sexuality and Gender Differences in Hildegarde of Bingen's 'Book of Compound Medicine,' " *Traditio* 40 (1984), 149–174. Cadden notes that for Hildegard, "the gender of the child appears to depend on the strength of the man's semen, while the character of the child depends upon the matrimonial devotion of both parents" (p. 155).

57. Albert, "Quaestiones" 10.1, p. 214.

power in the seed of the male tends to produce something like itself, perfect in masculinity. . . . But with reference to nature in the species as a whole, the female is not something *manqué*, but is according to the tendency of nature, and is directed to the work of procreation . . . [which] derives from God, who is the general author of Nature."[58]

Giles of Rome, a thirteenth-century scholastic and a member of the Order of Augustinian Hermits, produced an entire treatise on conception and embryology, or "the formation of the human body in the uterus."[59] Believing with Aristotle that the active male seed combined with the passive material of the menstruum to form a child, Giles was expressly concerned to oppose the Galenic theory of conception. The female seed, by which he meant the fluid emitted by a woman during orgasm, had no generative role, for women can and do conceive without orgasm. This "seed," analogous to male seminal fluid, existed only to facilitate generation by cooling the male seed and the womb and to increase the pleasure of intercourse, which was desirable, since it encouraged people to make love and have children.

Giles was interested in the growth and development of the fetus, particularly in the period of "formation" when it was "set," its parts organized. Following Aristotle, he thought that a male was formed (or "ensouled") in forty days after conception, a female in ninety days. Ensoulment came earlier for males because they were "of more compact and drier matter," whereas a female "consists of a slippery and fluid *materia* which can only retain the impress of the form in the womb when it is in the presence of the agent, the male semen." Like Albert, Giles believed that the cold and moist (therefore slippery) female nature made women unstable and untrustworthy. Females were formed more slowly in the uterus but grew and matured quickly after they were born, for nature was more deliberate about the development of males, who were supposed to reach perfection. After having children, how-

58. Aquinas, *Summa theologiae* 1a.92.1, p. 37.
59. See M. Anthony Hewson, *Giles of Rome and the Medieval Theory of Conception* (London: Athlone Press, 1975), esp. chap. 3.

ever, women aged quickly, rapidly losing their moisture, especially "those who have had intercourse frequently."[60] At any age, a female was at a moral and physiological disadvantage.

All these writers, even celibate men, must have been aware that pregnancy and childbirth were painful, difficult, and dangerous and that a great many women and infants died. By whatever means an infant was conceived and formed, its departure from the womb was fraught with pain and terror. Philosophers and biological theorists tended to ignore pregnancy and birth; their concern was with God and Man and Nature, not with women's problems. The medical writers, Soranus in particular, did pay attention to obstetrics, and medieval herbals and medical texts dealt with pregnancy and birth as well as menstrual difficulties. Soranus wrote about what should be done to avoid miscarriage, especially during the first vulnerable days and weeks of a pregnancy. He discussed diet, exercise, sex, bathing, and possible injuries to the fetus, and he urged women to follow a healthy regimen for the sake of their unborn children: "Even if a woman transgresses some or all of the rules mentioned and yet miscarriage of the fetus does not take place, let no one therefore assume that the fetus has not been injured at all. For it has been harmed: it is weakened, becomes retarded in growth, less well nourished, and, in general, more easily injured and susceptible to harmful agents; it becomes misshapen and of an ignoble soul."[61] He followed up the discussion of the preservation of pregnancy with comments about contraception, which he thought vastly preferable to abortion.

Soranus gave elaborate instructions on the preparations for a birth, including a description of the birthing stool, which provided the most satisfactory position for delivery. However, he thought

60. Ibid., p. 170. Hewson defends Giles against the charge of sexism, saying that his idea (and Aristotle's) of woman as imperfect man is "opposite to that often accepted today . . . at the present time the woman is often regarded as the general human type, or at least as a neutral form, of which the man is a specialized example." He cites no instance of such a belief but argues that Giles was, for his own time, "scientific": that is, "interested in seeking numerical proportions" (pp. 176–177).
61. Soranus, *Gynecology*, p. 48.

that a woman who was exhausted and frightened might be delivered "lying down since this way is less painful and causes less
fear."[62] He recommended that three helpers attend the birth to
calm and reasure the mother, who could be held on the lap of one
of them. These women were not midwives but attendants; the
midwife had to concentrate on the safe delivery of the baby, although she too was expected to concern herself with the patient's
emotional state. Soranus suggested that "the face of the *gravida*
should be visible to the midwife who shall allay her anxiety,
assuring her that there is nothing to fear and that delivery will be
easy." He was aware of the physical effects of fear and embarrassment: "The midwife should beware of fixing her gaze steadfastly
on the genitals of the laboring woman, lest being ashamed, her
body become contracted."[63] Before the natural childbirth movement of the twentieth century, few doctors were so conscious of
the physiological implications of the mother's emotions.

Trotula's instructions for the care of pregnant women were
sparse but included some attention to labor and delivery. Trotula
blamed obstetrical difficulties on the woman's pelvic structure,
or on her weakness or that of the fetus, and made several suggestions for easing a hard delivery: "Above all things when there is
difficulty in child-birth one must have recourse in God. Descend-
ing then to lower means, it is helpful to the woman in difficult
labor to be bathed in water in which has been cooked mallow,
chick peas, flaxseed, and barley. Let her sides, abdomen, hips, and
flanks be rubbed with oil of roses or oil of violets. . . . Let sneezing
be provoked. . . . Let the woman be led with slow pace through
the house." Like Soranus, Trotula was concerned that the new
mother not be troubled by the stares of onlookers "because women
are wont to be bashful in childbearing and after the birth."[64]

Hildegard's comments reflect her woman-centered perspective
and her sense of the enormous energy of creation. Birth, for Hildegard, was an explosive bursting-out of the infant (a rational being

---

62. Ibid., p. 73. This runs contrary to the views of the modern women's health
movement; the "lithotomy position" (lying down) is believed to be more difficult
for the mother but more convenient for the doctor.

63. Ibid., pp. 74–75.

64. Trotula, *Diseases of Women* 17, p. 23.

with a soul) together with its "cocoon," expelled by the same eternal forces that drew Eve from Adam's side. The mother's body is turned inside out, but it is strong enough to withstand these forces and return to itself when the child is born.[65] Of all the writings on labor and delivery, Hildegard's most powerfully and accurately convey a sense of the power of birth and the necessary, active participation of mother and child.

Learned writings of the later Middle Ages, including the encyclopedias, repeated Hippocratic and Galenic definitions and suggestions concerning pregnancy and birth. Bartholomew had little to say about either one, although he repeated the Hippocratic notion that a woman is healthier, of a better complexion, and happier if she is pregnant with a male child. That old idea is absent from the Woman's Guide, where the sex of the fetus is not the issue. Rather, pregnancy itself makes a woman happy and comfortable, and to lose any child is painful and sad: "Ache of the uterus is sometimes due to a stillborn child being born before his time. Because the mother has great contentment and happiness from the child inside her, when she loses it she naturally mourns and grieves just as a cow does when she has lost her calf, and that distress causes the ache of the uterus.[66] Bartholomew did express awareness of the misery and danger of childbirth, especially for younger women, but consoled himself and his readers with the familiar though unfounded notion that "the more woe and sorrow a woman had in labor with a child, the more she loves that child when he is born."[67]

The Woman's Guide distinguishes between natural and unnatural births: in the former,

> the child comes out in twenty pangs or within those twenty, and the child comes the way it should: first the head, and afterward the neck, and with the arms, shoulders, and other members properly as it should.

65. Hildegard, Causae et curae, p. 66.
66. Woman's Guide, p. 119.
67. Bartholomaeus, Properties of Things 6.7, p. 303. The little available evidence on this point indicates that the opposite is true: mother and infant get off to a better start after an easy labor.

Sixteen different presentations are described, with illustrative drawings and directions to the midwife for turning the infant in the uterus without harming mother or child. The drawings in Sloane 2463, which probably were derived indirectly from Soranus, accompany substantial information about the midwife's work. The third "unnatural mode," for example,

> is if the child's head is so bulky and large that he cannot emerge: the midwife should then push him back and anoint the orifice . . . with fresh May butter or with common oil, and then the midwife's hand, oiled first and then put in and the orifice enlarged, brings the child forth by the head.

The attendants are warned to be sure to deliver the afterbirth, known as "secundine,"

> a little skin that goes about the child while he is in his mother's womb, just as there is an inner skin that goes around the nut kernel. . . . [Sometimes] the secundine remains behind inside her because of the great weakness of her womb; and that may be the result of much fasting, great anger, wrath, beating, or some prolonged flux of the womb.

The primary patient was the mother; although the midwife's concern was with both, the child was second:

> Also, the root of iris put into the womb or fumigated underneath makes the woman lose her child, for iris roots are hot and dry and have the virtue of opening, heating, consuming, and wasting. For when the woman is feeble and the child cannot come out, then it is better that the child be killed than the mother of the child also die.[68]

Midwifery was recognized to require skill, training, and dedication. Soranus opened his gynecological text with the question "What persons are fit to be midwives?" He concluded that a successful midwife had to be smart, literate, hard-working, strong, and, "according to some people, endowed with long slim fingers

---

68. *Woman's Guide*, pp. 123, 125, 145, 97. See pp. 39–45 for Rowland's discussion of the birth drawings.

and short nails." She had to follow directions, be trustworthy in keeping household secrets, and use her intelligence and powers of observation to "prescribe hygienic regulations for her patients." She need not be a mother herself, but she must be sober, free of superstition, and "not greedy for money, lest she give an abortive wickedly for payment."[69] Even in a normal delivery, her role was active. At the right moment, the midwife "must insert the fingers gently at the time of dilatation and pull the fetus forward, giving way when the uterus draws itself together, but pulling lightly when it dilates. . . . Finally the midwife herself should receive the infant, having first covered her hands with pieces of cloth . . . so that it may neither slip off nor be squeezed, but rest softly."[70]

Trotula's instructions were briefer and simpler: the focus was less on normal delivery than on the consequences of difficult births, and the aim was to prevent such problems: "If difficulty in childbirth should result from tightness of the mouth of the womb, the cure of this is more difficult than anything else, therefore we subjoin this advice: let the woman take care the last three months in her diet that she so use light and digestible foods that through them the limbs may be opened." Unlike Soranus, Trotula wrote as a woman addressing other women—mothers and midwives. Citing Galen, she said that "'women who have narrow vulvas and tight wombs ought not to have husbands lest they die if they conceive.' But since they cannot all abstain they need our help." Instructions for the midwife blend into instructions for the baby's nurse, who had to cut and tie the umbilical cord, anoint and bathe and swaddle the infant, and keep it quiet and calm to recover from the delivery.[71]

Competent midwifery was essential to women's health and happiness. The *Woman's Guide* claimed that "different women experience great distress in giving birth through lack of a good midwife, and that distress is kept secret, and it requires assistance." Debilitating and embarrassing birth injuries, such as tears in the perineum, might be prevented or repaired, allowing women

69. Soranus, *Gynecology*, p. 5–7. The implication, of course, is that an "abortive" might be given for cause but not for money.
70. Ibid., p. 76.
71. Trotula, *Diseases of Women* 17, pp. 24–25; 11, p. 19.

to live longer and more comfortable lives. Prolapse of the uterus, which was believed to be incurable in older women, could be corrected in some young women by fumigation and anointing. The author's stated intention was to help women make the best of their circumstances—for example: "There are also other women whose womb often will come down and then sometimes go up for some reason, and such women cannot endure a man's penis because of the size of it, and sometimes they are forced to endure it whether they would or not. We give the previously mentioned medicine of the linen rag with tar to such women."[72] Women's lives were far from perfect; the midwife and her work helped to make them bearable.

Little documentation of the work of medieval midwives exists; there is much more evidence from the sixteenth and seventeenth centuries, when male doctors and clergy began to challenge their status, their effectiveness, and their near-monopoly of obstetrics. Maternal and infant mortality were consistently high throughout the Middle Ages and did not decline when men began to take over much of the responsibility for caring for mothers and delivering babies. The scanty information available about medieval midwives does not provide a basis for comprehensive assessment of their work, but it does reveal that they were presented in some texts as competent and essential persons. Before doctors began to compete with them and witch-hunters to denounce them, midwives were not associated with filth, evil, or incompetence. For centuries, women—ordinary relatives and neighbors as well as midwives—provided ante- and postnatal care, supervised and assisted in deliveries, and dealt with primary care of the newborn. Midwives supplied advice, medication, and therapy for women who wanted to conceive a child or to prevent conception, to fight off miscarriage or to abort an unwanted fetus. Just as war was men's business, pregnancy and birth were the responsbility of women—and equally dangerous.

Before modern times, every child depended for survival on the availability of some woman's milk—if not its own mother's, then

72. *Woman's Guide*, pp. 165, 167.

another woman's. Animal milk was unsafe and was believed to be unsuitable; the legend of Romulus and Remus was memorable in part because the children survived. Artificial feeding existed in rudimentary form; there were "nursing-horns" made of cows' horns, but they were only for emergencies. Human milk was essential to life, and women's breasts were perceived not as erotic playthings but as major organs of the reproductive system. In Hippocratic (and later) writings, the breasts indicated the health of a pregnant woman and a fetus: "Should the breasts of a woman with child suddenly become thin, she miscarries."[73] Bartholomew cited Hippocrates and Galen to support his belief that if the right breast of a woman carrying boy-girl twins diminished in size, the boy would be born prematurely.[74] (As usual, right and left were associated with superior/inferior, strong/weak, and male/female.) Aristotle pointed out that the *mammae* of quadrupeds were positioned in such a way as not to interfere with their mobility, but developed on the chest in human beings because "the parts around the heart need some covering."[75] Albert the Great took this a step further when he said that human beings, the noblest of animals, received their nourishment from the area of the heart and not from a place near the shameful organs of women.[76] Bartholomew commented on the admirable design of the breast, with its nipple "round . . . sinewy . . . [and] suited to the teeth of children." The breast was something more than a symbol of the mother; Bartholomew actually defined a mother as one who "puts forth her breast to feed the child."[77]

In ancient and medieval times, milk and blood were understood to be essentially the same substance: milk was a special form of blood, "concocted" for the nourishment of the young. Aristotle thought that when a child was born, the "residue" that was no longer needed to feed it in the womb was "bound to collect in the empty spaces" of the breasts. Women did not normally conceive

73. Hippocrates, "Aphorisms" 5.37, p. 167.

74. Bartholomaeus, *Properties of Things* 5.34, p. 235.

75. Aristotle, *Parts of Animals* 4.10, trans. A. L. Peck (Cambridge, Mass.: Harvard University Press, 1945), p. 377.

76. Albert, "Quaestiones" 2.13–16, p. 115.

77. Bartholomaeus, *Properties of Things* 5.34, pp. 235, 302.

or menstruate while they were nursing, because menstrual blood, fetal nourishment, and milk were different aspects of one vital substance: "If they do conceive, the milk dries up, because the nature of the milk is the same as that of the menstrual fluid, and Nature cannot produce a plentiful enough supply to provide both; so that if the secretion takes place in one direction it must fail in the other, unless some violence is done contrary to what is normal."[78]

Bartholomew explained that "nature" sent menstrual blood to the heart, and then to the breasts, by means of a "hollow vein."[79] Obviously, then, a child was better fed by its own mother's milk— the identical substance which sustained it in the womb—than by the milk of a wet nurse. There were various formulations, but all agreed that menstruation, pregnancy, and lactation represented different stages of one process and that a woman could or should not occupy more than one stage at a time. Furthermore, although Hildegard made the accurate observation that an infant's suckling increases the milk supply, it was generally assumed that a woman could not successfully nurse more than one child at a time— a reasonable assumption, given the nutritional status of most women.[80] This had serious implications: it meant that a wet nurse had to wean her own child, hand it over to someone else, or wait for it to die before she took on a client.

The association, based on appearance, between milk and semen was less common than that of milk and blood, but it lurked in the background of the general distaste for the notion of a nursing woman as sexually active. Sanctions against sexual intercourse for nursing women, including paid nurses, were couched in terms of moral disapproval but related to realistic fears about the milk supply and to the conviction that the same "blood" provided for fetus and for baby. Milk was a vital substance; its power and virtue

---

78. Aristotle, *Generation of Animals* 4.8, p. 473, 475.

79. Bartholomaeus, *Properties of Things* 5.34, p. 234.

80. Hildegard, *Causae et curae*, p. 111. See "Blood Parents and Milk Parents" in Christine Klapisch-Zuber, *Woman, Family, and Ritual in Renaissance Italy* (Chicago: University of Chicago Press, 1985), p. 137. Soranus (*Gynecology*, p. 94) assumed that a woman could nurse twins—but his patients were relatively prosperous and therefore perhaps well nourished.

were displayed in paintings of the nursing Madonna and in stories about miracles wrought by her milk. Legends of the saints also reported milk-related wonders; when a martyr was beheaded, for example, her neck might spurt milk instead of blood.[81] Hagiographers wrote of holy infants who refused to suckle after their mothers or nurses had sex.[82]

The absolute necessity of milk for survival, and its assumed identification with other bodily fluids, formed the basis for a powerful system of sanctions and taboos. Moralists and preachers, harping on a woman's obligation to nurse her own child, insisted that the qualities of mother or nurse were transmitted through milk, just as they had been conveyed to the fetus in its mother's blood. Bernardino of Siena warned: "The child acquires certain of the customs of the one who suckles him. If the one who cares for him has evil customs or is of base condition, he will receive the impress of those customs because of having sucked her polluted blood."[83] The identification of blood and milk and the association of blood with social class are mingled in his threats and warnings.

Regardless of doctors and preachers, parents did hire wet nurses for their children. There was general agreement that a nurse must be carefully chosen, and her desirable characteristics changed little over the centuries. Soranus thought the ideal nurse was between twenty and forty, had more than one child, was healthy, "self-controlled, sympathetic and not ill-tempered, a Greek, and tidy." He disapproved of sexual activity for her because "coitus cools the affection toward [the] nursling by the diversion of sexual

81. E.g., in Jacobus de Voragine's story of St. Katherine of Alexandria, "when her head was cut off, milk gushed forth from her body instead of blood"; see *The Golden Legend of Jacobus de Voragine*, ed. Granger Ryan and Helmut Ripperger (New York: Arno Press, 1969), p. 714 (hereafter, *Golden Legend*).

82. Katarina of Sweden is the best-known example: see Chapter 5, n. 84, below. Instances of infants refusing the breast are discussed by Donald Weinstein and Rudolph M. Bell in *Saints and Society* (Chicago: University of Chicago Press, 1982), pp. 24–25.

83. Quoted in James Bruce Ross, "The Middle-Class Child in Urban Italy," in *The History of Childhood*, ed. Lloyd De Mause (New York: Harper & Row, 1974), p. 186. Klapisch-Zuber ("Blood Parents," p. 162) argues that middle-class men in fifteenth-century Tuscany believed—against the teaching of medical and clerical authorities—that their "blood" predominated in their children, prevailing over the milk of mother or nurse.

pleasure and moreover spoils and diminishes the milk or sup-
presses it entirely."[84]

Soranus offered a complete regimen for the nurse, who had to
exercise in order to keep her milk of the proper consistency. She
could play with a ball to exercise her upper body; "for those who
are too poor, however, rowing or drawing up water in a vessel,
winnowing and grinding grain, preparing bread, making beds and
whatever is done with a certain bending of the body" would suf-
fice. Her food must be nourishing and digestible and her diet
accommodated to the needs of a growing child. In the wealthy and
well-run households attended by Soranus, considerable attention
was focused on children's needs, emotional as well as physical.
He would have liked each child to have several nurses, for "it is
precarious for the nursling to become accustomed to one nurse
who might become ill or die, and then, because of the change of
milk, the child sometimes suffers from the strange milk." When
a baby cried, the nurse had to make sure it was not hungry or wet
and then "hold it in her arms, and soothe its wailing by patting,
babbling, and making gentle sounds, without, however, in addition frightening or disquieting it by loud noises or other threats.
For fright arising from such things becomes the cause of afflic-
tions, sometimes of the body, sometimes of the soul."[85]

Trotula, whose requirements were somewhat less stringent,
expected the nurse to be young, clean, healthy, and moderately
fat. Bartholomew, who defined the mother as the one who put
forth her breast, apparently believed that whoever put forth her
breast *became* the mother: "The nurse is instead of the mother
. . . glad if the child is glad and sorry if the child is sorry, and takes
him up if he falls, and gives him suck if he cries, and kisses him
if he is quiet."[86] The woman who performed the vital function of
supplying a child with milk, and hence with life, was its "mother";
her emotions were expected to flow in the direction of her milk.

No systematic physiology of motherhood emerges from this
sketch of prevailing themes in ancient and medieval texts dealing

84. Soranus, *Gynecology*, pp. 91–92.
85. Ibid., pp. 94, 98, 113.
86. Bartholomaeus, *Properties of Things* 6.9, p. 304.

with women's bodies and with reproduction. The texts come from widely separated centuries and parts of the world and are dissimilar in design, authorship, and intended audience. The Hippocratic writings are brief medical treatises; Soranus's *Gynecology* is a handbook by a working physician that survived to influence gynecological writings throughout the Middle Ages. Aristotle, of course, was not only "the Philosopher" but the most significant scientific thinker for the West until early modern times; his influence on Christian thought can be seen most clearly in the integrative work of the thirteenth-century scholastics. The medical writings of the Middle Ages are entirely different in spirit, content, and intention from those of the philosophers. Whether or not Trotula was a professor, her treatises were models for later texts of a practical bent—for example, Sloane 2463, the *Woman's Guide*. Hildegard's writings cannot be grouped with any of these; her physiological ideas were unique, and her work is included for its originality and inherent interest.

The ancient writings are significant here because they were widely copied, quoted, and imitated, and each of the medieval writings exemplifies some aspect of what was thought and written (and practiced, we assume) during the Middle Ages. Given the enormous differences in intention and provenance, these works are startling for the similarity and persistence of certain ideas. Familiar notions and associations appear again and again, including the identification of male and female with strong and weak, right and left, hot and cold, dry and wet, good and bad. Attitudes toward menstruation vary from disgust to appreciation, but almost all sources, even those most confused about the nature and function of the "menstruum," consider it essential to women's health and to female identity. In all sources, milk is associated with blood, and the absolute necessity of lactation and breastfeeding to human life is accepted without question.

The sources exemplify the organization of scientific discussions in relation to the perspectives and starting points of the discussants. Arguments over "one seed or two seed" theories of conception were conducted for the most part by learned, celibate men who ascribed all power and activity to the male, reducing women's contribution to lifeless matter and questioning the very necessity of women's existence. Such theorists, even when they wrote about mothers and children, were interested primarily in fathers and sons. But writers who knew, lived, or worked with women (or *were* women) were inclined to believe that both parents contributed something vital to the generation of their children.

Texts that deal with the work of midwives and nurses present a "high" view of those professions. Large demands were placed on those who cared for pregnant women and delivered and cared for babies, and the importance of their work was recognized to a degree not apparent in traditional historical and theological sources. To read denunciations of midwives by witch-hunters and male doctors, and of wet nurses by popes and preachers, is to listen only to men who were not at all involved with women and children. The medical writings balance the didactic and homiletic literature, providing a different and presumably more realistic view of the medieval midwife and nurse.

In histories of medieval women and Christianity we depend very much on the *Lives* and legends of saints; stories about ordinary women are much more rare. The saints were exceptional by definition, and to make sense of their extraordinary experience— especially of the heroic asceticism that so impressed their contemporaries—we make informed guesses about the implications of being "exceptional." The medical literature helps us to see what was believed and taught about the relationship of diet and rest and peace of mind to health, particularly reproductive health. It is apparent at least that "health" and "holiness," as these states were defined in relation to women, were markedly incompatible and that motherhood demanded a regimen antipathetic to the regimen of the saint.

CHAPTER THREE

Spiritual Motherhood: Extraordinary Women in the Early Middle Ages

In late antiquity and the early Middle Ages, Christians added new shades of meaning to the notion of "mother" and to inherited ideas about motherhood. This does not imply that there were fundamental alterations in traditional medical definitions or physiological assumptions, which changed very little between the fourth and the tenth centuries. The legacy of Greek biological science was preserved in the learned tradition, although attenuated in the West by the general loss of educational and intellectual resources and confined increasingly to a narrowing group of literate people. By the sixth century, almost the only people in western Europe who could read were monks and nuns, so that monastic ideologies assumed an ever larger place in Christian consciousness. Within monastic institutions and through the writing and preaching of those associated with them, a new ideology of "spiritual" motherhood was constructed alongside ancient ideas about what mothers were. Crucial distinctions between physical and spiritual maternity were introduced, with far-reaching implications for women and children distant from centers of monastic learning and devotion.

By the end of the fourth century, Christianity was the established religion of the Roman world. No more Christian martyrs were persecuted in the western empire, and existing legal, administrative, and other institutions adapted gradually to the new faith and order. Christian emperors, challenged and advised by Christian bishops, ruled in Rome and Constantinople. The Church began to assume the majestic proportions that it would maintain for more than a millennium as the predominant institution of western Europe. As the higher clergy moved into positions of social, political, and educational as well as religious leadership, they acquired new duties and assumed roles much more extensive than those of the early shepherds of the flock. Later, with the decline of the empire and its institutions, the enormous prestige of Church and clergy compensated for severe practical limitations on ecclesiastical authority and effective means of control.

As a persecuted sect was transformed into a dominant and later an established church, conversion became a mass movement. Missionaries were free to make converts by teaching and preaching; Christian allegiance became helpful or even essential to success in many kinds of endeavor. Inevitably, some of the new Christians appeared shallow or lukewarm to their co-religionists. Membership in a state church bears little resemblance to identification with a persecuted minority, and significant losses accompanied the overall triumph of Christianity—chief among them a steady erosion of the intimacy and intensity of the earlier "family" of the beleaguered followers of Jesus. The rough equality of hard times, the comradeship across class and gender lines experienced by (for example) Perpetua and Felicitas, vanished along with persecution. Christians were quickly redivided into classes and degrees based on sex and status; the zeal once shared by all, with their willingness to die for the faith, became the property of a new elite. In the fourth and fifth centuries some heroic men and women continued to flee to the "desert"—now suggesting physical hardship and isolation rather than a specific place—while significant numbers entered monastic institutions, where they struggled to live perfect lives in community. Like their models and predecessors, the martyrs and the desert saints, these extraordinary Christians suffered for the faith and renounced "this world," including the comforts, obligations, and affections of traditional domesticity.

Monks and nuns built new families to replace the families left behind. They carried into the cloister images and meanings attached to such designations as "sister," "brother," "mother," and "father" and returned new definitions and relationships to the wider community. The language and imagery of an elite carry weight far beyond its numbers, particularly when it holds a near-monopoly of the education and written records of a society. The renunciation of sexual activity and conventional family ties was essential to monastic ideology and practice, and the writers and thinkers and preachers who shaped Christian teaching in these centuries were, for the most part, monks. Their special perspectives played a critical part in forming Christian attitudes toward sexuality and domesticity, and because their words were written down, preserved, and taken seriously, they are critical still.

Many people, not only monks and nuns but those who supported them and depended on their prayers and services, believed that monasticism offered the "best" life for a Christian. It aimed at perfection, which was thought to be within the grasp of a celibate monk or nun but out of the reach of persons distracted from devotion to God by the things of this world, including families. St. Jerome, for one, believed that too much affection for one's children weakened one's love of God.[1] In its everyday physical and social meanings, parenthood was excluded from the monastic world; candidates for the religious life were expected to eschew it if possible or, if they were already parents, to find a new focus for their interests, energies, resources, and affections. (This was true to an extent for both sexes but had different implications for men and women; I am concerned here with its significance for women and for motherhood.)

In the ancient world, maternity was women's sole or primary claim to status and significance. There were exceptional situations, but in general—and in societies as diverse as those of the Jews and the Romans—women without children were pitied, ignored, or despised. The earliest Christians upset these traditional values so that motherhood was neither an avenue nor an obstacle to honor and sanctity. In time, as Christian communities became increasingly hierarchical and their leadership exclusively male,

---

1. Jerome, letter 39 to Paula on the death of Blesilla, in *Sancti Eusebii Hieronymi Epistulae*, ed. Isidore Hilberg (Leipzig: G. Freytag, 1910), 1:293–308; CSEL, vol. 54.

women who aspired to holiness were restricted to forms of religious life in which physical motherhood was actually incompatible with devotion to God. Within the convents, however, and in influential circles outside, the world "mother" began to acquire new kinds of significance. If physical maternity was devalued, spiritual maternity soon took its place, so that "motherhood," transformed, retained a high status in medieval Christian ideology.

St. Jerome, writing near the turn of the fifth century, was an articulate and extreme representative of monastic views of family, sexuality, and the Christian life. He easily dismissed traditional filial piety when it got in the way of "higher" goals. His letters to friends and disciples are filled with concrete warnings about family burdens that interfere with the ascetic vocation. To a young man—not married but carrying heavy domestic responsibilities— Jerome wrote:

> I know full well the fetters which you will say impede you. . . . Your widowed sister clings to you to-day with loving arms. . . . Your old nurse and her husband, who have the next claim to your affection after your own father, exclaim, "Wait for a few months till we die and then give us burial."[2]

The duty to bury one's parents properly was one of the most serious and sacred obligations of a Roman son, but Jesus called Christians to new responsibilities when he said, "Follow me, and leave the dead to bury their own dead" (Matt. 8:22). Like the martyr Perpetua, Jerome insisted on the superior claim of the new family:

> But, you will say, the Scripture bids us to obey our parents. Nay, whosoever loves his parents more than Christ loses his own soul. The enemy takes up his sword to slay me: shall I think of my mother's tears? . . . The battering-ram of affection which shakes faith

2. *St. Jerome: Select Letters*, trans. F. A. Wright (Cambridge, Mass.: Harvard University Press, 1980), letter 14, p. 33. Here Jerome takes for granted the quasi-parental status of a nurse.

must be beaten back by the wall of the Gospel: "My mother and my brethren are these, whosoever do the will of my father which is in heaven."[3]

Family affection is the devil's weapon, a battering-ram wielded by the powers of darkness; the mother's tears, summoning conventional sentiment, only weaken the resolve of a son of the true Father. Images of pathetic, clinging family members, which could be powerfully moving in another context, signify danger and treachery here; the passage from the Gospel is skillfully employed to shape the meaning of this collage of touching scenes.

The advice quoted above was written to a young man, but many of Jerome's fiercest admonitions were intended to persuade women of the advantages of virginity and celibacy over marriage and motherhood. He wanted young women to remain unmarried and widows to avoid remarriage, and he vehemently stated his indifference and contempt for the traditional duties and pleasures of a Roman matron—to carry forward her husband's "line" and gratify her father in his old age. He wrote to Furia, a widow: "Are you afraid that the line of Camillus will cease to exist and that your father will not have a brat of yours to crawl upon his breast and soil his neck with nastiness?"[4] To Furia, Jerome trivialized the rewards of motherhood; this argument lacks the weight and force of the "battering-ram" that threatened the vocation of the young monk.

When Jerome wrote to Paula, his favorite Roman matron, however, he expressed the most profound admiration and respect for her choices. When she left Rome for Bethlehem, Paula chose a new life in Christ over "this world," including the children who remained in it. Jerome drew a poignant picture of Toxotius, the youngest, standing on the shore, hands outstretched toward his departing mother.[5] Paula hardened her heart for Christ's sake, and Jerome responded with love and praise. He congratulated Paula and Melania (another widow who left her home and child in order to live in Jerusalem) for "scorning their wealth and deserting their

3. Ibid., pp. 33, 35.
4. Ibid., letter 54, p. 233.
5. Jerome, *Epistulae*, letter 108.6, 2:311; CSEL, vol. 55.

children [as they] lifted up the Lord's cross."[6] To Jerome, wealth and children alike were "goods" to be left in the world unless they could be brought into religious life. Paula took some of her property to help establish her community in the Holy Land, and she took her daughter Eustochium, who was committed to virginity. She left behind her husband's property, her younger daughter, who was about to be married, and her son, who "belonged" to his father.[7] (The attitudes toward children and property expressed in these letters were, of course, Jerome's. Evidence of Paula's feelings comes only from what he tells us and what we can infer from her behavior.)

A daughter offered a second chance to a mother who had missed her own opportunity: "Why, mother, grudge your daughter her virginity? She has been reared on your milk, she has come from your body, she has grown strong in your arms. Your watchful love has kept her safe. Are you vexed with her because she chooses to wed not a soldier but a King? She has rendered you a high service: from to-day you are the mother by marriage of God."[8] The mother of that passage is nurturing, strengthening, protective, and loving, but those qualities are celebrated only in relation to the production and preservation of a virgin child. Jerome was sympathetic to mothers, but he found much of their work unappealing: "She carried you long, and she nursed you for many months; her gentle love bore with the peevish ways of your infancy. She washed your soiled napkins and often dirtied her hands with their nastiness. She sat by your bed when you were ill and was patient with your sickness, even as she had before endured the sickness of maternity which you caused."[9] Jerome wrote almost nothing about his own family; we do not know his mother's name. Physical maternity, for him, was difficult and heartbreaking, even disgusting, unless redeemed by a new relationship to virginity.

6. Jerome, *Select Letters*, 45, p. 183.
7. Here I follow the analysis of Jo Ann McNamara in "Cornelia's Daughters: Paula and Eustochium," *Women's Studies* 11 (1984), 9–27. See also Elizabeth A. Clark, "Friendship between the Sexes: Classical Theory and Christian Practice," in *Jerome, Chrysostom, and Friends* (New York: Edwin Mellen Press, 1979), pp. 35–108.
8. Jerome, *Select Letters*, 22, p. 95.
9. Jerome, *Epistulae*, letter 117.4, 2:319.

Such devaluation and disregard for conventional family ties did not express simply a desire to withdraw from the world the better to serve God. The attitudes of Christian intellectuals toward the human body and human relationships were strongly colored by the environment of late antiquity—a world in which many learned and serious people, Christian and pagan alike, tended to distrust the physical world and their own physical being. There are conflicting interpretations of the dualism and antimaterialism of the Mediterranean world in the second to fourth centuries of the Christian era, but all agree at least about the existence of a widespread detachment or distaste for human bodies and conventional human relationships.[10] In the Neoplatonic tradition of patristic Christianity, body and soul were distinct and separate, and spiritual reality was valued far above the material. Indeed, in significant respects the spiritual world *was* the real world: St. Augustine remembered that "by reading these books of the Platonists I had been prompted to look for truth as something incorporeal."[11]

Dualism could go far beyond orthodoxy, as Augustine knew very well. Christians were bound to a God who not only created the material universe but entered it: their God was born, suffered, and died a human being. Nonetheless, the holiest men and women in the ancient world seemed to act out in their bodies and lives the intellectual dualism of the elite. One of the Desert Fathers accounted for his abuse of his body by saying: "I am killing it because it is killing me."[12] The "it," the body, was separate from

---

10. See esp. E. R. Dodds, *Pagan and Christian in an Age of Anxiety* (Cambridge: Cambridge University Press, 1985), chap. 1. For a different interpretation, see Peter Brown, *The Body and Society: Men, Woman and Sexual Renunciation in Early Christianity* (New York: Columbia University Press, 1988). Brown argues that the emphasis on virginity and celibacy should be understood in part as a social phenomenon—that ascetics, by "dying" to the family and the state, disqualified themselves for childbirth and for military service and thus escaped society and its demands.

11. Augustine, *Confessions* VII.20, trans. R. S. Pine-Coffin (London: Penguin Books, 1961), p. 154.

12. *Heraclidis Paradeisos* 1, cited in Dodds, *Pagan and Christian*, p. 30. Harry Stack Sullivan's notion of the "not-me," constructed out of unbearable anxiety, helps to describe, if not to explain, the "awe, dread, loathing, and horror" expressed toward the body, sexuality, and women in some of these writings; see *The Interper-*

the "me," the soul. The body detracted from goodness and wisdom and closeness to God and endangered the soul; "it" required discipline. Men like Jerome, who feared the power of their bodies and especially of their sexuality, easily transferred their fear and disgust to the women who were objects of longing and occasions of conflict. Their interpretations of the Fall captured a psychological truth, for they distinguished the "self"—Man, or soul, or the rational aspect of human nature—from the Other: Woman, or body, or the carnal aspect. The rejected aspect of human nature was assigned to Eve, a creature like and unlike her "mother," Adam.

The desert saints did not privilege motherhood; female parents did not escape the fear and disgust attached to women's bodies. Among their tales is the following:

> A certain brother was going on a journey, and he had his mother with him, and she was old. They came to a certain river, and the old woman could not cross it. And her son took off his cloak and wrapped it about his hands, lest he should in any wise touch the body of his mother, and so carrying her, he set her on the other side of the stream. Then said his mother to him, "Why didst thou so cover thy hands, my son?" He answered, "Because the body of a woman is fire. And even from my touching thee, came the memory of other women into my soul."[13]

Only women who remained entirely apart from sex and physical maternity avoided the identification of the female with flesh and sin and death. The descendants of Eve were punished by subjection to men and by suffering in childbirth, but because virginity was the state of our original creation, a virgin could escape the double curse. Jerome told Paula's daughter Eustochium:

---

sonal Theory of Psychiatry, ed. Helen Swick Perry, Mary Ladd Gawel, and Martha Gibbon (New York: Norton, 1953), p. 315. Margaret Miles believes that beginners in the ascetic life were especially likely to feel the need to "discipline" their bodies; see Fullness of Life: Historical Foundations for a New Asceticism (Philadelphia: Westminster Press, 1981), p. 60.

13. The Desert Fathers, Helen Waddell, ed. (Ann Arbor: University of Michigan Press, 1981), p. 7.

You must not be subject to the sentence whereby condemnation was passed upon mankind: 'In pain and in sorrow shalt thou bring forth children.' Say to yourself: "That is a Law for a married woman, but not for me." . . .

Eve in Paradise was a virgin: it was only after she put on a garment of skins that her married life began. . . .

That you may understand that virginity is natural and that marriage came after the Fall, remember that what is born of wedlock is virgin flesh and that by its fruit it renders what in its parent root it had lost.[14]

Death came into the world with the Fall, making sexual reproduction necessary to replenish the human race, but only until the birth of Christ. For the patriarchs and their wives, fruitfulness was a blessing and barrenness a curse. Before Christ, "the world was empty of people, and . . . the only benediction possible was the gift of children." All that changed with the second Adam, born of the second Eve—another virgin, like Eve before the Fall: "Death came through Eve: life has come through Mary. For this reason the gift of virginity has been poured most abundantly upon women, seeing that it was from a woman it began."[15]

The Church Fathers, as a group and as individuals, were as inconsistent as other human beings, and the work of each was shaped by his unique experience—social, intrapsychic, and material as well as religious. Unlike Jerome, St. Gregory of Nyssa came from a prominent family of bishops and saints. (One of his brothers was Basil the Great, the most important of the eastern monastic founders and the author of an influential monastic rule.) Among Gregory's writings are a treatise on virginity and a life of his sister Macrina, who founded a community of ascetic women. The treatise catalogues the horrors of marriage and parenthood, including widowhood and parental bereavement. Mortal children, according to Gregory, were born to die:

For the bodily procreation of children . . . is more an embarking upon death than upon life for man. Corruption has its beginning in birth

14. Jerome, *Select Letters*, 22, pp. 91, 93.
15. Ibid., pp. 97, 99.

and those who refrain from procreation through virginity themselves bring about a cancellation of death by preventing it from advancing further because of them, and, by setting themselves up as a kind of boundary stone between life and death, they keep death from going forward.[16]

The common identification of sexuality and reproduction with death is particularly striking here. Special horrors awaited mothers, and Gregory noted their terrible fear and suffering: "Children born and not born, living and dying, are alike the source of pain."[17]

The argument of "On Virginity" is extreme, and extremely dualistic, but internally logical and consistent if its premises are accepted. When it is placed beside Gregory's "Life of St. Macrina," however, major inconsistencies are revealed. Macrina was a virgin saint of incomparable wisdom and virtue, a woman so holy that Gregory was not sure it was "right to use that natural designation for one who went beyond the nature of a woman." As "the earliest flowering of our mother's womb," Macrina was the oldest of nine siblings in this remarkable family.[18] The mother herself was a pure and holy woman. Although she would have preferred to remain unmarried, as a beautiful orphan she was in danger of abduction and rape, so she selected a husband as a kind of "guardian for her own life."[19] When Macrina was about to be born, her mother fell asleep and: "seemed to be holding in her hands the child still in her womb, and a person of greater than human shape and form appeared to be addressing the infant by the name of

16. Gregory of Nyssa, "On Virginity," 14, in *Saint Gregory of Nyssa: Ascetical Works,* trans. Virginia Woods Callahan (Washington, D.C.: Catholic University of America Press, 1966), p. 48.

17. Ibid., 3, p. 19.

18. Gregory of Nyssa, "The Life of St. Macrina," in *Ascetical Works,* p. 163.

19. Ibid., p. 164. The assumption that women without fathers or husbands were vulnerable to rape and abduction lives in the background of ascetical writings; women based their choices on harsh realities. In the very different (perhaps harsher) world of the seventh-century Franks, a royal widow—convinced that her daughter would be raped or seduced after the king's death—had the girl tonsured and built a convent to which they both retired; see "Vita Sanctae Geretrudis," in SRM, Vol. 2, ed. Bruno Krusch (Hanover: Hahn, 1888), pp. 455–456.

Thecla . . . as she awoke from her sleep she saw the dream realized.[20]

The mother's dream foretold the daughter's greatness, and the name "Thecla" identified her sanctity with virginity through association with the heroic Thecla of the Apocryphal Acts. Macrina was betrothed at an early age, but when her young fiancé died, she refused to marry anyone else, claiming a widow's status. She protected herself from suitors by "a resolve never to be separated for a moment from her mother, so that her mother often used to say to her that the rest of her children she had carried in her womb for a fixed time, but this daughter she always bore, encompassing her in her womb at all times and under all circumstances."[21]

The relationship of mother and daughter came to resemble that of an abbess and a nun, although their roles kept shifting throughout their lives together: "Certainly, the companionship of her daughter was not burdensome or disadvantageous for the mother, because the care she received from her daughter surpassed that of many of her maidservants and there was an exchange of kindly offices between them. The older woman cared for the younger woman's soul and the daughter for her mother's body, fulfilling in all things every desirable service." Macrina baked her mother's bread, shared her worries, and ultimately involved her in the life of "philosophy, drawing her on little by little to the immaterial and simpler life."[22] In the new family of religion, Macrina became the spiritual mother of her own mother as well as her physical caretaker; the humbler chores were elevated by humility and love.

Gregory greatly admired the woman who had raised her children to be saints and whose life ended so beautifully: "Having come to a rich old age, [she] went to God, taking her departure from life in the arms of . . . her children."[23] Macrina is the protagonist of the "Life," but the mother is central too—blessed in her motherhood and in her children, whose sanctity made her a benefactor to the world. Sorrow and trouble could not prevail over such gifts; the

20. Gregory, "Life of Macrina," p. 164. For the uses of stories about Thecla, virgin and teacher, see MacDonald, *The Legend and the Apostle.*
21. Gregory, "Life of Macrina," p. 166.
22. Ibid., pp. 166–167.
23. Ibid., p. 172.

sons and daughters whom she bore and educated became in turn her parents. The message of the "Life," which deals with Gregory's own family and was shaped by his experience and deep emotion, runs almost directly counter to the message of "On Virginity." Two kinds of motherhood are represented, and Gregory's distaste for physical maternity, expressed so strongly in the treatise, is overpowered by experience in the family memoir. There, the physical motherhood of one woman is transformed into the spiritual motherhood of the other; physicality is redeemed by association with holiness. Because the two works belong to different genres with different conventions, Gregory never had to address the inconsistency, but it is apparent that he perceived his mother, as well as his sister, as wholly exceptional and her motherhood therefore inapplicable to the experience of other women.

Inconsistency and ambivalence notwithstanding, in their theoretical writings and explicit valuations the Church Fathers prized virginity as the best way of life for any Christian. They frequently cited the parable of the sower and the seed to measure the relative status of marriage, widowhood, and virginity: the goodness of marriage was thirtyfold; of widowhood, sixtyfold; of virginity, a hundredfold. For Augustine of Hippo, the three fruits of marriage were the mutual fidelity of the partners, the procreation and Christian upbringing of children, and the representation in the marital bond of the indissoluble relationship of Christ and the Church. Augustine held a higher view of marriage than either Jerome or Gregory, but not a higher view of procreation. Offspring were not essential to the goodness of marriage; indeed, its highest form might be based on a mutual vow of continence. He knew from experience that children were not born Christian; they had to undergo a second birth through their true mother, the Church.[24]

Augustine's thoughts and feelings about motherhood are not fully revealed in his theoretical statements about the value of procreation or the status of virgins. Like Gregory, he was the son of a remarkable woman, and he wrote at length about his mother, their relationship, and her role in his life. He saw Monica as the

---

24. Augustine (*Confessions* 1.7, p. 28) said of babies that if they "are innocent, it is not for lack of will to do harm, but for lack of strength."

agent of his conversion and perhaps of his salvation: "In the flesh she brought me to birth in this world: in her heart she brought me to birth in your eternal light."[25] Like the mother of Gregory of Nyssa, Monica was entirely exceptional, achieving spiritual as well as physical maternity. The power and grace of her maternal passion were recognized by the Church in the person of the bishop who said "It cannot be that the son of these tears should be lost." For such a woman, evangelism begins when her child is born and becomes more intense as he grows: "Words cannot describe how dearly she loved me or how much greater was the anxiety she suffered for my spiritual birth than the physical pain she had endured in bringing me into the world." Augustine shared the contemporary belief that moral and spiritual qualities were ingested with the milk of mother or nurse. Monica's milk, and her tears, kept him afloat in the "hissing cauldron of lust"[26] in which he spent his recalcitrant adolescence.

Augustine's *Confessions* offer an intimate, extended account of his childhood, his early relationships and their significance to him, and his experience of Monica from the close and passionate perspective of a favorite child. As a historical document his autobiography is unique: there was nothing like it in its own time, or for hundreds of years thereafter. It would be wrong to attach too much significance to the experience of such an unusual mother and son; we cannot assume that the *Confessions* is descriptive of motherhood in general. Nonetheless, its portrait of two extraordinary individuals helps to balance the other surviving sources from their era and environment—treatises, arguments, and polemics about the status of marriage and the hierarchy of souls.

By the fifth century, Christian thinkers and writers had transformed values and attitudes derived from their Jewish roots, the Roman environment, and the late classical thought-world into complex but identifiable Christian ideologies of family and sexual-

25. Ibid., 9.8, p. 192. See Clarissa W. Atkinson, " 'Your Servant, My Mother': The Figure of St. Monica in the Ideology of Christian Motherhood," in *Immaculate and Powerful: The Female in Sacred Image and Social Reality*, ed. Clarissa W. Atkinson, Constance H. Buchanan, and Margaret R. Miles (Boston: Beacon Press, 1985), pp. 139–172.

26. Augustine, *Confessions* 3.12, p. 70; 5.9, p. 102; 3.1, p. 55.

ity. It is much more difficult to establish a corresponding transformation in people's experience, although we may surmise that to bear and raise a child where motherhood was always considered a lesser good was to assume a special psychological burden, and perhaps a social and economic burden, even for women who did not receive letters from Jerome. Little of our information comes from mothers; most of it reflects the views and experience of the celibate, learned men who shaped Christian faith and morals in the first centuries. For these men, procreation—and therefore motherhood—was an aspect of Creation and Fall. Human sexuality, deeply flawed by sin, was redeemed to a degree by parenthood. Eve, and through her all women, might be saved "through bearing children" (1 Tim. 2:15). Children were among the "goods" of marriage, and maternity a necessary contribution to the economy of salvation. And yet by the fifth century virginity was much more holy than motherhood. An individual mother—Monica, or the mother of Gregory and Macrina—might be a paragon or even a saint, but only in the context of her relationship with extraordinary children and only when that relationship shifted from the ordinary into the spiritual realm. Early medieval Christians received from their Fathers a profound ambivalence about sex, family, and motherhood, a legacy they carried into the extensive missionary enterprises that occupied the western Church in the early Middle Ages.

In the fourth, fifth, and sixth centuries of the Christian era, the churches and their bishops moved into the power vacuum created by the deterioration and collapse of imperial institutions in the West. Shifting principalities ruled by petty kings could not establish a stable political system, and the failure of Justinian's attempt to reunite the empire only confirmed the split between Rome and Byzantium. Western Catholics were left on their own to confront heresy, disorder, famine, and plague. At the end of the sixth century, the bishop of Rome responded to the crisis by turning the face of his church toward the West, where he hoped to find new resources and new allies. The gradual conversion to Christianity and cultural assimilation of the Germanic peoples of northern and western Europe had begun long before, but under Gregory the

Great, mission became ecclesiastical policy. Bede, the eighth-century Anglo-Saxon historian, identified Gregory as the apostle who "transformed our still idolatrous nation into a church of Christ."[27] Bede's careful, detailed account of the conversion of the Anglo-Saxons and the establishment of Roman Christianity in England supplies much of what is known about the encounter of cultures that created medieval Christianity. His *Historica Ecclesiastica* lays bare the complex processes of mission, conversion, and acculturation.

Among the valuable documents incorporated in Bede's history are letters exchanged by Gregory the Great and the missionary bishop Augustine of Canterbury—correspondence that illuminates the establishment of a foreign institution and ideologies within a host culture and society. Among the questions that worried the bishop were those relating to rules and customs governing marriage, family, and sexual behavior. "To what degree may the faithful marry with their kindred?" he asked. "And is it lawful for a man to marry his step-mother or sister-in-law?"[28] With respect to family and motherhood, Augustine's eighth question is especially relevant:

> May an expectant mother be baptized? How soon after childbirth may she enter church? And how soon after childbirth may a child be baptized if in danger of death? How soon after child-birth may a husband have relations with his wife? And may a woman properly enter church at the time of menstruation? And may she receive Communion at these times? And may a man enter church after relations with his wife before he has washed? Or receive the sacred mystery of Communion? These uncouth English people require guidance on all these matters.[29]

The questions and answers provide some information about the new "people of God" but much more about the missionaries. They set out to carry the Gospel to the pagans, but their Gospel was

27. Bede, *History* 2.1, p. 94.
28. Ibid., 1.27, p. 74.
29. Ibid., pp. 76–77. The last comment reveals a sense of superiority that was harmful to Augustine's relations with his see, although Gregory warned him particularly to beware of pride (1.31, p. 88).

embedded in six hundred years of history and supported by a framework of cultural norms and assumptions that included a specific set of distinctions between sacred and profane. The Romans' notions of pollution and taboo were not like those of their hosts. Their sexual and marital arrangements were different, and interactions between the two groups were affected by the missionaries' commitment to celibacy.[30] Augustine described the Anglo-Saxons as "uncouth" in sexual matters; unfortunately, we have no record of Anglo-Saxon opinion of the habits and behavior of the Romans. As always, the first opportunities for historical interpretation belonged to the conquerors and their successors. In this instance they belonged to Bede, an Anglo-Saxon Christian monk who traced his significant ancestry, his true lineage, to the Roman pope rather than the English converts.

The correspondence of pope and bishop is one-sided in relation to the Anglo-Saxons but still revealing. Gregory's answers show him to be a moderate in matters of sex and marriage. Reminding Augustine that "the fruitfulness of the flesh is no offence," he asserted that expectant mothers *could* be baptized. God's "gift of grace," by which he meant a pregnancy, was not "contrary to the sacred mystery by which all guilt is washed away." Making use of an allegorical interpretation of Scripture, the pope tempered the Law. The Hebrew rule of thirty-three days of "pollution" following the birth of a male child, sixty-six for a female, "is to be understood as an allegory, for were a woman to enter a church and return thanks in the very hour of her delivery, she would do nothing wrong." Neither pregnancy nor childbirth was to be treated as pollution; even a menstruating woman was allowed in church, "for the workings of nature cannot be considered culpable, and it is not just that she should be refused admittance, since her condition is beyond her control." The favor shown by Jesus toward the bleeding woman was extended to others of her sex. Nature was fallen, and its "workings" were understood to be especially difficult and painful for women. Their pains were acceptable; their

---

30. For a discussion of some of the differences between Germanic-pagan and Roman-Christian ideas about marriage, see Raoul Manselli, "Vie familiale et éthique sexuelle dans les pénitentiels," in *Famille et parenté dans l'Occident*

suffering entitled them to compassion and consideration from church and clergy.[31]

Yet there was a darker side to Gregory's message concerning women and sex. "The fault," he wrote, "lies in the bodily pleasure, not in the pain; the pleasure is in the bodily union, the pain is in the birth, so that Eve, the mother of us all, was told: *'In sorrow thou shalt bring forth children.'* "[32] Pleasure was the enemy, and the special enemy of married people; the pope spelled this out in his *Book of Pastoral Care*:

> The married must be admonished to bear in mind that they are united in wedlock for the purpose of procreation, and when they abandon themselves to immoderate intercourse, they transfer the occasion of procreation to the service of pleasure . . . though they do not then pass beyond the bounds of wedlock, yet in wedlock they exceed its rights. Wherefore it is necessary that they should efface by frequent prayer what they befoul in the fair form of intercourse by the admixture of pleasure.[33]

Writing to the Canterbury mission, Gregory stated that parents should postpone the resumption of sexual relations after childbirth until the child was weaned, and he took the opportunity to comment on the "bad custom" of wet-nursing.[34] His objections apparently were based on the mother's motives rather than the child's welfare; he castigated women whose "incontinence" prompted them to hand over their babies to nurses. The issue was sexual pleasure, and the pope's tone was harsh and critical, unlike the gentle tone of his sympathy with menstruating and pregnant women.

Like other moralists and preachers, Gregory moved back and forth between a reasonable, pastoral approach to women, whose special sorrows and difficulties he appreciated, and his fear of

médiéval, ed. Georges Duby and Jacques Le Goff (Rome: Ecole Française de Rome, 1977).

31. Bede, *History* 1.27, pp. 77–78.

32. Ibid., p. 77.

33. Gregory the Great, *St. Gregory the Great: Pastoral Care*, trans. Henry Davis, S.J. (Westminster, Md.: Newman Press, 1950), 3.27, pp. 188–189.

34. Bede, *History* 1.27, p. 78.

"Woman," who was fatally associated with pleasure. "The Serpent suggested the first sin, and Eve, as flesh, took physical pleasure in it, while Adam, as spirit, consented."[35] When Eve was not suffering, bringing forth children in sorrow, she was identified with pleasure and with sin. Gregory had no intention of falling into Adam's fatal mistake of consenting to her sin; it was one task of the Church to limit and control tragic reenactments of the primal drama. Suffering women—usually mothers or potential mothers, who suffered in their reproductive capacity—were welcome in church and entitled to pastoral care. Women who were not suffering, women experiencing and tempting men with physical pleasure, represented a continual threat to the well-being of all people, but particularly of celibate men. Gregory's writings, especially his *Book of Pastoral Care*, which was given to every bishop at his consecration, were extremely influential in the development of moral theology in the West. His profound ambivalence about women and Woman, pain and pleasure, has had a long life in the history of Christianity and of motherhood.

The subordination and protection of women were characteristic of the social relations and legal arrangements of Germanic societies long before the arrival of the missionaries. A woman lived within the *mundium* (protection and control) of her father or husband or another kinsman, whose status determined her social and legal position. Germanic societies controlled violence by making perpetrators pay compensation to the victims or their kin; the amount of this *wergild* varied with the status of the victim and the nature of the crime. Heavy sanctions were placed on rape, abortion, and the murder of women, with compensation paid to the men in whose *mundium* they belonged. Such efforts to protect women against violence and to discourage offenders may have been related to a significant imbalance in the sex ratio. Men outnumbered and outlived women throughout late antiquity and the early Middle Ages. In the eleventh or twelfth century, the balance was restored and began to move in the other direction; after the twelfth century, women outnumbered men.

Scholars agree that demographic reality shapes social relations

35. Ibid., p. 83.

but do not agree about the implications of the early medieval sex ratio. David Herlihy argued that the scarcity of women made them valuable, especially as potential mothers. He pointed to the laws of the Salian Franks, in which the *wergild* of a free female child was the same as that of a free man but tripled when the girl reached puberty and increased still more when she was pregnant; at menopause, her "value" reverted to that of a young girl or a man. In some cases the protection of females extended still further: among the Alemanni, the person responsible for causing an abortion was fined twice as heavily if the fetus was female.[36]

Persistent attention to the safety of women and girls may also imply that they were not so much valuable as vulnerable, objects of continual violence. Literary sources depict a society of warriors whose ethical system honored physical courage, loyalty from men to their leader, generosity from the leader to his men. In the world of *Beowulf* the only active female figure was Grendel's horrible mother. The important relationships were those of the heroes who fought side by side in battle and slept side by side in the lord's hall. Women, even the queen, were peripheral, and women of the lower classes had no existence, at least in the literary remains of the culture. Certain clauses of the legal codes reflect similar values: the Burgundian code, under the heading "Of Women Violated," required a "native freeman" who assaulted a maidservant to "pay twelve solidi to him to whom the maidservant belongs."[37] Nothing we know about the societies of Germanic Europe is incompatible with the need to protect women against violence.

Most of the data for early medieval demographic studies come from ninth-century materials arising in societies very unlike those that produced either *Beowulf* or the laws of the Burgundians or Salian Franks. The surviving Carolingian documents served practical purposes as surveys or census reports of peasant households in agricultural communities. Figures taken from such documents indicate a strikingly uneven sex ratio, which has provoked varying interpretations. Female children may have been underreported by

---

36. Herlihy, "Life Expectancies," pp. 8–9.
37. *The Burgundian Code*, trans. Katherine Fischer Drew (Philadelphia: University of Pennsylvania Press, 1972), p. 44.

their parents or ignored by census takers, although that explanation does not support the notion that their value was enhanced by scarcity. Men may have migrated into these relatively well-organized farming communities to find work, and women may have emigrated to work as domestic servants or to marry, but migration alone was probably not sufficient to account for the sex ratio.

On the basis of the ninth-century census of households dependent on the abbey of St. Germain-des-Pres, Emily Coleman argues that girls may have been at special risk of infanticide. She found that the more numerous the family and the smaller the holding, the greater the preponderance of males. When the family was smaller and the holding larger, the sex ratio tended toward equality. Coleman believes that "too many" daughters could be disastrous in a marginal property: the holding was endangered if its resources were stretched to provide for each child, and young men with sisters at home could not marry and bring home wives. More comfortable families with fewer children could afford to keep all their daughters; the sex ratio evened out with prosperity.[38] Given the high infant mortality of medieval Europe, a child who was not actively helped to live might easily die without provoking comment or intervention. Infanticide did not require much activity on the part of the parents. Of course it was forbidden by the Church, along with contraception and abortion, but such prohibitions are rarely effective; their existence testifies to a problem, not a solution.

It is generally assumed that the preponderance of males in early medieval Europe was somehow related to the death of women in childbirth or through complications of pregnancy. The reversal of the sex ratio later in the Middle Ages, however, occurred without significant advances in obstetrics or gynecology; maternal mortality is not in itself an adequate explanation for the demographic shift. It has been suggested that dietary deficiencies may help to account for the discrepancies.[39] Until the eleventh century, when

38. Emily Coleman, "L'infanticide dans le Haut Moyen Age," *Annales E.S.C.* 29 (1974), 315–335.

39. This discussion is based on Vern Bullough and Cameron Campbell, "Female Longevity and Diet in the Middle Ages," *Speculum* 55 (1980), 317–325. See also

more meat became available and iron cooking pots came into general use, most people consumed very little iron. The iron requirements of menstruating, pregnant, and lactating women are much higher than the requirements of men, too high to have been adequately supplied by the iron available in the diet of the earlier period. It is likely that women's lives were shortened by anemia, which usually does not cause death directly but significantly complicates blood loss—as in miscarriage, abortion, or childbirth—and contributes to the mortality rate from respiratory disease. Iron deficiency cannot account for a preponderance of male *infants*, which appears in some documents and not in others,[40] but it does answer some questions raised by the sex ratio in age groups past puberty. It helps to explain the stability of the European population before the eleventh century, when the increase in population overall may have been stimulated by an increase in dietary iron. Women who are seriously anemic do not menstruate or become pregnant, and thus anemia serves as a physiological mechanism for the adjustment of population to food supply. That interpretation of the demographic data does not exclude social interpretations, such as female infanticide or the underreporting of women and girls, but it does shed some light on a puzzling aspect of the history of motherhood in the medieval West.

Christian bishops and missionaries in the underdeveloped world of the early Middle Ages confronted the multiple challenges of converting, teaching, and supervising the faith and morals of illiterate people widely dispersed in rural areas—indeed, in wilderness—and powerfully attached to ancient social and religious cus-

the essential work of Lynn White on the agricultural revolution of the Middle Ages and its implications in *Medieval Technology and Social Change* (Oxford: Oxford University Press, 1982), pp. 69–76.

40. Using the polyptych of the abbey of St.-Germain-des-Pres (gathered between 801 and 829), Coleman, "L'infanticide," found the preponderance of males stable throughout the age groups; it varied with the size of the holding and the household, not with age. Using the surveys of the church of St. Victor of Marseilles and the monastery of Farfa, David Herlihy, "Life Expectancies," found that the preponderance of females among infants disappeared as the population aged: among adults, males predominated.

toms. There were never enough priests, nor were most parish priests significantly better educated than the people they served. In this environment, the clergy made use of penitentials—teaching and disciplinary codes first developed by Irish monks—to assist them in parish work among lay people. Penitentials were produced in Ireland and England from the sixth century on, and later on the Continent. Sins were catalogued by subject and penances prescribed for each offense. The penitentials resembled Germanic legal codes in that penances varied according to the status of the offender: most sins were taken more seriously when committed by clerics than by lay people, by adults than by children, and so forth. As guides for the behavior of men and women in the world, the penitentials were not very appropriate: the penances themselves, which included prolonged bread-and-water fasts, were more suited to monks than to undernourished peasants. As historical sources they contribute less to our knowledge of lay people than to our understanding of the attitudes and morality of early monasticism.

The penitentials reflect a physical and intellectual environment far removed from that of the late Roman Empire. Pollution was a constant concern, and the eating and drinking of unclean things.[41] The physical and moral health of the community were not sharply differentiated, and the clergy took responsibility for both. Strict rules protected sacred persons and objects against the perpetual danger of contamination. The "Bigotian Penitential" of the early eighth century warned clerics:

> The penance of one who drinks what has been contaminated by a layman or a laywoman, one day on bread and water.
> The penance of one who drinks what has been contaminated by a pregnant serving-woman, or for cohabitation with her, forty days on bread and water.[42]

41. E.g., the "Canons of Adamnan" ruled that "a cistern in which is found either the corpse of a man or [the carcass] of a dog or of any animal is first to be emptied, and the slime in it, which the water has moistened, is to be thrown out, and it is clean"; see *The Irish Penitentials*, ed. Ludwig Bieler, (Dublin: Dublin Institute for Advanced Studies, 1983), p. 177.

42. *Irish Penitentials*, p. 217.

The pregnant woman, apparently, was believed to be forty times less clean than the ordinary layperson; it is not clear whether her pregnancy or her social status was more dangerous.

Authors of penitentials frequently cited the Church Fathers. They taught the same faith and followed the same moral code, but their world, their concerns, and their reasons for writing were entirely different. They did not produce sermons or theology, and their works lacked the nuances of the writings of Jerome and Augustine. The authors were preparing handbooks—practical tools for confessors and religious leaders—and theological subtlety was neither necessary nor desirable. But these documents were strikingly unlike their patristic models, less in style than in cultural background. In speaking of marriage and motherhood they did not contradict the Church Fathers but placed their emphases differently. The later writers tended to focus on sexual and other kinds of pollution and on "magic"—that is, the use of herbs or spells for reproductive purposes, whether to promote fertility or impede conception or produce abortion. Various medical-religious practices were forbidden: the seventh-century "Penitential of Theodore" warns that "if any woman puts her daughter upon a roof or into an oven for the cure of a fever, she shall do penance for seven years."[43]

The conversion of the Germanic peoples to Christianity was not accomplished at once, and the clergy knew very well that many persons, especially in country places, followed the practices of their ancestors. (Indeed, this was still the case in the seventeenth century and later.) Medicine and religion were closely identified, and the Church tried hard to discourage attempts to control nature through supernatural means—unless, of course, such means were sanctioned by the Church, as were the relics and shrines of the saints. The writings of Christian historians and hagiographers are filled with tales of children who were taken, usually by their mothers, to saints' shrines, where they were cured of disorders ranging from birth defects to high fevers. Gregory of

---

43. *Medieval Handbooks of Penance*, ed. John T. McNeill and Helena M. Gamer (New York: Columbia University Press, 1938), p. 198. We do not know why daughters but not sons were treated by this method.

Tours tells of one young girl, mute from birth, whose mother took her to the tomb of St. Martin, where her first word—"Good"—was spoken in response to a question about the smell of incense at the shrine. Hearing that first sound, the mother tried another test: she placed holy water in her daughter's mouth and asked about the taste, and the girl again answered "Good." The joyful mother then took her child home, leaving her grief and anxiety at the saint's tomb.[44] Such miraculous healings were perceived as direct interventions by the holy dead, whereas a woman who put her daughter on the roof was doing the devil's work.

Caesarius of Arles, a sixth-century bishop who with Gregory the Great formed an essential link in the transmission of patristic theology in the West, was a strict constructionist in sexual ethics. His attitude toward married lay people was unyielding: he equated contraception with homicide and threatened women with damnation if they did anything to impede conception. Chastity was the only acceptable way to avoid pregnancy.[45] Leaders of the Church were concerned about concubinage and about the persistence of "superstitious" practices, not about the gynecological and social consequences of sexual activities inside or outside of marriage. Authors and compilers of penitentials, in contrast to such bishops as Caesarius, showed a certain appreciation of the complexity of human circumstances and made some distinctions:

> A woman who causes miscarriage of that which she has conceived after it has been established in the womb, three years and a half of penance. If the flesh has formed, it is seven years. If the soul has entered it, fourteen years' penance. If the woman dies of the miscarriage, that is the death of body and soul, fourteen cumals [are offered] to God as the price of her soul, or fourteen years' penance.[46]

44. Gregory of Tours, "De virtutibus S. Martini" II.38, in *Gregorii Turonensis opera*, vol. 1, pt. 2, ed. Bruno Krusch (Hanover: Hahn, 1885), SRM, 1:172. I am indebted to Rosemary Hale for her interpretation of this story.

45. Caesarius said, "Chastity is the sole sterility of the Christian woman" (quoted in Noonan, *Contraception*, p. 146).

46. *Medieval Handbooks*, p. 166. A "cumal" was a female slave, defined as "a measure of value. . .equivalent to three cows or twelve fatted fowls" (p. 119 n.19). Regard for human life, especially female life, is always relative to class and status.

Aristotle thought the fetus was "formed" and became human after a period of forty days for males and ninety for females. Most Christian thinkers adopted his views, although some believed that "ensoulment" occurred at conception. The author of this "Old Irish Penitential" apparently believed that the soul entered the fetus after its flesh was "formed."[47]

Although writers and compilers of penitentials did tend to copy older works, it is still safe to assume that repeated condemnations of certain practices indicate that such practices continued to exist and to cause problems. Variations and intriguing anomalies occasionally appear among the repetitions. In the "Penitential of Theodore," for example, a distinction is made in cases of infanticide:

> If a mother slays her child, if she commits homicide, she shall do penance for fifteen years. . . .
> If a poor woman slays her child, she shall do penance for seven years.[48]

The distinction is based on class and resources, with no explicit statement about the relative morality of the two mothers. In an eighth-century version of this clause, pejorative language alters the meaning of the text and introduces a further distinction:

> A mother who kills her child before the fortieth day shall do penance for one year. If it is after the child has become alive, [she shall do penance] as a murderess. But it makes a great difference whether a poor woman does it on account of the difficulty of supporting [the child] or a harlot for the sake of concealing her wickedness.[49]

A "harlot," of course, is assumed not to be poor!

In at least one document the consistent emphasis on the preservation of fetal life was turned around. From the sixth-century "Penitential of Finnian":

47. For a discussion of "formation" and "ensoulment," see Noonan, *Contraception*, pp. 89–91.
48. *Medieval Handbooks*, p. 197.
49. Ibid., p. 225.

If a woman by her magic destroys the child she has conceived of somebody, she shall do penance for half a year with an allowance of bread and water, and abstain for two years from wine and meat and fast for the six forty-day periods with bread and water.

But if, as we have said, she bears a child and her sin is manifest, [she shall do penance] for six years [with bread and water], as is the judgement in the case of a cleric, and in the seventh year she shall be joined to the altar, and then we say her crown can be restored and she may don a white robe and be pronounced a virgin.[50]

The text suggests that abortion was taken less seriously than "illegitimate" pregnancy and birth, which involved public shame. The clause probably was designed for nuns, and the possibility of full restoration to "virginity" may account for the harsh penalty for bearing a child.

Interference with reproduction was taken very seriously, but so was marital intercourse; rules governing the behavior of husbands and wives were colored by the horror of contamination that pervades these documents. Gregory the Great had "accepted" menstruation as an unavoidable burden carried by women since the Fall, but authors of penitentials were inclined to equate it with pollution:

He who is in [the state of] matrimony ought to be continent . . . after conception, and during the menstrual period to its very end.

After a birth he shall abstain, if it is a son for thirty-three [days]; if a daughter, for sixty-six [days].[51]

Despite Gregory's insistence that menstruating women were welcome in church, the "Bigotian Penitential" states that "during their monthly period women should not enter a church nor receive holy communion."[52]

The penitentials offer a rich, if somewhat bizarre, picture of the fears, interests, and passions of early medieval monks who were attempting to serve lay people as well as members of their own communities, and they naturally reveal more about the monks

---

50. *Irish Penitentials*, pp. 79, 81. I have not found similar suggestions in other penitentials.
51. Ibid., p. 117.
52. Ibid., p. 223.

than about the men, women, and children who were their penitents. Most of the texts address matters such as aggression, gluttony, and pride; many of them were associated with problems that arose in communities of men, with fears about eating and drinking and the danger of pollution of the Host. Mothers and children were present in the writers' consciousness but—with certain important exceptions—more as threats to monastic purity than as subjects of pastoral responsibility.

Early medieval historians, from Gregory of Tours and Bede to Paul the Deacon, historian of the Lombards, incorporated a great variety of stories into their works—tales of kings and queens, saints and villains. Occasionally, as in the case of Gregory's wicked queens and some of Bede's saints, the stories involve mothers and children. They rarely tell us much about the experience of motherhood, and they never are told from the mother's point of view, but they do represent certain attitudes of the historian and his society.

Gregory of Tours wrote about powerful, ambitious queens as well as holy female saints. Royal and aristocratic Merovingian society observed no significant distinctions between private and public; family dynamics and Frankish politics were one. The royal power rested on the king's strength and physical courage, his treasury, his family possessions, and his ability to attract and reward warrior companions. Power within a royal or noble family provided access to power outside. Royal women could more easily acquire and wield such power through motherhood than through marriage; the king's mother was much more secure than his consort. The Church had not yet imposed monogamy on its royal sons, and a wife or concubine could easily be supplanted by a rival. A king might have several wives, but only one mother. Furthermore, women inherited property and ruled their lands; often they were the guardians of fatherless children and of the children's property. Suzanne Wemple has commented: "loyalty to the uterine line was inculcated in aristocratic males in their early childhood, and hence we should not be surprised that Clotild asked her sons, not her husband, to avenge the murder of her parents."[53]

53. Suzanne F. Wemple, *Women in Frankish Society: Marriage and the Cloister, 500 to 900* (Philadelphia: University of Pennsylvania Press, 1985), p. 60.

Without monogamy or primogeniture, loyalty was directed primarily toward mothers, children, and siblings; marriage was not the principal or exclusive bond that it later became. The tie between mother and child was likely to be the central relationship for both. When St. Monegund's daughters died, she left her husband and retired to a cell; she could bear her grief only by changing her life entirely.[54] With her children gone, nothing kept her in the world—certainly not the needs or companionship of her husband. Monegund's story was not unique or even very unusual.

Children in stories about miraculous cures frequently appear to belong exclusively or especially to their mothers. (Of course, such children generally had something serious wrong with them.) St. Martin cured a child with terrible birth defects; both the mother and the author, Gregory of Tours, blamed the mother for the child's difficulties, for he had been conceived on a Sunday.[55] Parents of both sexes were sternly warned of the possible consequences of such a sin, but it was clear that this child was his mother's responsibility. A powerful relationship existed between the moral and religious nature or status of parent and child and the physical processes of conception and birth. Gregory's own mother suffered from severe pains in her leg from the time of his birth until thirty-four years later, when Gregory was ordained and she came to visit St. Martin's shrine.[56] Gregory did not explain the connection, but evidently he believed that his own changed status, as well as the saint's disposition to help sufferers, contributed to his mother's recovery, just as his birth was associated with the onset of her pain.

Women were responsible for the children born to them, and a woman who abandoned or killed her child was assumed to be promiscuous as well as desperate. Infanticide was associated with sexual depravity; the histories do not acknowledge the distinctions of wealth and poverty noted in some of the penitentials. With little sympathy to spare for women who gave birth outside of supportive social structures, historians usually characterized them as monstrous or "unnatural." In the eighth century Paul the Deacon told a story in which the mythic archetype of the fostering

54. Gregory of Tours, "Liber vitae patrum" XIX, 1, in *Opera*, SRM, 1:286.
55. Gregory of Tours, "De virtutibus" II.24, p. 167
56. Ibid., III.10, p.185.

of the hero illustrates the "protection" of women and children in early medieval Europe:

> At this time a certain prostitute had brought forth seven little boys at a birth, and the mother, more cruel than all wild beasts, threw them into a fish-pond to be drowned. . . . It happened therefore that when King Agelmund had stopped his horse and looked at the wretched infants, and had turned them hither and thither with the spear he carried in his hand, one of them put his hand on the royal spear and clutched it. The king moved by pity . . . ordered him to be lifted from the fish-pond and commanded him to be brought to a nurse to be nourished with every care.[57]

The king was not kind enough to rescue the other six babies, but Paul does not call him cruel for "turning them over" with his spear. The *mother* was cruel and unnatural; the king was exceptionally compassionate and well rewarded by the heroic destiny of his foster child.

In recent years the lives of saints have been enthusiastically exploited as sources for many kinds of historical research. Their exemplary protagonists embody the ideals of a society, or at least of the hagiographer's particular segment of a society; and the background and context illuminate aspects of medieval life, including family and class relationships, that may not have been important to the hagiographer but are of great interest to historians.

The stated purpose of Rudolf, the monk who wrote "the Life of St. Leoba" in the ninth century, was to celebrate the holiness, learning, and power of Leoba, abbess of Bischofsheim and close friend of St. Boniface. As a foil to Leoba's virtues, the author told a story about another woman, "a certain poor little crippled girl." (In medieval stories, physical deformity or ugliness frequently exhibits moral evil—but not always: great saints such as St. Ber-

57. Paul the Deacon, *History of the Lombards*, ed. and trans. William Dudley Foulke (Philadelphia: University of Pennsylvania Press, 1974), 1.4, p. 26. On the exposure of infants, see John E. Boswell, *The Kindness of Strangers: The Abandonment of Children in Western Europe from Late Antiquity to the Renaissance* (New York: Pantheon Books, 1988).

nard were praised for triumphing over physical weakness and illness.) The poor woman lived near the convent and was given food and clothing by the nuns. When she conceived a child, she concealed her pregnancy, and when the baby was born, she "cast it at night into a pool by the river which flowed through that place." A woman who came to draw water discovered the body and assumed that the child had been born to one of the nuns. She was utterly enraged, first at the hypocrisy of those who preached morality but did not practice it and then at the pollution of the pool. She spoke with furious irony:

> How admirable is the life of nuns, who beneath their veils give birth to children and exercise at one and the same time the function of mothers and priests, baptising those to whom they have given birth. For, fellow-citizens, you have drawn off this water to make a pool, not merely for the purpose of grinding corn, but unwittingly for a new and unheard-of kind of Baptism. Now go and ask those women, whom you compliment by calling them virgins, to remove this corpse from the river and make it fit for us to use again.[58]

The story reveals powerful resentment on the part of the community served by these missionary nuns. Apparently they were believed to think themselves better than other people, and they may also have been seen as outsiders. (Leoba was an English-woman called by Boniface to help in the conversion of the Germans.) The concern about pollution, so prevalent in the penitentials, is prominent here too. When the mother threw her baby in the pool, "she added crime to crime, for she not only followed fleshly sin by murder, but also combined murder with the poisoning of the water."[59]

In the end, Leoba forced a confession from that "wretched little woman, the dupe and the tool of the devil."[60] The spiritual power of the abbess conquered the Father of Lies, who had arranged the

---

58. Rudolf, "The Life of Saint Leoba by Rudolf, Monk of Fulda," in *Anglo-Saxon Missionaries in Germany*, trans. C. H. Talbot (London: Sheed & Ward, 1954), pp. 216–217. The *topos* of the nun who hides her pregnancy under her habit became a staple of U.S. anti-Catholic propaganda in the nineteenth century.

59. Ibid., p. 216.

60. Ibid., p. 218.

ugly situation in order to discredit the convent. For Leoba, the entire series of events was a matter of public standing and reputation. She performed a public miracle: flames surrounded the victim and drove her to confess. The point was to restore the good name of the nuns—indeed, to enhance their standing through evidence of divine favor. Neither the author nor, as far as we know, the nuns were interested in the private tragedy that produced the public spectacle.

In almost all early medieval lives of female saints, monastic authors presented "real" or significant motherhood as a spiritual rather than a biological relationship. Leoba had two mothers: the first was Aebbe, who gave birth long after "the onset of old age had deprived [her] of all hope of offspring." Aebbe conceived after a miraculous dream interpreted by her old nurse—another maternal figure—to mean that a daughter would be born and must be consecrated to God. The biblical *topoi* of elderly parents and miraculous dreams, common in saints' lives, marked Leoba as extraordinary. Such a child required supernatural as well as natural parenting, and when she was old enough, "her mother consecrated her and handed her over to Mother Tetta to be taught the sacred sciences."[61]

Tetta was abbess of Wimbourne, a strict and holy teacher, an appropriate mother for a saint. Like her mentor, the virgin Leoba became a perfect mother: as an abbess she was responsible for the nuns entrusted to her care and leadership. The miracle that cleared their name was a spiritual labor that called forth "tears and groans." When her "children" were ill she cared for them; one had been given up for dead when Leoba "blessed milk and poured it drop by drop down the throat of the sick nun."[62] The patient recovered and outlived Leoba, as was fitting for a daughter.

The historian Bede, a great admirer of holy women, set forth some of the connections betwen virginity and spiritual motherhood. One of his favorites was Etheldreda, an East Anglian princess who was married to the king of the Northumbrians, with whom she lived for twelve years in "the glory of perpetual virginity."

61. Ibid., pp. 210, 211.
62. Ibid., pp. 218, 221.

When finally Etheldreda persuaded the king to allow her to retire to a convent, she became "the virgin mother of many virgins vowed to God."[63] Bede's ode to Etheldreda illustrates the relationship between virginity and "true" motherhood, realized and represented by the Virgin Mary:

> Fair maid, who gav'st the whole world's
> Parent birth,
> God gave thee grace. And by that grace empowered
> How many virgin blossoms since have flowered![64]

A woman could emulate Mary by remaining a virgin and acquiring spiritual offspring.

Bede wrote most admiringly of Hilda, abbess of the double monastery at Whitby, where kings went for counsel and future bishops learned their Scripture and theology. Hilda's father was sent into exile during her mother's pregnancy and died before she was born, a situation reflected in another wonderful dream presaging the birth of a saint. Hilda's mother dreamed that "he was suddenly taken away, and although she searched everywhere, she could find no trace of him. When all her efforts had failed, she discovered a most valuable jewel under her garments; and as she looked closely, it emitted such a brilliant light that all Britain was lit by its splendour." The jewel, of course, was Hilda, "whom all her acquaintances called Mother because of her wonderful devotion and grace."[65]

The term "Mother" carried overtones of profound respect, almost awe, in the writings of men whose stories celebrated holy virgins who presided over communities of women, and even of men (double monasteries, ruled by an abbess, were not uncommon in Anglo-Saxon England). For some privileged women, spiritual motherhood was an attractive alternative to the relentless biological cycle that brought weakness, illness, and early death to so many others. Poor women had no such opportunities, however, except in extraordinary circumstances; Bede's female saints came

63. Bede, *History* 4.19, pp.238–239.
64. Ibid., 4.20, p. 242.
65. Ibid., 4.23, p. 248.

from royal or noble families. These sources do not reveal exactly how vocational choices were made, but we observe that it was not unusual for the mother of a saint to predict or perceive in a dream her daughter's future. The saints were preternaturally holy as children: Leoba "had no interests other than the monastery and the pursuit of sacred knowledge."[66] Infant sanctity certainly was read back into the lives of these women by hagiographers, but it is likely also that parents, nurses, and teachers did what educators do in every age: that is, plant and nourish and discover in children the traits they hope and expect to find. "Exceptional" children are quick to reward the expectations of significant adults, and the medieval mothers who dreamed of their daughters' excellence and singularity had a substantial part in making their dreams come true.

Histories, legal codes, penitentials, and saints' lives present fragmented images of women and children, formulaic in style and shaped by the wishes, fears, and fantasies of their (male, and usually clerical) authors. It is very difficult to find direct evidence about the experience of women in the early Middle Ages. We piece together scraps, and our speculation is highly colored by our own experience and imagination. Apart from a few letters, prayers, poems, and lives (usually of abbesses by nuns), women's writings are scarce, and writing by laywomen—that is, by biological mothers—even scarcer. For that reason, as well as its intrinsic interest, Dhuoda's *Manual* is enormously valuable.

Dhuoda belonged to a noble Frankish family. She married Bernard of Septimania, a cousin of the Carolingian kings, who was assigned to guard and govern the Spanish March by Louis the Pious in the 820s. Bernard sent his wife and son William, born in 826, to live apart from him—perhaps because, according to court gossip, he was the lover of the empress. He visited Dhuoda at least once, for a second son was born in 841, the year when Bernard fought on the losing side of the battle in which Charles the Bald defeated his rivals and became the new emperor. After the defeat, Bernard sent William to Charles's court as a hostage and took his

66. Rudolf, "Life of Leoba," p. 211.

infant son back to his own headquarters. Dhuoda—her older son dismissed to the dangerous life of a royal captive, her baby removed even before his baptism—was left alone. Clearly, the power and authority of the royal and noble mothers of Merovingian times were not available to her. Whether because her kin could not help her, or because of Bernard's status or character, or because of the changed times, Dhuoda was unable to protect herself or her children. It is significant that her writing betrays no sense that she was entitled to protection, and her advice to William does not urge loyalty to herself and her family. Dhuoda was no Merovingian queen; she regarded William as his father's child.

Dhuoda's *Manual* was written as William left to take up his paternal legacy of royal politics, war, and violence. His mother's fears were realistic: Bernard was put to death for treason in 843, and William followed him four years later. All Dhuoda could do, her only way of touching her son or taking part in his life after their separation, was to write. She chose a form that William could read and reread, a guide or handbook to keep beside him. The work was entirely for him: "From the beginning of this little book until the end, in style and in meaning . . . all of it, in every way, as you know, was written for the health of your soul and body."[67] The *Manual* gave her a common project with her son, a way to remain a presence in his life.

Dhuoda built her book around a core of traditional suggestions for a Christian life lived in the world. Unlike most of our sources, the *Manual* is not monastic in spirit; William was raised to be a soldier, the father of a family, a vassal and a lord. His mother directed him to love and obey his father, to pray for his father's ancestors, to take his place in the line of warriors from which he was descended. Dhuoda's French translator, Pierre Riché, points out that her faith was a "religion of fatherhood,"[68] and Peter Dronke has described Dhuoda's universe as one "in which the bonds of loyalty to the human father, to the emperor, and to a Father God are seen concentrically."[69] Mother and son alike were

67. *Dhuoda: Manuel pour mons fils*, ed. and trans. Pierre Riché (Paris: Cerf, 1975), p. 68.
68. Ibid., p. 27.
69. Dronke, *Women Writers*, p. 38.

born into patriarchy; their choices were limited to the possibility of doing well or badly within that system. Dhuoda expected her son to come into his masculine power and hoped that he would use it well. She did not complain of Bernard's cruelty, and she allowed her sadness to break through only once or twice, observing "that most women in the world rejoice in living with their children, and that I, Dhuoda, am kept far away from you, my son William."[70] She was a wife without a husband, a mother without children, but her losses did not weaken her passion and conviction.

The *Manual* belongs to the genre of the "Mirror for Princes," guides for young Christian noblemen, but the mirror reflects the features of the parent, not those of the child. The work gave Dhuoda a means of expression and a way to exert her maternal authority in the narrow sphere that remained. Even as she apologized for weakness, she claimed her strength: "In spite of my weakness, living unworthy among worthy women, I am still your mother."[71] Begging God to endow William with grace and virtue, she prayed:

> Let him be generous and prudent, loyal and brave,
>   let him never abandon moderation.
> He will never have one like me to tell him this,
>   I who, though unworthy, am also his mother.
> I who always, at all moments and all hours, am
>   asking you with all my strength: have mercy on him.[72]

Dhuoda's sense of her own authority was independent of her ability to control her own situation or protect her child. In the circumstances, her assurance was extraordinary. When she told William that although she had written the book, he must put it to use, she quoted St. Paul: "I have planted, Apollos watered; but God gave the increase" (1 Cor. 3:6). She had done all she could: "I have fought a good fight, I have finished the course, I have kept the faith" (2 Tim. 4:7). At the end she spoke with the crucified

70. Dhuoda, *Manuel*, p. 72.
71. Ibid., p. 80.
72. Quoted in Dronke, *Women Writers*, p. 42.

Christ: "It is finished."[73] The power of love, and the conviction that her relationship with William was unique, made possible her identification with Paul and with Christ.

Dhuoda's *Manual* is one of the rare expressions of maternal consciousness that survives from medieval Europe and one of the most poignant of any age. Unlike the monastic authors, Dhuoda did not dismiss physical motherhood, but it was not the primary source of her love and confidence, which came from the intimacy of sixteen years. She was no Paula, abandoning her children to do God's work; nor Monica, whose special status derived from a remarkable son. Her understanding and experience of motherhood were not at all similar to those of her contemporary, St. Leoba, as perceived and described by Leoba's biographer. Dhuoda could not spare William or herself their patriarchal destiny, but she spoke for herself; she was not a creation of legend or fantasy or memory or imagination. Unlike most extant documents of the early Middle Ages, the *Manual* records the voice of an individual woman speaking to her child.

Dhuoda's *Manual* offers a glimpse of the world outside the limitations of monastic sources. By the ninth century, in the ideology of Christian monasticism, spiritual motherhood had replaced biological motherhood as a woman's most valuable work. The companionship of the early communities and the arena, where marital status and parenthood were of little consequence compared with faith and commitment, was long vanished. Through the intense ascetic zeal of the Church Fathers, it had been accepted in theory that marriage and motherhood disqualified women for heroism and spiritual grandeur, except for the mothers of exceptional children. Production and reproduction were separated, with "production" defined (in the spiritual and ecclesiastical realm) as active holiness, the work of prayer and charity, teaching and mission. Ordinary mothers could not be "productive" in this sense; their work was reproduction—a lesser sphere. Holy women were not deprived of the status of marriage and motherhood, however, for they were brides of Christ and mothers

73. Dhuoda, *Manuel*, p. 70.

of holy persons and communities. Spiritual motherhood was the only religious leadership permitted to women; the term "mother," transformed, retained its ancient power.

Within the sphere of monastic ideology, the construction of spiritual motherhood was extremely significant, although its implications in the world outside are much less clear. Dhuoda's *Manual* reveals that at least among the noble classes, women had actually lost effective power in relation to their children during the centuries in which the Church was establishing its authority in western Europe. Dhuoda's plight was not mitigated by clerical reverence for spiritual motherhood, which was irrelevant to her and her children. Neither Church nor clergy came to her assistance—nor, as far as we know, did she expect that they would. Dhuoda, in fact, became one of the unfortunate women described by Jerome and by Gregory of Nyssa: a mother whose love for mortal children ended in sorrow and in loss.

CHAPTER FOUR

Theological Motherhood: The Virgin Mother of God

In most of the world's religions, sacred beings exist within familiar, usually familial, structures and relationships. Sexed and gendered deities, motivated by attraction and hostility, jealousy and friendship, parental and erotic love, are linked to one another as spouses, siblings, lovers, parents, and children. Complex and ambiguous affections characterize the relationships of gods and goddesses as well as those of men and women.

The most significant exceptions to these polytheistic norms are the great monotheistic traditions that arose in the Middle East. The God of Jews and Muslims is One, without child or consort, and theoretically without sex or gender—although that claim has been challenged and shaken.[1] The God of Christianity also is One, but Christianity is an extraordinary monotheism based upon a divine relationship—not among its gods but within its God. The One of Christianity is Three, and although one is a Spirit, the others are a Father and a Son. The mother of the Son is not one of the Persons of the Trinity, although she is a member of the Holy Family, which also includes three persons. Jesus Christ partici-pates in both triads: as the Second Person of the Trinity he remains

---

1. See, e.g., Nawal El Saadawi, "Man the God, Woman the Sinful," in *The Hidden Face of Eve: Women in the Arab World*, ed. and trans. Sherif Hetata (Boston: Beacon Press, 1982), chap. 12; also Judith Plaskow, *Standing Again at Sinai: Judaism from a Feminist Perspective* (New York: Harper & Row, 1990).

fully human, and as the son of Mary and Joseph, fully divine. Christian stories and the theologies constructed upon them leave ample room for speculation about the mother of God.

Such stories and speculation, and the cult of the Virgin Mother, have been crucial in the experience of Christian women and the formation of Christian ideologies of motherhood. The genius of Christianity is its incarnate god, born as a baby to a human woman in historical time. That event and that relationship stand at the center of Christian faith: Christ's humanity, taken from his mother, enabled him to save his fellow human beings.[2] Physicality—birth, embodiment, death—is the source and secret of the Savior's relationship to all men and women. But the language of late antique philosophy, in which the credal definitions of Christianity were asserted, could not completely capture or define the figure of the human mother of Jesus or her role in the faith and experience of believers. Myths and stories and devotional practices flourished along with doctrine; some of the difficult questions in the history of Mary arise from discrepancies between the resounding abstractions of learned Mariology and the passionate expressions of devotion to a beloved mother who participates in the lives of her children.

The legends and the cult of Mary, as well as dogmatic statements about her nature and status, have long divided Christians, and division persists through the earnest ecumenical efforts of modern times. Such difficulties are not easily resolved, for they emerge not only in attitudes toward Scripture and tradition but in differences of nation, class, and culture. Attachment to Mary— and the reverse, contempt for "Mariolatry"—runs very deep. Over two thousand years her cult has acquired songs, stories, liturgies, miracles, visions, memories, and works of art. It continues to exert

2. On the atonement, Anselm of Canterbury wrote: "The unbelievers deride our foolishness and claim that we offer God injury and scandal when we say he descended into the womb of a woman, was born of a woman, was nourished by milk and the food of human beings, and suffered fatigue, hunger, and thirst and died hanging on the cross between two thieves. ... But if unbelievers would carefully consider how suitably the restoration of humanity was accomplished in this way, they would not laugh at our foolishness but with us would praise God's wisdom and goodness"; see "Cur Deus Homo" 1.3, in *S. Anselmi opera omnia*, ed. F. S. Schmitt (Edinburgh: Thomas Nelson, 1946), 2:50–51.

a powerful pull on the aspirations, experience, and imaginative creations of people all over the world. The magnetic field of the Virgin is shaped by her theological position, but its power is generated by the emotional and psychological status of the Mother of God and of Christian people.[3] The figure of Mary evokes feelings about human mothers as well as faith in a divine Son.

In order to examine theological motherhood, an essential element in historical Christianity and in the history of motherhood, I begin by looking very briefly at the mother of Jesus in the Scriptures and at the construction of the figure of "the Virgin Mary" in early Christianity.[4] From the abundant material available for the study of the medieval Mary, I have chosen to investigate the figure, status, and activities of the Virgin in selected religious literature of the twelfth century. At that time, devotion to Mary found expression in new artistic, liturgical, and literary works, including prayers, homilies, and treatises by men in religious life—notably, but not exclusively, by Cistercian monks. Along with contemporary autobiographical writings, these works shed light on attitudes toward God's mother, on feelings and assumptions about ordinary human mothers, and on the relationship between the two.

Twelfth-century European Christians also produced numbers of new stories and collections of stories about the miraculous appearances and activities of Mary. The miracle tales, which include significant folkloric elements, were for the most part "written" (or collected and transcribed) by clerical men but were shaped also by the interests and attitudes of people outside the cloister. Members of the literate elite gathered and retold tales that had circulated for centuries in Europe and the East, making them newly available to preachers and storytellers and through them to lay people. Individual tales and collections were formed in part by

3. Henry Adams puzzled over the force field of Mary; see "The Dynamo and the Virgin (1900)," in *The Education of Henry Adams* (Boston: Houghton Mifflin, 1910).

4. Theologically, of course, Mary's motherhood is significant only for Christians, but their long political and cultural dominance has made their ideologies influential for others as well—for Jews in medieval Europe, and for people all over the world after the fifteenth century.

the tastes and responses of audiences, so they reveal certain values and assumptions of those who heard them. Because much of this literature deals with mothers and motherhood, it discloses ways in which the figure of Mary, and Marian devotion, shaped maternal ideologies and thus affected the experience of women and children in medieval Europe. Unlike other monotheistic religions, Christianity claims a central, sacred figure who is a woman and a mother; her history illuminates much that is perplexing in the history of motherhood in the West.

Students of Mary usually begin with Scripture, perhaps because her appearances in the New Testament are few and deceptively simple. They certainly do not provide a full or detailed picture of the mother of Jesus. Roman Catholics and Protestants differ over the interpretation of various texts but agree that the canonical Scriptures offer little information about the historical Mary or her relationship to the earliest Christian communities. For the New Testament writers, the mother of Jesus was primarily a vehicle for their Christologies, their community loyalties, and their special concerns—a pattern of writing about Mary that has endured for two thousand years.

In the earliest books of the New Testament, the letters of Paul, Mary is not mentioned by name. Writing to the Galatians in the context of the assertion of Christ's humanity and identification with the children of Abraham, Paul said, "God sent forth his Son, born of woman, born under the law" (Gal. 4:4). The characteristics of this nameless woman, even her sexual and marital status, were not of interest to the Apostle. Mark, earliest of the synoptic gospels, begins with Jesus' baptism and public ministry and has little to say about his mother. Of the three synoptic accounts of the scene in which Jesus asked, "Who is my mother, or my brothers?" Mark's is the most harsh and distinguishes most clearly between the physical kin of Jesus and the eschatological family of discipleship. Matthew and Luke soften the force of the distinction and the severity of the question.[5]

5. See Raymond E. Brown, Karl P. Donfried, Joseph A. Fitzmyer, and John Neumann, eds. *Mary in the New Testament* (Philadelphia: Fortress Press, 1978), pp. 51–58.

Matthew presents the virginal conception of Jesus as the ful-fillment of Isaiah 7:14: "Behold, a young woman shall conceive and bear a son." The prophecy was confirmed with the conception and birth of Jesus; nothing was said about Mary's continued virgin-ity. References to younger children apparently did not contradict Matthew's understanding of the function of Mary's antepartum virginity or compromise the messianic status of Jesus.[6] In later times these brothers and sisters were explained away, but for Matthew they were not problematic: Mary's virginity signified only in terms of her fullfilment of the prophecy.

The infancy narrative of Luke is the richest canonical source for the history of Mary and includes the unique passages in which she speaks her own words. It is difficult to imagine modern Chris-tian piety, or the history of Western art, without the first two chapters of Luke: Annunciation, Visitation, Nativity—angels, shepherds, swaddling clothes. (Later Christians imagined that St. Luke heard these stories from Mary herself when he painted her picture, harvesting the fruit of her years of reflection on sacred history.) The author of Luke and Acts constructed a history of salvation from the conception and birth of Jesus through his minis-try, Passion, and Resurrection and the foundation of the Church. He understood Mary's discipleship as a vital aspect of redemption. The assertion of her obedience to the will of God, which became such a powerful theme in the ideology of Christian motherhood, was derived mainly from Luke's sense of the response appropriate to divine command. He associated Mary with the poor in Israel—humble people who hear and obey God's word, who may not understand the marvels that occur but have the faith to believe and accept them. Luke's gospel established Mary as primary among the disciples, a significant theme in modern Mariology.[7]

The gospel of John contributed the figure of the Woman at the Cross. Entrusted to the beloved disciple, Mary became the mother

---

6. Ibid., pp. 83–87. See also John J. Saliba, S.J., "The Virgin-Birth Debate in Anthropological Literature: A Critical Assessment," *Theological Studies* 36 (1975), 428–454.

7. See, e.g., Patrick J. Bearsley, S.M., "Mary the Perfect Disciple: A Paradigm for Mariology," *Theological Studies* 41 (1980), 461–504. The "discipleship" model allows questions about virginity to be put to one side.

of an eschatological household, of all faithful followers of Christ. In later medieval piety, the Woman at the Cross served as a model for weeping women, and the Pietà—the mother holding her dead son—became a central figure in art, liturgy, and the imagery of Christian motherhood. The salvific tears of mothers over lost children, generally sons, are persistent religious and sentimental elements in Western literature.

The most prolific early sources for the medieval cult of Mary were never accepted into the canon of the New Testament. The apocryphal gospels of the second and third centuries, which represented the passions and world views of groups excluded from "orthodox" Christianity during that period, reflected a growing interest in the family of Jesus. The central text for the construction of the medieval Mary, the second-century Protevangelium of James, supplied a full biography for the mother of Jesus. Born miraculously to the aged, barren couple Joachim and Anna, Mary was consecrated to virginity in infancy and spent a supernaturally holy childhood at the Temple in Jerusalem. At twelve, when even the holiest female became a potential source of pollution, she entered a chaste marriage with the aged widower, Joseph. Mary is the central figure in this complex and elaborate tale, as she is not in the canonical gospels, and her virginity is presented as essential to the history of redemption—even though consecrated virginity had no place in first-century Judaism, nor was virginity regarded as a desirable status for an adult woman. Nevertheless, by the second century C.E. it was sufficiently significant to certain Christians to be read back into the origins of their faith.

Although some Christians in the early centuries used the apocryphal gospels to nourish and support their insistence upon virginity and sexual asceticism, the same material supplied an idealized domesticity for the different interests of Christians a thousand years later. The great medieval cult of St. Anne was built out of materials in the apocryphal writings: Mary's mother became the exemplary, stable, and loving grandmother for a new age (see Chapter 5). Despite exclusion from the canon, these writings shared the power and immediacy of the Gospels and provided lavish embellishment for the creations of artists, preachers, and storytellers. The apocrypha made an important contribution to the imaginative resources of medieval Christians in the construction of theological motherhood.

During the early centuries of the development and expansion of Christianity, interest in Mary was shared among all classes, including the intellectuals. It was the task of theologians to define the role of Christ's human mother in the work of redemption and to participate as apologists in the mission of the churches. Christianity was a missionary faith, seeking to teach and convert and preach its good news to the world. The perception and presentation of Mary and her relationship to Christ were adapted to the religious and cultural systems of potential converts and transformed in turn by those systems.

When proselytizing Christians encountered a mother goddess, they responded by insisting on the One God who required neither mother nor consort. Christian monotheism was challenged by the Great Goddess of the ancient Mediterranean and the polytheistic pagan religions of Asia and Europe, and the exhortations of teachers and bishops did not always succeed in establishing a "pure" monotheism. The figure of Mary acquired characteristics of the old goddesses, whose ancient shrines were revived in some of Mary's holy places.[8] The Virgin was credited with some of the capacities, if not the name, of a fertility goddess; in medieval Europe her girdle was prized above all other relics by women who longed to conceive a child. While preachers fulminated against the old religion, devotion to Mary increasingly resembled devotion to the goddess. In the late fourth century, for example, Epiphanius wrote disapprovingly of women who set up altars and made offerings of food and drink to Mary at shrines once sacred to Astarte.[9]

Christian apologists modified and elaborated their teaching in the face of challenges from many different theological systems and sacred figures. When they encountered gnostic dualism, with its relegation of the material world and of human bodies to the

8. In *The Goddess Obscured* (Boston: Beacon Press, 1985), Pamela Berger speculates about the gradual transformation of the ancient protectress of grain into various female saints and the Virgin Mary.

9. Epiphanius, *Panarion* 79.1, cited in Hilda C. Graef, *Mary: A History of Doctrine and Devotion* (New York: Sheed & Ward, 1963), 1:73.

sphere of darkness, they proclaimed the reality of the Incarnation. To emphasize and celebrate Christ's humanity, they stressed his "real" birth from a "real" woman. In the face of gnostic pessimism about world and flesh, they portrayed a material world created by the one good God and redeemed by the participation of the same God in Jesus Christ. Against pagan intellectuals, who tended to dismiss Hebrew and Christian Scriptures as exotic trash, they continued to insist upon the reality and dignity of the birth and death of Jesus. The One of Greek philosophy required no mother and was not subject to pain and suffering and humiliation: Hellenized intellectuals objected not to the oneness of the Christian God but to the humanity of Christ. Their conversion, like that of the gnostics, demanded that they be persuaded of the reality and necessity of the Incarnation, and thus of the birth of Christ to Mary.

Early apologists adjusted the figure of Mary to reinforce their developing doctrines of Christ, but their teachings did not always prevail in the sphere of symbolic representation—in art and worship. Mariology is an aspect of Christology; dogmatic theological assertions about Mary are derived from the implications of assertions about Christ. This is not necessarily true of expressions of devotion or of artistic and literary representations, where the primary focus is Mary herself.[10] The approaches of the theologian, the artist, and the worshiper are not always compatible; their divergent paths may require adjustment or reconciliation. In the history of Christianity, Mariology has frequently followed in the path made by devotion.[11]

10. Both kinds of statement are also "about" the hopes and wishes and fears of the believer, although theological argument may appear to be more "objective" than painting or praise.

11. The title Theotokos, accepted at the Council of Ephesus in 431, was used in Western liturgies long before its theological implications were addressed during the adoptionist controversy of the eighth and ninth centuries; in fact, such usage was one argument against adoptionism. Similarly, the Assumption of Mary was celebrated on August 15 during the Middle Ages, even though the official dogma was not proclaimed until 1950. The Immaculate Conception was debated by theologians and taught by preachers long before it was accepted officially. See Jaroslav Pelikan, The Christian Tradition: A History of the Development of Doc-

Ignatius of Antioch, writing early in the second century C.E., was the first theologian to describe Mary's role in salvation. To counter the gnostic, docetic view of Christ as an impassible God who "assumed" human flesh without truly experiencing human life or death or affliction, Ignatius stressed Christ's double parentage from God and Mary: "There is one Physician, who is both flesh and spirit, born and yet not born, who is God in man . . . both of Mary and of God, first passible and then impassible, Jesus Christ our Lord."[12]

The theme of the Second Eve, which became a persistent analogy in the theological construction of Mary's motherhood, appeared in the writings of Apostolic Fathers later in the second century. Paul had identified Christ as the Second Adam; for theologians after him, Mary was the Second Eve, whose obedience reversed the damage done by the disobedience of the first. By implication, just as Eve was Adam's partner in the Fall, Mary was Christ's partner in redemption. Irenaeus said: "For as Eve was seduced by the word of an angel to flee from God, having rebelled against his Word, so Mary by the word of an angel received the glad tidings that she would bear God by obeying his Word. . . . As the human race was subjected to death through [the act of] a virgin, so was it saved by a virgin, and thus the disobedience of one virgin was precisely balanced by the obedience of another."[13] The Eve/Mary theme, tenacious in the history of Christianity, has reinforced the tendency of some men to perceive women as either "good" or "bad," and to venerate or punish them accordingly.[14]

Commentators on the analogy rarely remark that Eve was Ad-

---

trine, vol. 3, *The Growth of Medieval Theology (600–1300)* (Chicago: University of Chicago Press, 1978), pp. 68–69, 172.

12. Ignatius of Antioch, "Letter to the Ephesians" 7.2, p. 181.

13. Irenaeus, "Adversus Haereses" 5.19, in *Sancti Irenaei adversus haereses*, vol. 2, ed. W. Wigan Harvey (Ridgewood, N.J.: Gregg Press, 1965), p. 376.

14. Commentators frequently present Adam as a good and well-meaning man with a tragic flaw, Eve as all bad—a wicked seductress, or an amoral woman ruled by her appetites. The Eve/Mary dichotomy reflects the phenomenon of "splitting" noted by psychologists: children tend to see their mothers as entirely good or frighteningly bad—to "split" the angry or punishing mother from the loving mother necessary for emotional health.

am's wife but Mary was Christ's mother; little significance is attached to the difference in these relationships.[15] Conflation of the roles and identities of consort and mother, typical of early and medieval devotion to Mary, characterizes the other great Marian theme adumbrated by the Apostolic Fathers: Mary as representation of the Church. Like the Church, she was steadfast and patient, enduring to the end, bride of Christ and mother of Christians. The blending of erotic and maternal characteristics, and of the roles of bride and mother, was a vital element in the construction of the medieval Mary and in her contribution to Christian ideologies of motherhood. Maternal-erotic language and imagery, accessible to the imagination of medieval Christians through these early theological metaphors, allowed the Virgin Mother to be associated with the Lady of romance.

While Mary became Christ's bride and consort as well as his mother, she was simultaneously transformed into the "ever virgin" Mary of patristic theology and ascetic spirituality. The biblical infancy narratives established the virginal conception of Jesus through the Matthean emphasis on prophetic fulfillment and the Lukan association of the virginity of Mary with the holiness of her child: "The Holy Spirit will come upon you, and the power of the Most High will overshadow you; therefore the child to be born will be called holy, the Son of God" (Luke 1:35). The early Fathers wove Mary's virginity into their theological systems: Ignatius believed that along with Christ's birth and death it was one of God's three secrets from the Devil.[16]

Neither scripture nor theology could have constructed the medieval Virgin Mary without the energy and impetus of the ascetic movement of the third and fourth centuries. Athanasius, the premier theologian of the Incarnation, was also a great publicist of the monastic ethos. His *Life of Antony* was an essential model for the new heroes of the desert and the cell, for whom sexual asceticism was intrinsic to holiness and virginity a blessed condition to which human beings might aspire. In his treatise on the

15. Rosemary R. Ruether notes this point in *Mary: The Feminine Face of the Church* (Philadelphia: Westminster Press, 1977), esp. pp. 19–23.
16. Cf. Ignatius, "Letter to the Ephesians" 19.1, p. 193.

Incarnation, Athanasius said that God "took our body, and not simply that, but from a pure and unspotted virgin ignorant of a man, a body pure and truly unalloyed by intercourse with men."[17] Mary was not "simply" human but human in a particular way—a virgin. In Athanasius's *Letter to the Virgins*, Mary—the first-century Jewish wife and mother—appeared in the guise of a fourth-century Christian nun.

When new rules were developed for virtuous women in the post-Constantinian church, a new Mary was required for their edification, a Mary characterized by a quiet voice and demure behavior. Jerome interpreted her terror of the Annunciation as offended modesty: "She had never been greeted by a man before."[18] The Fathers agreed that Christ's birth from a virgin transformed motherhood. Eve's children were born in pain and anguish; Mary's triumph lifted that ancient curse. Unlike married women, said Jerome, virgins had the possibility of conceiving Christ, and the most deserving might aspire to the ultimate prize: "He having been conceived grows to manhood, and as He becomes older regards you not as His mother but as His bride."[19] Mary became the spouse not of the old man, Joseph, but of the young man, Jesus. The metaphors of filial, maternal, and erotic love are closely entwined; the romantic character of Mary's motherhood is no less passionate for its association with virginity.

The ideology of spiritual motherhood, firmly established in monastic communities and spheres of influence by the late fourth century, was developed in imitation of the fruitful motherhood of Mary. Even though it was precisely her *physical* motherhood that accomplished the Incarnation, still—and increasingly—the differences, not the similarities, between the birth of Christ and all other births were elaborated and celebrated. As the ascetic ideal spread and flourished, it became impossible to imagine God's mother giving birth like other women. Persistent gnostic influences may have contributed to the atmosphere of difference sur-

---

17. Athanasius, "On the Incarnation of the Word" 1.18, in *Contra gentes and De Incarnatione*, ed. and trans. Robert W. Thomson (Oxford: Clarendon Press, 1971), p. 153.

18. Jerome, *Select Letters*, 22, p. 147.

19. Ibid., p. 149.

rounding Christ's Nativity. In Ode 19 of the second-century Syrian *Odes of Solomon,* the "masculinity" of Mary reinforces a sense of her awesome power:

> So the Virgin became a mother with great mercies.
> And she labored and bore the Son but without pain,
> because it did not occur without purpose.
> And she did not seek a midwife,
> because he caused her to give life.
> She bore as a strong man with desire,
> and she bore according to the manifestation,
> and possessed with great power.
> And she loved with salvation,
> and guarded with kindness, and declared with greatness.
> Hellelujah.[20]

To medieval Christians it became increasingly obvious that Mary was *always* a virgin—during and after, as well as before, the birth of Jesus. Sexual activity was unthinkable for her, as was a ruptured hymen: perfection was incompatible with the loss of bodily integrity, and despite evidence to the contrary (such as menstruation), medieval people believed that the hymen served as a kind of seal.[21] Mary gave birth without the pain, immodesty, and disarray of ordinary female experience, and the miraculous nature of Christ's birth was emphasized ever more strongly. In the fourteenth century, Birgitta of Sweden (see Chapter 5) described her own vision of the Nativity, in which Mary knelt reverently in prayer while the stable filled with light from the divine infant.[22]

---

20. *The Odes of Solomon,* in *The Old Testament Pseudepigrapha,* vol. 2, ed. James H. Charlesworth (New York: Doubleday, 1985), pp. 752–753. Gail Paterson Corrington discusses the male and female metaphors of Ode 19 in "The Milk of Salvation: Redemption by the Mother in Late Antiquity and Early Christianity," *Harvard Theological Review* 82 (1989), 393–420.

21. See Clarissa W. Atkinson, " 'Precious Balsam in a Fragile Glass': The Ideology of Virginity in the Later Middle Ages," *Journal of Family History* 8 (1983), 131–143; also Charles T. Wood, "The Doctors' Dilemma: Sin, Salvation, and the Menstrual Cycle in Medieval Thought," *Speculum* 56 (1981), 710–727.

22. Birgitta of Sweden, *Den Heliga Birgittas Revelaciones,* ed. Birger Bergh, SUSF, ser. 2, vol. 7, Lat. skrifter (Uppsala: Almqvist & Wiksells, 1967) chap. 21, pp. 187–190.

Artists and their patrons were inspired by Birgitta's revelation, which shaped later representations of the Nativity. Birgitta was the mother of eight children; her vision demonstrated radical discontinuity between Mary's experience and her own.

Learned Christians taught, with Ambrose, that "he who came from the Father took flesh from the Virgin; he took this disposition from his mother so that he could bear our infirmities."[23] Mary might be unlike all other mothers in her virginity and mode of giving birth, but the conception of Jesus was in other respects compatible with the paradigms of Aristotelian biology. Fathers were thought to be the active agents in procreation, and like other children, Jesus received his spirit from his Father, his flesh from his mother. Over time, Christian thinkers came to believe that human conception was clouded by original sin, transmitted in the male seed from father to child. Christ, having no human father, was conceived without original sin. In response to the Pelagians, Augustine strengthened the identification of original sin with sexuality and with the father's seed. Augustine was primarily concerned with sin, grace, and the unity of the human race, but he worked out these themes within an inherited framework of biological opinion. Within that system it was easy to understand that Christ was joined to Adam, and thus to all human beings, through his mother's flesh, and to God through his paternity. Augustine persisted in the belief that a father was the parent of a child's spirit, even though his own experience indicated something quite different. He repeatedly praised his mother's role in his conversion, but neither contempt for his father's earthbound materialism nor appreciation of his mother's spiritual gifts forced him to revise his intellectual and theological heritage concerning gender, spirit, and flesh.

In the early fifth century, long-standing disagreement about the two natures of Christ crystallized in sharp controversy over the Marian title *Theotokos* (bearer of God). The Council of Ephesus was convened in 431 in part to determine whether Mary carried and gave birth to the true God or simply to the human Jesus.

---

23. Ambrose, "Explanatio Psalmi 61" 5, in *Sancti Ambrosii opera*, pt. 6, ed. M. Petschenig (Leipzig: G. Freytag 1919), p. 380; CSEL, vol. 64.

Among the sparks that set off the conflict was an inflammatory sermon preached in Constantinople by Proclus, who venerated Mary as *Theotokos*. The imagery and language of his sermon display the high Mariology of some eastern Christians:

> We have been assembled by the holy Mary, the stainless jewel of virginity, the rational paradise of the second Adam, the workshop of the unity of the natures, the scene of the saving contract, the bridal chamber, in which the Word espoused the flesh . . . the only bridge between God and men. . . .[24] Emmanuel has, indeed, opened the gates of nature, because he was a man, but he did not break the seals of virginity because he was God . . . he was born as he was conceived; he had entered without passion, he went forth without corruption.[25]

The theologians' enthusiasm for the title *Theotokos*, which reinforced the unity of the two natures of Christ, was echoed by crowds of monks and lay people who shouted in the streets while the council deliberated. The crowds were rallied by ecclesiastical pressure groups, but their rowdy participation may also be associated with Ephesus itself—the old city of Diana, with its tradition of sacred female power.

In the wake of the council, enthusiasm for Mary was proclaimed in passionate prayer and preaching, and images of the Virgin were placed in churches and added to shrines once sacred only to Christ and the apostles. Representations of the Adoration of the Magi, in particular, served as opportunities to depict in stone and paint the majesty of God's mother.[26] In the large churches of the East and of Byzantine Italy, the sovereignty of the Virgin was celebrated in monumental statues of the Madonna and Child, frontal sculptures presented in an attitude and style denoting majesty. In the great mosaics of Ravenna, Christ and Mary share the glory of earthly and divine kingship with the imperial family.

With the expansion of Charlemagne's empire and the Carolingian Renaissance of the ninth and tenth centuries, the influence

---

24. Note that Mary, not Christ, is the "bridge."

25. Proclus of Constantinople, "Oratio I, De laudibus Sanctae Mariae," cited in Graef, *Mary*, 1:102.

26. See Marie-Louise Thérèl, "Les visages de Marie," *Bullétin de la Société Française d'Etudes Mariales* 33 (1975–76), 5–20.

of Italian and other Byzantine works of art began to be reflected in the sculpture and architecture of western Europe. The grandeur of Christ and Mary suited the theology and spirituality of the early Middle Ages, when Father and Son were closely identified, and Christ was preeminently king and judge, distant from this world and its people. Christ reigns in majesty or presides over the Last Judgment on the portals of Romanesque churches, and his mother is portrayed as Queen of Heaven. In French Romanesque wood sculptures of the Madonna and Child, Mary's lap offers not maternal comfort and intimacy but a throne for the God-child; both figures are majestic and mature, and both face forward.[27] Images of Mary reflect the lordship of her divine son. Maternity remained the source of her power, but its majesty and uniqueness were stressed at the expense of intimacy and familiarity. Early medieval Christians depended on approachable local saints and their tangible relics for comfort and protection; Mary was the queen-empress, presiding over heaven and earth with the Father and his awe-inspiring Son.

However, the mighty and remote Queen of Heaven of the year 1000 represented only one strand in the construction of the mother of God. Within that complex figure monks found their Virgin Mother, theologians their *Theotokos*—key to Incarnation and Redemption—and Christian people, including monks and theologians, a sacred maternal being who incorporated certain powers and qualities of the ancient goddesses. The protean "Mary" changed her shape to accommodate the requirements of her devotees. Early theologians, artists, and worshipers painted her portrait with a brush broad enough to leave a rich and ambiguous legacy to medieval people. When the society and religious culture of Europe entered a period of radical change at the beginning of the second millennium C.E., Mary began to participate in new ways in Christian faith and experience.

By the latter part of the eleventh century, profound alterations were under way in almost every aspect of European society and

27. On these figures and their significance, see Ilene Forsyth, *The Throne of Wisdom: Wood Sculptures of the Madonna in Romanesque France* (Princeton, N.J.: Princeton University Press, 1972).

culture. Trade increased within Europe and around the Mediterranean, enhancing the growth and prosperity of cities and towns; new urban centers, in turn, fostered commerce in many kinds of goods. More fundamental, perhaps, were the accumulated effects of long-term developments in agriculture and technology. Eleventh-century Europeans ate more food and better food than their ancestors. Thanks to higher agricultural yields and improved techniques in animal husbandry, they consumed more vegetable and animal protein and dietary iron. Women conceived more easily, carried more babies to term, and kept more children alive to adulthood. Agricultural surpluses appeared in some areas, stimulating markets and fairs that brought people and goods together. Urban and commercial growth encouraged sociability and stimulated political and cultural change; for the first time in half a millennium, opportunities for education and cultural expression existed outside of monasteries. Artists and artisans exerted themselves in the construction of large churches in new towns and cities; schools grew up around teachers and libraries attached to cathedrals. In relation to the history of Mary, the rebirth of literacy was especially significant. Writing and texts began to dominate many forms of discourse, with implications for politics, theology, and culture[28]—including the construction and circulation of new literary representations of the Virgin Mary.

In the late eleventh century, the "Church"—meaning, in this instance, significant members of the Roman Curia and their supporters among bishops and monks all over Europe—undertook a major campaign of self-criticism, reform, and reorganization. Pope Gregory VII and his associates determined to put an end to the domination by lay magnates that had characterized early medieval ecclesiastical polity. Concentrating on the issues of lay investiture, simony, and clerical celibacy, they set out to purify the Church, to distinguish it sharply from "the world," and to make its clergy worthy to lead all Christendom. The Gregorian reformers believed that the Church and its clergy ought to be dissociated as

28. See Brian Stock, *The Implications of Literacy: Written Language and Models of Interpretation in the Eleventh and Twelfth Centuries* (Princeton, N.J.: Princeton University Press, 1983).

far as possible from worldly things and worldly people, including women and families.

In the reformers' vision of the Church, it was inappropriate for priests to marry or have children. Most of the leading Gregorians were monks, and they wanted the entire clergy to be monastic in ethos and ideology. Peter Damien used Mary's virginity to argue for clerical celibacy: "For because the Lord's body grew together in the temple of a virgin's womb, even now he asks of his ministers the purity of continence." Assuming that Christ's earthly father as well as his mother was a virgin, Damien asked, "By whom then, I ask you, does he want his body to be handled now except also by virgins?"[29] In art, theology, and devotion the Lord's body became an object of enormous interest. The meaning and mode of the Eucharist were subjected to intense discussion during the twelfth century, when renewed emphasis on the Mass reinforced respect for the power and sacredness of those who handled Christ's body. In all aspects of secular and religious life, the Gregorian reformers stressed differences between clergy and lay people. They promoted separate clerical living arrangements and special legal and educational systems and institutions, adamantly resisting secular interference in the lives and business of the clergy.

In the century after the reform, the Roman Church grew steadily more powerful, more ambitious, more centralized, and more "rational" in its procedures. The popes tightened their own authority within the Church, which sought first independence and then authority in the world outside—authority based not only on reform but also on the rediscovery of Roman law and the development of canon law and ecclesiastical procedures. As one element in its program of centralization, legalization, and order, the Curia claimed exclusive control over the making (or recognition) of saints; shrines and monasteries were no longer permitted to canonize local wonder-workers. Popes and reformed religious orders, with their international identity and membership, encouraged increased attention to the universal figures of Christ and Mary. The centralized church of the twelfth century and the new "Chris-

29. Peter Damien, *Opuscula* 18.1, 17.3, in *S. Petri Damiani opera omnia*, vol. 2; PL 145, col. 384.

tendom" of the Crusades required unifying symbols. Mary gradually took the place of old, familiar, and beloved local saints and acquired some of their characteristics—intimacy, immediacy, and parental concern for the affairs of her children.

The passionate, single-minded enthusiasm of the reformers helped to bring about a widespread revival in the life and piety of monastic institutions, with corresponding changes in the form and feeling of prayer. In the ninth century most worship revolved around collective recitation of the liturgy; hymns and prayers were based mainly on psalms. By the eleventh century devout monks had begun to create new forms, making use of tender, pathetic, personal language and imagery. They paid attention to their own feelings and to the imagined feelings of Christ and Mary and the saints, dwelling less on the majesty of the distant Lord Christ than on the sufferings of the man Jesus and his family and friends. Inevitably, there was a corresponding shift in the perception and praise of Mary. Near the end of the century, Anselm of Canterbury composed a meditation on the Virgin that worked through fear, shame, and sadness toward love and joy. Anselm exulted in his own relationship, through Mary, with his Savior:

> The mother of God is our mother. The mother of him in whom alone we hope and who alone we fear is our mother. The mother, I say, of him who alone saves us, alone damns us, is our mother. . . .
>
> If you, lady, are his mother, then are not your other sons his brothers? . . .
>
> Therefore our judge is our brother. The saviour of the world is our brother. Finally our God is made our brother, through Mary. . . .
>
> Mary, how much we owe to you! Lady mother, through whom we have such a brother, what thanks, what praises, should we return to you?[30]

The traditional theological emphasis on Christ's salvific humanity exploded in passionate gratitude to Mary as mother—Christ's mother, but the mother also of those to whom she had provided hope for redemption.

30. Anselm of Canterbury, "Oratio 7," in *Opera omnia* (Schmitt) 3:23–24.

The affective piety of the eleventh and twelfth centuries was in part a product of the Gregorian reform and, like the reform itself, was monastic in origin and ethos. R. W. Southern noted that Anselm's friend and biographer Eadmer of Canterbury was the first to use the rhetoric of "historical rhapsody" to argue for Mary's immaculate conception, deducing the "necessity of otherwise unknown historical events from arguments of theological propriety."[31] The archbishop's nephew, another Anselm, was involved with the production of one of the earliest English collections of "Miracles of the Virgin."[32] The literature of Marian devotion was generated in reformed monasteries in England and on the Continent, in intense communities of men who loved Mary, Jesus, and one another.

Anselm of Canterbury was only one of many twelfth-century monks who manifested passionate adoration of the Virgin in sermons, prayers, meditations, and theological treatises. Chief among her monastic devotees was the Cistercian Bernard of Clairvaux, who believed that God became human so that human beings could love God. The human motherhood of Mary, essential to Bernard's theology of love, was completely different from that of ordinary women. According to Bernard, Mary rejoiced in childbirth "not for itself, but in him whom she has borne. God . . . was careful to prepare her on earth with a special grace; whereby she conceived undefiled beyond all telling and unspoiled she gave birth. Only this mode of birth was becoming to God—to be born of a virgin."[33] To Bernard, the humility of Mary reflected the humility of Christ, who became the lowest and weakest of crea-

---

31. R. W. Southern, *St. Anselm and His Biographer* (Cambridge: Cambridge University Press, 1963), p. 289. Eadmer argued that since God *could* and *should* have created Mary without sin, he *must* have done so: "De conceptione B. Mariae Virginis." *S. Anselmi opera omnia*, vol. 2, PL 159, col. 305.

32. Southern argues that the first English collections were made in monasteries with a "strong old English tradition by men admiring Anglo-Saxon piety"; see "The English Origin of the Miracles of the Virgin," *Medieval and Renaissance Studies* 4 (1959), 177.

33. Bernard of Clairvaux, *Magnificat: Homilies in Praise of the Blessed Virgin Mary by Bernard of Clairvaux and Amadeus of Lausanne*, trans. Marie-Bernard Saïd and Grace Perigo (Kalamazoo, Mich.: Cistercian Publications, 1979), 2.12, p. 15.

tures—a little child whose helplessness and lowliness was manifested in obedience to his mother. "Just imagine! Double marvel! God does what a woman says—unheard-of humility. A woman outranks God—unparalleled sublimity!"[34]

Bernard believed that the daughter, Mary, reconciled her mother, Eve, with the Father and thus liberated all women from "the hard burden and heavy yoke laid on every daughter of Eve. If they bear children, they are in anguish: if they are childless, then they are cursed." All mothers ought to rejoice in Mary's work, but "you more especially, mother Eve, exult."[35] Because of Mary, men no longer condemn and reproach women: "Eve is pardoned through her daughter, and the complaint of men against women is put to rest."[36] The "pardon" remained theoretical: Bernard always distrusted women. He discouraged the spiritual direction of nuns by Cistercian monks on the grounds that "to be always in a woman's company without having carnal knowledge of her—is this not a greater miracle than raising the dead? You cannot perform the lesser; do you expect me to believe that you can do the greater?"[37]

This greatest of Mary's praise-singers was the son of a remarkable mother who dreamed, discerned, and shaped his destiny. According to the *Golden Legend*, Bernard's mother Aleth refused for her children their aristocratic legacy of pride, luxury, and war: "As long as they remained in her care she bred them for the cloister rather than for the court, giving them coarse and common goods as if they were to be sent off to the desert." Defying the noble custom of employing wet nurses, she would not "allow her children to be suckled at the breasts of other women, but imparted to them, with the maternal milk, the nature of the mother's vir-

34. Ibid., 1.7, p. 11.

35. Ibid., 3.7, p. 38; 2.13, p. 16.

36. Bernard of Clairvaux, "Sermo in nativitate Beatae Mariae," in *S. Bernardi opera*, vol. 5, ed. Jean Leclercq and Henri Rochais (Rome: Editiones Cistercienses, 1968), p. 278.

37. Bernard of Clairvaux, *On the Song of Songs III*, sermon 65.4, trans. Kilian Walsh, O.C.S.O., and Irene M. Edmonds (Kalamazoo, Mich.: Cistercian Publications, 1979), p. 184. See Sally Thompson, "The Problem of the Cistercian Nuns in the Twelfth and Early Thirteenth Centuries," in *Medieval Women*, ed. Derek Baker (Oxford: Basil Blackwell, 1978), pp. 227–252.

tue."[38] Aleth died when Bernard was seventeen. He entered a period of depression and disillusion from which he was restored, apparently, by commitment to the spirit and tough regime of the Cistercians and by a passion for the Virgin Mother. According to contemporary stories, Mary rewarded his devotion with three drops of her milk.[39]

Bernard's sister, Aleth's only daughter, married despite her mother's intention to consecrate all her children to religious life. When she visited her brothers in the monastery, Bernard would not look at her, and another brother called her a "bedizened dung-hill." Bursting into tears, the unfortunate woman reminded them that Christ died for sinners and that they as Christ's servants were responsible for the care of souls: "If my brother despises my flesh," she said, "let not the servant of God despise my soul."[40] The story is a vivid representation of Cistercian ambivalence; in spite of Mary's victory over the curse of Eve, women were feared and despised as sources of evil unless they were consecrated virgins or the mothers of exceptional men. Caroline Walker Bynum has demonstrated that although Cistercian men frequently attributed to themselves the "feminine" and "maternal" characteristics of tenderness and patience, such attributions occurred most often in the context of issues about authority.[41] Their use of the vocabulary of motherhood reveals some of the assumptions and expectations that surrounded idealized motherhood in the twelfth century but has little to do with actual mothers.

The English Cistercian Aelred of Rievaulx composed loving, personal meditations on Christ and Christ's lovers, including the Virgin. The Gospels offered little to nourish the Cistercian hunger for intimate details of Jesus' life, and the monks tended to focus on certain familiar incidents to the point of sentimentality. Aelred

38. "Saint Bernard," in *Golden Legend*, p. 465.
39. Cf. the fresco by Filippino Lippi, *The Vision of St. Bernard*, from the Bardi church in Florence, reproduced by Marina Warner in *Alone of All Her Sex: The Myth and the Cult of the Virgin Mary* (New York: Vintage Books, 1983), fig. 31.
40. *Golden Legend*, p. 470.
41. Caroline Walker Bynum, "Jesus as Mother and Abbot as Mother: Some Themes in Twelfth-Century Cistercian Writing," in *Jesus as Mother: Studies in the Spirituality of the High Middle Ages* (Berkeley: University of California Press, 1983), pp. 110–169.

employed a meditation on Jesus at twelve to ask questions about the relationship of mother and son. Why was Jesus so inconsiderate as to disappear during the visit to Jerusalem? Why did Mary worry, like an ordinary mother, when she knew he was God? On the other hand, why was she so careless as to lose sight of the precious boy? Why (and this, of course, is the Christological point) was God a child at all, and thus subject to parents? Who took care of him during the three days' separation? "Who provided you with food and drink? Who made up a bed for you? Who took off your shoes? Who tended your boyish limbs with oil and baths?"[42]

The subject is a boy of twelve, almost an adult by medieval standards. The care and service mentioned are those required by a toddler, but they serve the author's purpose by creating a context of concrete tenderness: "not theological speculation but devotion; not something to sharpen your tongue but something to arouse your affections."[43] Vivid reminders of the physical presence of a young child awaken lively thoughts and feelings, and this is a major impulse and purpose of affective piety. Taking hold of our response to a child too young to remove his own shoes, Aelred glides without interruption into another set of powerful images and feelings—the erotic. He attributes to Mary, discovering her son among the rabbis, the language of the Song of Solomon (3:4): " 'I found,' she says, 'him whom my soul loves. I held him fast and would not let him go.' "[44] Maternal tenderness and sexual yearning—the passions aroused by Christ's humanity—carry the Christian closer to God.

Guerric of Igny wrote a series of sermons dealing with themes of childhood and maternity. Even more than his fellow-Cistercians, he perceived women in terms of extreme good and evil. Since mothers were defined as good, Eve could not be a mother at all; "not so much a mother as a stepmother since she handed on to her children an inheritance of certain death. . . . She is indeed called the mother of all the living, but she turned out to be more

---

42. Aelred of Rievaulx, "Jesus at the Age of Twelve" 6, trans. Theodore Berkeley, O.C.S.O., in *The Works of Aelred of Rievaulx*, vol. 1, *Treatises: The Pastoral Prayer* (Spencer, Mass.: Cistercian Publications, 1971), p. 10.
43. Ibid., 11, pp. 13–14.
44. Ibid., 8, p. 11.

precisely the murderer of the living . . . since the only fruit of her child-bearing was death."[45]

The conventional opposition of church and synagogue was especially vicious in Guerric's usage. He identified these female *personae* with the two mothers in the story of Solomon and the contested infant (1 Kings 3:16–28): "The evil harlot in her rivalry would rather the infant were killed than given to me alive, but the judgment of our Solomon . . . made no mistake in finding the mother. Give to the Church, he says, the living infant, for she is its mother." Like church and unlike synagogue, a conscientious abbot is a good mother. Guerric promised to "show myself a mother by love and anxious care . . . this name of mother is not restricted to prelates, although they are charged in a special way with maternal solicitude and devotion."[46]

The Virgin was the best mother, and Guerric preached on the feast of her purification: "Neither conception nor childbirth violated your integrity. . . . Why then, as if you had suffered something of what is the common lot of woman in conceiving or giving birth, do you thus seek the remedies of a cleansing which was provided for woman's weakness?"[47] That question was frequently asked, mainly in order to point up the vast difference between Mary and all other women, and the answer was always the same. Mary submitted to purification out of her extraordinary humility—the quality, above all others, that women were urged to emulate.

It is sometimes asserted that medieval women found strength and support through identification with the maternal status and power of the Virgin. This may be true, but it cannot be demonstrated from the writings of twelfth-century Cistercians. These works were intended for monks, and sometimes for nuns, and were probably unknown or irrelevant to laywomen—that is, to mothers, whose concerns were not of interest to the authors. It would have been more natural for laywomen to identify with Eve, charged by Cistercians with bringing death into the world, than

45. Guerric of Igny, *Liturgical Sermons* (Spencer, Mass.: Cistercian Publications, 1971), 2:168.
46. Ibid., 1:52.
47. Ibid., p. 120.

with the "Mary" of these texts. In reality, of course, the death that came into the world in medieval childbirth was the death of women and their infants, but that reality does not intrude in these writings. For these twelfth-century Cistercian male authors, "true" motherhood belonged to the Church, the Virgin, and themselves.

At least one twelfth-century woman did write extensively about Mary, a woman who was theologian and visionary, counselor and healer, abbess and preacher. Hildegard of Bingen held strikingly original views on obstetrics and gynecology (see Chapter 2). When she wrote about the mother of God, however, she was concerned not with Mary's individual human nature and maternity, but with her theological status in relation to the Creation and Redemption of the world. Barbara Newman describes Hildegard's Mary as "the capstone of the arch formed by the celestial foreshadowing of Wisdom on the one side and the embodied fertility of Eve on the other . . . through her the Incarnation is accomplished and God becomes man. Thus she unites the celestial with the earthly, the divine with flesh . . . Mary together with her Son is the supreme theophany, the revelation of God's ultimate will."[48]

Hildegard's appreciation of the female and maternal aspects of humanity informed her high Mariology and her proclamation of the feminine aspects of the divine. Assumptions about female inferiority, which she shared with her contemporaries, did not diminish her self-esteem or deflect her vision of God and Creation. Hildegard's appreciation of the gender of Wisdom and the maternal nature of God was unique in her time and much later. Her works remind us that twelfth-century attitudes—toward Mary or motherhood or any other matter—cannot be confined to a summary; they were as varied and complex as our own.

Just as medieval devotional and theological works that deal explicitly with Mary reveal the writers' assumptions about human motherhood, autobiographical writings that deal explicitly with human parents and children reveal the authors' perceptions of the

---

48. Newman, *Sister of Wisdom*, p. 158.

Virgin. Both genres disclose a wide range of associations between Marian ideologies and Christian motherhood. When Guibert of Nogent, taking Augustine's *Confessions* as a model, set out to write the story of his life, he thanked God for "a mother who was beautiful, yet chaste, modest, and steeped in the fear of the Lord."[49] Like Augustine, Guibert was his mother's favorite child. The details of his birth were fixed in his imagination and sense of destiny. His mother labored all through Good Friday but was unable to give birth. His despairing family went to church to ask for Mary's help, and: "in the place of an offering this gift [was] laid upon the gracious Lady's altar: that should a male child be born, he should be given up to the religious life in the service of God and the Lady, and if one of the inferior sex, she should be handed over to the corresponding calling. At once a weak little being, almost an abortion, was born."[50]

When Guibert was twelve, his adoring mother left to enter religious life. Abandoned, he was furious and desperate: "She knew that I should be utterly an orphan with no one at all on whom to depend, for . . . there was no one to give me the loving care a little child needs at such an age; though I did not lack for the necessities of food and clothing, I often suffered from the loss of that careful provision for the helplessness of tender years that only a woman can provide.[51] As in Aelred's portrait of Jesus, Guibert saw himself not as the young man his society expected a twelve-year-old to be, but as a helpless child. His models failed him: Monica, as perceived and presented by Augustine, was entirely identified with her son; her spiritual destination was his conversion to Catholic Christianity. In the scheme of the *Confessions*, it would have been inconceivable for Monica to leave her

---

49. Guibert of Nogent, *Self and Society in Medieval France: The Memoirs of Abbot Guibert of Nogent*, ed. and trans. John F. Benton (New York: Harper & Row, 1970), p. 38. An insightful psychohistorical interpretation of Guibert and his mother is Nancy F. Partner, "The Family Romance of Guibert of Nogent" (unpublished paper, 1987). See also Mary M. McLaughlin, "Survivors and Surrogates: Children and Parents from the Ninth to the Thirteenth Centuries," in De Mause, *History of Childhood*, pp. 101–181.
50. Guibert, *Self and Society*, p. 40.
51. Ibid., p. 42.

son before his triumphant maturity. Later children of devout mothers experienced different outcomes, even when their mothers' behavior was consciously modeled upon that of Monica.[52]

In Guibert's adult judgment, his mother behaved correctly and deliberately in choosing God and her own salvation over her son's happiness. She was confronted with a clear choice between the responsibilities of physical motherhood and her spiritual health: "She knew for certain that she was a cruel and unnatural mother . . . tenderness would then have been her ruin if she, neglecting her God, in her worldly care for me had put me before her own salvation." At twelve, however, Guibert had no mature perspective on his mother's choice. He reacted, predictably, by making trouble at school and at church, associating with rowdy companions, and indulging his depression by sleeping so much that he became ill. As he must have known it would, word reached his mother, who was "struck half dead by what she heard." She arranged for him to enter monastic life, and like Bernard he discovered in the cloister a resolution of his suffering. He did well until puberty, when "the life of this world began to stir my itching heart with fleshly longings and lusts to suit my stature." His mother intervened again, persuading him to confess his harmful feelings and to make amends.[53] Then he settled down—if that can be said of such a troubled spirit, for he remained subject to violent and disturbing fantasies.

Guibert did grow up and turn his attention away from his mother, although he held on to the comforting notion that she never *really* left him, even after death. Her virtues remained available for his salvation: "Through her merit next to Jesus and His Mother and the Saints, while I still live in this evil world there remains to me the hope of that salvation which is open to all. . . . And now that she is dead . . . she is not ignorant of the miseries in which I am entangled, and, blessed as she is, she bewails my wanderings when she sees my feet go astray from the path of goodness marked out by her recurrent warnings.[54] Among the

52. See Atkinson, "Your Servant, My Mother," esp. pp. 155–158.
53. Guibert, *Self and Society*, pp. 74–75.
54. Ibid., p. 41.

persistent ideologies of Christian motherhood is the conviction that mothers can—and therefore should—be good enough to "save" their children. In Guibert as in Bernard, confidence in maternal virtue and spiritual power was combined with an experience of loss and abandonment. The conflict was resolved in part through a passion for the mother of God, but also, in both men, by a profound and permanent distrust of women.

The best-known autobiographical writing of the twelfth century, Peter Abelard's "History of My Calamities," is in form and content very different from Guibert's memoirs; Abelard was more interested in adult achievement than in youthful development. He believed that his career had been determined by one crucial choice between scholarly and military pursuits. (Although he chose philosophy, he remained within the family tradition by becoming an intellectual champion—a fighter in the schools.) Abelard was his parents' first-born and his father's favorite child. Autobiographical writing was uncommon in that era; it may be that the experience of a parent's special attention persuaded both Guibert and Abelard that their individual experience must be of general interest.

Unlike Guibert and most other literate persons in the twelfth century, Abelard was a parent as well as a child, although his son Astralabe was handed over to relatives immediately after his birth. To judge from their famous letters, Abelard and Heloise were not much interested in their child, whose conception provided the occasion for their marriage. Pregnant, Heloise still insisted on the incompatibility of philosophy and marriage or, more accurately, of philosophy and parenthood: "What harmony can there be between pupils and nursemaids, desks and cradles, books or tablets and distaffs, pen or stylus and spindles? Who can concentrate on thoughts of Scripture or philosophy and be able to endure babies crying, nurses soothing them with lullabies, and all the noisy coming and going of men and women about the house? Will he put up with the constant muddle and squalor which small children bring into the home?"[55]

---

55. Peter Abelard, *The Letters of Abelard and Heloise*, ed. and trans. Betty Radice (New York: Penguin Books, 1974), p. 71.

Heloise rejected marriage as a degraded state unworthy of great love; Abelard insisted upon it from fear of reprisals. Neither of them used the existence or well-being of their child to make points in the discussion, nor was Heloise's entry into religious life discouraged on Astralabe's account. Their personal letters do not mention him, although after Abelard's death Heloise did ask the Abbot of Cluny to find a position for her son.[56] None of this was extraordinary: twelfth-century children frequently were raised by relatives or by other families, and parents of young children did enter convents. It may be more significant that Astralabe did not figure in Abelard's attempt to console Heloise for her unhappiness by reminding her of her spiritual offspring: "What a hateful loss and grievous misfortune if you had abandoned yourself to the defilement of carnal pleasures only to bear in suffering a few children for the world, when now you are delivered in exultation of numerous progeny for heaven! Nor would you have been more than a woman, whereas now you rise even above men, and have turned the curse of Eve into the blessing of Mary."[57] Abelard was following his favorite, St. Jerome—but Jerome had no children. In this passage, Astralabe's father seems to have forgotten that Heloise ever did bear a child; their living son was subsumed in the abstract representation of the curse of Eve.

It would be wrong to make too much of attitudes expressed or implied in the letters of Abelard and Heloise. Their shared conviction of Abelard's unique genius shaped all their activities and relationships, including parenthood. Neither of them was interested in motherhood as a concept or a reality, and the "nurturing, affectivity, and accessibility" attributed to mothers by contemporary monks[58] were irrelevant to the relationship of Heloise and Astralabe. As parents, Heloise and Abelard did not ask very much of themselves. They found a home for their infant son, and when he was old enough, his mother helped him find a job. Among the legacies of these remarkable letters are an implicit warning

56. Peter the Venerable, letter to Heloise, in ibid., p. 287: "I will gladly do my best to obtain a prebend in one of the great churches for your Astralabe, who is also ours for your sake."
57. Ibid., p. 150.
58. See Bynum, *Jesus as Mother*, p. 154.

against overgeneralization from the writings of one group of people and a reminder that the notion of "motherhood" maintained by Cistercian monks was not necessarily shared by actual parents.

These world-famous lovers, obviously unaffected by Cistercian ideas about motherhood, were also untouched by the contemporary phenomenon known (much later) as "courtly love." Their passionate affair bore no resemblance to the idealized yearnings of the troubadours, and their gender roles reversed those of the courts, where young men worshiped unattainable, godlike older women. Abelard and Heloise belonged to Paris, not Provence; to the university and the cathedral, not the court. Furthermore, they existed, whereas no one is certain that courtly lovers ever lived outside of songs and stories.[59]

If courtly love had any reality beyond literary convention, it was confined to the new leisure class of twelfth-century Europe. An improved climate, increased food production, and substantial population increase made possible, for the first time in the West since late antiquity, the existence of persons with energy to spare from "work"—defined in the early Middle Ages as fighting, prayer, and agricultural labor. In some parts of Europe the constant burden of war and preparation for war was lightened by improvements in material conditions and by the long-term efforts of Church and Crown to channel and control endemic violence. The Crusades and the ecclesiastical peace movements limited the extent and duration of hostilities within Europe, and at certain courts war games and tournaments replaced battles. An aristocracy based on land-ownership and lineage rather than military achievement came into being; noble status could be reflected and displayed in manners and behavior, creating a market for discussions of style. *The Art of Courtly Love* does not necessarily describe real situa-

59. John F. Benton suggested that "The study of love in the middle ages would be far easier if we were not impeded by a term which now inevitably confuses the issues. As currently employed, 'courtly love' has no useful meaning. . . .I would therefore like to propose that 'courtly love' be banned from all future conferences"; see "Clio and Venus: An Historical View of Medieval Love," in *The Meaning of Courtly Love*, ed. Francis X. Newman (Albany: State University of New York Press, 1968), p. 37.

tions, but it does mark a new attention to the social relations of upper-class men and women.[60]

Twelfth-century romance, like twelfth-century religious culture, was rooted in demographic change. Men no longer outnumbered women; upper-class men tended to marry late and to marry women much younger than themselves, creating a situation in which wives occupied a middle, mediating position between husbands and children. Young widowed mothers and distant older fathers were commonplaces of aristocratic life and literature; a son might easily become the "lord" of his widowed mother. Women who interceded for their children with authoritative men and women who bowed before their sons were familiar figures in feudal society as well as religious art.[61] And with the establishment of primogeniture in some parts of Europe came increasing friction among the male members of aristocratic families. Eldest sons waited impatiently to inherit land and position; younger brothers were excluded from family estates and from the opportunity to take over their fathers' roles. Whether they entered religious life or became landless knights, they remained unmarried and childless, perpetually "young" and dependent on patronage. For these men, it may have been useful and appropriate to direct emotional energy toward unattainable women—the Virgin of the monks, or the knight's lady. An older woman with power derived from close relationship to a lord aroused complicated passions in the "young."[62]

60. Andreas Capellanus said, "If you should, by some chance, fall in love with a peasant woman, be careful to puff her up with lots of praise and then, when you find a convenient place, do not hesitate to take what you seek and to embrace her by force"; see *The Art of Courtly Love by Andreas Capellanus* 1.9, trans. John Jay Parry (New York: Ungar, 1957), p. 24. Scholars debate whether this treatise is intended to be satirical, but in none of the courtly literature is there evidence of respect, let alone adoration, for peasant women.

61. See David Herlihy, "The Generation in Medieval History," *Viator* 5 (1974), 347–364; also Doris Desclais Berkvam, *Enfance et maternité dans la littérature français des XIIe et XIIIe siècles* (Paris: Librairie Honoré Champion, 1981), p. 139.

62. See Georges Duby, "Au XIIe siècle: Les 'Jeunes' dans la société aristocratique," *Annales E.S.C.* 19 (1964), 835–846. Christianne Marchello-Nizia argues that the energy of courtly love derived from the relationship of young men to older, more powerful men: the lady was a convenient device for the expression of a

There are significant analogies between the cult of the Lady and that of the Virgin. In striking respects, not least her "maternal" characteristics (which included youth and beauty), the Lady of the troubadours resembled the Lady of hymns and prayers. What is not clear is the degree of resemblance between either lady and any real woman, the extent to which these phenomena influenced the status or experience of women, or the positive and negative implications of such influence.[63] Was the figure of the Lady drawn from real situations, however limited in social context, or was it entirely a projection of fantasy, a creation of the "male gaze"? Julia Kristeva believes that a common origin in the male psyche links courtly love to the cult of the Virgin: "Even in its carnal beginnings courtly love had this in common with Mariolatry, that both Mary and the Lady were focal points of men's aspirations and desires."[64] Whether or not she existed, the lady of secular and religious romance was a significant figure in twelfth-century Christian ideologies. Men brought to the new cults and the new romantic literature their filial-erotic passion for the older woman– young mother. The Mary of the *Planctus* (the lament of the Virgin at the Cross) mourns Jesus her son, her lover, and her father.[65] The intertwined feelings distinguished by twentieth-century people as "filial," "maternal," and "erotic" were expressed with the forceful passion that characterized the age.

---

passion that had more to do with ambition than with heterosexual love; see "Amour courtois, société masculin, et figures du pouvoir," *Annales E.S.C.* 36 (1981), 969–982.

63. Once hailed as the supreme European contribution to the elevation of the status of women, courtly love (and "chivalry" in general) has recently been perceived as the base of that "pedestal" whose shadow is the stake. See E. William Monter, "The Pedestal and the Stake: Courtly Love and Witchcraft," in *Becoming Visible: Women in European History*, ed. Renata Bridenthal and Claudia Koonz (Boston: Houghton Mifflin, 1977), pp. 119–138; also Penny Schine Gold, *The Lady and the Virgin: Image, Attitude, and Experience in Twelfth-Century France* (Chicago: University of Chicago Press, 1985).

64. Julia Kristeva, "Stabat Mater," in *The Female Body in Western Culture*, ed. Susan Rubin Suleiman (Cambridge, Mass.: Harvard University Press, 1986), p. 106.

65. See John R. Secor, "The *Planctus Mariae* in Provençal Literature: A Subtle Blend of Courtly and Religious Tradition," in *Spirit of the Court*, ed. G. S. Burgess and R. A. Taylor (Cambridge: D. S. Brewer, 1985), pp. 321–326.

After the middle of the eleventh century, literary images of Mary began to be affected by the interests and values of persons and groups outside the elites of court and cloister. The dignified Queen Mother of the early Middle Ages grew to incorporate the joyful young mother of Bethlehem and the tragic old woman at the Cross. Her portraits in paint and stone and song represented many phases of life: youth and beauty and tenderness, age and suffering and death. Monks continued to produce devotional and theological writings but turned also to genres and materials that were subject to influence from outside the monastic world. Mary's legend and cult received inspiration from new sources, including the collections of tales and legends that were gathered, written down, and circulated first inside and then far outside the monasteries and convents of western Europe.

Stories about the Virgin and her miracles, many of which originated in the East, had always been told in medieval Europe: as early as the sixth century, Gregory of Tours included six such tales in his *Book of Wonders*. By the late eleventh century, however, the context in which the stories were known was very different from that of the sixth. With the new literacy and interest in texts and in writing, monks and others began to record old stories—in Latin at first, but soon in the vernacular languages. Collections were made for the edification of monks and nuns, for the satisfaction of various communities and interest groups, and for the use of preachers and storytellers, who carried the tales far from their monastic homes.[66] The interests of readers (more often, of listeners) became more significant in the construction of individual tales and the shaping of collections. "Reader response," the enthusiasm or indifference and special tastes of audiences, had an impact on the writers and tellers, and folkloric elements in the legends blended with monastic Mariology. The written miracles are not "popular" stories in the literary sense, for they were told to and by clerics and composed by a literate elite. Nonetheless, as the stories grew more and more "popular" in the sense of "well-liked," and widely available, audiences included lay people as well as monks, women as well as men, the nonliterate as well as the

---

66. See, e.g., Southern, "English Origin."

educated, parents as well as celibates. Through their likes and dislikes, their values and concerns, these persons and groups took part in the construction of the new "Mary."

To read medieval "Miracles of the Virgin" is to be struck by the force and scope of Mary's powers in contrast to the helplessness and contingency of human beings. The men and women in the tales could not protect themselves or their children against sickness, death, or the consequences of sin. Their only recourse against harsh circumstances was to appeal to Mary, whose power was never in doubt, although she had to be persuaded to act. The keys to such persuasion were simple: supplicants had to prove single-minded devotion by prayer, constancy, and the performance of ritual acts of service. Mary did not come to the aid of suffering humanity out of the "unconditional love" ascribed to good mothers by modern psychologists; she required devoted attention. She did not expect heroism of her servants, or even good behavior, but she did demand faithfulness.[67]

Even a thief could be faithful, as demonstrated in the often-repeated story of "the hanged man":

There was once a very great robber, a most wicked man. . . . Yet he had this good in him that he scrupulously fasted on bread and water during the vigil of the blessed Mary; and, when he went out to rob he used to salute her with such devotion as he could, asking her not to allow him to die in mortal sin.

But, being caught and brought to the gallows, he hung for three days and could not die. And when he called to those passing by and asked them to bring a priest, one came with the judge and the people and he was taken down from the gallows. Then said he that it was the blessed Virgin who kept him alive; and so he was set free, and afterwards he finished his life in praiseworthy fashion.[68]

67. The protagonists of the miracle stories, who ask for and receive help from the Virgin, are in that respect unlike courtly lovers, who were supposed to expect no favors in return for their devotion. See Frederick Goldin, "The Array of Perspectives in the Early Courtly Love Lyric," in *In Pursuit of Perfection*, ed. Joan M. Ferrante and George D. Economou (Port Washington, N.Y.: Kennikat Press, 1975), p. 55. The miracles represent a steady stream of transactions between Mary and her suitors: it is assumed that services will be exchanged.

68. Johannes Herolt, *Miracles of the Blessed Virgin Mary: Johannes Herolt*, trans. C. C. S. Bland (London: George Routledge, 1928), pp. 22–23. Other versions

The thief's crimes paled in significance beside his devotion to Mary; she protected much more vicious sinners than he.[69] The stories frequently end with the sinner's reform, but the reform is a by-product of the miracle, not its purpose. The stories are about Mary's mercy and power, not about the conversion of sinners.

Medieval paintings, theological writings, and visionary literature tend to emphasize Mary's mediating role: interceding for sinners, she uses her maternal influence to plead for mercy from Christ the Judge, or God the Father, who is the central figure.[70] In the stories, Christ appears less frequently and then typically as a little child. Mary uses her own strength on behalf of her servants—she spares the hanged man without help from her son.[71] Like the warrior chiefs and patron saints of the early Middle Ages, she rewards her followers with her own gifts, taking care of her people. The ethical system of the tales has the character of the earlier period, when loyalty (from follower to lord) and generosity (from lord to follower) were normative virtues of the ruling class. Certainly Mary's power was understood to come from God and from her relationship to God, but in the tales she is active and independent: God remains in the background, or in his mother's arms.

The "miracles" include stories about kings and queens, knights and ladies, monks and nuns, criminals and poor old widows. In many of the tales, hierarchical assumptions and expectations are overturned, reinforcing the theme of the "Magnificat." A monk who knows no Latin and can learn none save the "Ave Maria" is despised by his brothers and superiors. When he dies, a fabulous

---

of the story are recounted in The "Stella Maris" of John of Garland, ed. Evelyn Faye Wilson (Cambridge, Mass.: Medieval Academy of America, 1946), pp. 209–210 (hereafter Stella Maris).

69. Even perpetrators of incest and infanticide were protected: in several stories, when a mother who loves her son "too well" and bears a child-grandchild whom she kills, Mary saves her from execution for murder. See Stella Maris, pp. 176–177.

70. In artistic representations of the "double intercession," Mary displays her breast, Jesus his wounds, to persuade God to show mercy to sinners. See, e.g., Warner, Alone of All Her Sex, fig. 26; and Bynum, Holy Feast, figs. 28, 29. Cf. also Birgitta's vision of Mary pleading for the soul of Karl, in Chapter 5.

71. My interpretation differs from the thesis of Mary Vincentine Gripkey, The Blessed Virgin Mary as Mediatrix in the Latin and Old French Legend prior to the Fourteenth Century (Washington, D.C.: Catholic University of America, 1938).

lily—the words "Ave Maria" engraved on every leaf—grows out of his grave.[72] Humility triumphs; the mighty are put down; Mary's servants are justified.

The curious tale of "the hostage," which appears in many of the collections, illustrates the relationship of image and reality in medieval Europe. A mother whose child is in imminent danger of death prays for help to a statue of the Madonna. When no help comes, the woman snatches the image of the Christ Child from the statue and threatens to keep it until her own child is returned. Mary then sets to work to rescue the other mother's child.[73] There is never any doubt about her ability to do so, but she must be begged or bullied into action. Hostages, usually children, were commonly given and taken in medieval Europe, and Mary did not become angry when her own child was taken—perhaps because she recognized maternal desperation. The question "Why doesn't she simply take back the Christ Child?" was not asked or answered; after all, she did not take him back from the Cross.

The numerous children and infants in the stories present a poignant and complicated glimpse of medieval childhood. Children faced mutilation and death by fire and water, disease and accident; they were promised to the Devil by wicked or careless parents; they were neglected and abused as well as loved and cherished by parents and parental surrogates. Their presence in such numbers, with the assumption that they and their circumstances are touching and pitiful, argues against the "indifference" to children sometimes attributed to medieval adults.[74] On the

72. In a pleasant rendering of this common theme, a feeble-minded priest was prohibited by his bishop, Thomas Becket, from saying mass. Mary ordered the priest restored to his office, reminding St. Thomas that she had once helped him repair his hair shirt. Becket obeyed immediately. See Caesarius of Heisterbach, *Dialogue on Miracles*, ed. G. G. Coulton and Eileen Power (London: George Routledge, 1929), 1:458–459.

73. In the *Golden Legend* version (p. 527), the mother returns the image of Christ, saying, "Thanks be to thee, Lady, for that thou has returned my only son to me; and now I do the same for thee."

74. In *Centuries of Childhood: A Social History of Family Life*, trans. Robert Baldick (New York: Knopf, 1962), Philippe Ariès asserted that emotional ties between parents and children were weak until the seventeenth century. Similarly, in *The Family, Sex, and Marriage in England, 1500–1800* (New York: Harper & Row, 1977), Lawrence Stone finds weak emotional bonds in English family life

other hand, the stories do not supply evidence of careful and empathic parenting—far from it: Mary is a much more satisfactory parent than any of the adults.

The collection of miracles from the shrine of the Virgin of Chartres is a rich source of stories about children spared from horrible fates. Little Guillot discovered a girl from his village in the arms of a knight, who cut out the child's tongue so he would not report what he had seen. The Virgin restored the boy's speech three days after Easter and replaced his tongue at Pentecost.[75] A babysitter gave a crying infant a piece of glass to play with; the child swallowed the glass, choked, and died. When the mother returned, she set out for Chartres with the baby, and even before they reached the shrine, it coughed up the glass and returned to life.[76] A lady was godmother to her servant's child; when he drowned in a ditch, the lady promised to make an annual pilgrimage to Chartres if the child was restored to life, and she kept that promise to the end of her life.[77] A couple longed for a baby, prayed to Mary, and had a son. The father went on a pilgrimage of thanksgiving, and while he was gone, the mother—bathing with the baby—fell asleep and let him drown. She was convicted of infanticide and sentenced to burning, but her husband returned in time to ask for Mary's help. Just before the fire was lit, the mother asked permission to kiss her dead infant one more time—and with

---

before early modern times, when the "closed domesticated nuclear family" replaced the "open lineage family" of the Middle Ages. Edward Shorter, in *The Making of the Modern Family* (New York: Basic Books, 1975), pp. 168–204, extends Ariès's position and finds widespread parental, especially maternal, indifference to children well into the eighteenth and early nineteenth centuries. Recently, many historians have rejected this characterization of medieval families: e.g., David Herlihy, *Medieval Households* (Cambridge, Mass.: Harvard University Press, 1985), esp. pp. 112–130; David Hunt, *Parents and Children in History: The Psychology of Family Life in Early Modern France* (New York: Basic Books, 1970); Klaus Arnold, *Kind und Gesellschaft in Mittelalter und Renaissance: Beitrage und Texte zur Geschichte der Kindheit* (Cambridge, Mass.: Harvard University Press, 1985).

75. *Miracles de Notre-Dame de Chartres*, Pierre Kunstmann, ed., (Ottawa: Editions de l'Université d'Ottawa, 1973), p. 36.

76. Ibid.

77. Ibid., p. 40.

the kiss, he came back to life. Unable to leave well enough alone, the couple then set out on another pilgrimage of thanksgiving.[78]

The insecurity and real dangers of medieval childhood created powerful, persistent fantasies of protection and rescue by an omnipotent, loving mother. In that age of high infant and child mortality, parents could not protect their children from illness or from sudden, violent death. Through that harsh reality as well as the neglect and abuse common in every age, children suffered greatly. The tale of the child promised to the Devil by parents who later repent and regret the bargain appears in many collections; its representation of parental ambivalence must have struck a significant chord. At adolescence, the child—like the protagonist of a folktale—must go out into the world to find someone to rescue him; his parents cannot. Various powerful religious men (pope, patriarch, holy hermit) try to help, but in the end it is Mary—the unambivalent mother—who saves him from the Devil.[79] The innocent child, carrying the burden of his parents' sin, depends on the Virgin for redemption.

A significant number of the miracles that focus on children are also anti-Jewish tales; these themes were linked to each other and to Mary. Chaucer's Prioress told the well-known story of the little "clergeon," or schoolboy, in a version filled with the language and imagery of mothers and children.[80] Like so many of the young protagonists, the clergeon was a widow's son and thus especially pitiful, vulnerable, and Christlike. As he walked to school through the ghetto he sang the "Alma Redemptoris": the Jews hated the song and killed the singer, cutting his throat and dropping his body in a sewer. When the widow could not find her child she prayed to Mary, who caused him to sing again (with his throat cut) until the Christians discovered the body and slaughtered the

78. *Etudes sur les miracles de Notre-Dame par personnages*, ed. Marguerite Stadler-Honegger (Geneva: Slatkine Reprints, 1975), pp. 51–53.

79. Several versions of the story appear in *Stella Maris*, pp. 201–202. In this folkloric tale, the hero must leave home to make his way in the world—thus the protagonist is inevitably male.

80. Nikki Stiller makes this point in *Eve's Orphans: Mothers and Daughters in Medieval English Literature* (Westport, Conn.: Greenwood Press, 1980), p. 114.

Jews.[81] The opposite number of the clergeon was the Jewish boy who innocently received the Eucharist with his Christian schoolmates. When his father found out, he put the child in a furnace, where the Virgin protected him from harm until he was rescued by a Christian friend. Then the father was killed—by crucifixion in some versions, and in others by taking his son's place in the furnace.[82] Representing all Jews, the father was made to suffer the fate of the "victim"—the young protagonist of the story or the Christ Child himself.

Anti-Jewish stories were written with grim zest; strategies for getting the better of Jews were reported with vengeful delight. In one of the nastiest tales, a young Jewish woman is seduced and made pregnant by a clerk. She fears her parents' anger, and the clerk persuades her to tell them that she is a virgin. He then speaks to them at night through a hollow reed, announcing that their daughter "hath conceived a son, who shall be the deliverer of your people Israel." (When that promise turns to bitter disappointment, according to the author, it is "fitting that they whose forefathers had been troubled by Herod by the birth of the Son of God . . . should in these times be mocked.") The family and the community, believing the girl, take care of her and gather for the birth: "The hour came in which the unhappy one should be delivered, and there ensued the usual pains, groans, and cries. At last she brought forth an infant, not indeed the Messiah, but a daughter. When this became known, there was much confusion and trouble among the Jews, and one of them, wild with indignation, seized

81. See Geoffrey Chaucer, "The Prioress's Tale," in *The Riverside Chaucer*, ed. Larry Benson (Boston: Houghton Mifflin, 1987), pp. 209–212. Lester Little notes the association of money, Jews, and filth and the scatological details in medieval anti-Jewish writings; see *Religious Poverty and the Profit Economy in Medieval Europe* (Ithaca: Cornell University Press, 1978), esp. pp. 51–57.

82. This often repeated story was told by Evagrius Scholasticus in the sixth century about a glassblower's son—hence the furnace. It was translated from Greek in the ninth century and appears in most of the major collections (e.g., *Stella Maris*, pp. 157–159). In a Middle English version, the boy fell in love with an *image* of Mary, which protected him in the furnace; he and his mother were saved (and converted) when the father was killed. See *The Middle English Miracles of the Virgin*, ed. Beverly Boyd (San Marino, Calif.: Huntington Library, 1964), pp. 38–43.

the poor baby by the foot and dashed it against the wall."[83] The very notion of a female Messiah, like that of a female pope, is inconceivable and contemptible, provoking hideous revenge on mother and infant.

In some stories Mary is represented as sympathetic to Jewish women as mothers, although her protection and their survival always depend upon their conversion. Vincent of Beauvais, among others, told of a woman in childbirth who saw a heavenly light and heard a voice telling her to call on Mary. She obeyed and gave birth safely and painlessly, but then had to leave her family and community and flee to a church for baptism and protection against the furious Jews.[84] In another tale, a Jewish wife reported her husband for damaging a holy image—an image of Christ alone in the original Greek story but, in the later western version, an image of Christ in Mary's lap: by the twelfth century, certain kinds of story were unthinkable without the Virgin. Stories about the defacement of images generally ended with the capture and brutal punishment of the perpetrator, or with a conversion effected by the miraculous events surrounding discovery. Blood gushes from mutilated images, identifying the villains and demonstrating the powers of Mary and of Christ.[85]

The persistence and cruelty of anti-Jewish stories, which were widely circulated in the twelfth century and later, reflect a level of hatred and resentment maintained at simmering point and ready to break into overt violence when there was an incident, or a Crusade. Such stories held profound meanings for their audiences, for they were repeated over and over for centuries. Helpless, fragile children were presented as logical victims of Jewish aggression; they were identified with Jesus, portrayed in Christian teaching as the victim of the Jews. Children were seen as simple, innocent, and pure, like most of Mary's favorites. As the custodian of Christ's infancy, the only human being with whom he was physically intimate, Mary was also the custodian of all children

---

83. Caesarius, *Dialogues*, 1:104–106.
84. *Stella Maris*, pp. 189–190.
85. Ibid., p. 203.

threatened by enemies of her son. The stories demonstrate the phenomenon of reversal, characteristic of hate literature: while Christians, especially Christian children, were depicted as the victims of Jews, Jews in medieval Europe were in fact being persecuted and killed by Christians.[86]

Jews were portrayed as faithless betrayers (of Christ); Mary's help and protection were contingent upon absolute fidelity to her. She brooked no competition with any other relationship or with ties of family, faith, or community and fiercely resisted her lovers' attempts to form other romantic associations. The boy who betrothes himself to Mary (usually to an image of Mary) and then is pushed toward marriage by insistent parents is always sharply reminded of the earlier vow. It most versions he escapes at the last minute and becomes a monk, preserving his commitment to the Virgin.[87] Because she demanded utter fidelity, her consistent preference was for men in religious life, who were not distracted from her service. The monks who wrote down these stories presented themselves as Mary's favorites.

Although some of the legends were very old in the twelfth century, others were new, and many of the new stories originated in the cloister. A major theme of Caesarius of Heisterbach's *Dialogue on Miracles* was Mary's passion for the Cistercians, displayed by public protection of the order and intimate service to its members. She visited sick monks in the infirmary, blessing the virtuous brothers while they slept; one monk "saw in the dormitory a woman of wonderful beauty. She went round the beds of the sleepers and gave a blessing to each one, leaving out only one monk from whom she turned away her eyes . . . he confessed that he had lain that night somewhat carelessly, relaxing from the strict rule of the order." The work and piety of good monks received Mary's encouragement, affection, and maternal care. Another reported seeing "Our Lady one night go around the choir while they were singing the psalms and wipe the faces of all the

86. Little makes this point in *Religious Poverty*, pp. 51–52.

87. This group of stories, varied in detail and setting, is one of the oldest; it descends from Roman tales of a young man betrothed to Venus. See *Stella Maris*, pp. 161–166.

monks but two. Of these two, one soon became an apostate and it is not yet known what became of the other."[88]

The Virgin even recruited for the Cistercians. A monk struggled to persuade the abbot to accept a younger brother who was too young, according to the rules, but his brother was worried about him. The abbot's favorable decision was influenced by a vision of a lovely woman "before the monastery gate, holding a beautiful boy in her arms; and when he asked her whose boy it was, she replied, "He is the son of the monk———," mentioning the older brother by name.[89] Motherhood, in that context, was defined by care and protection, and the novice had two "mothers": Mary, and his older brother.

Caesarius's interlocutor asked whether the Virgin loved and visited religious women as well as men. The monk, claiming that she made no distinction based on sex, reported two visits to convents but quickly returned to stories about Mary's love for the monks. His indifference to the fate of women, even religious women, was revealed in the story of the youth who "violated a certain nun, and urged both by shame and fear, because she was nobly born, he took the vows in our Order. So that what the devil had prepared for his ruin became for him an occasion of salvation."[90] Caesarius says nothing more about the nun, or about the spiritual and practical consequences of the seduction. His attitude illustrates the difficulties faced by women who wanted to be Cistercian nuns or were directed by Cistercian monks.

The often repeated tale of the pregnant abbess is usually set among nuns who suspected their superior of hypocrisy and resent her strictness. The abbess has an affair, becomes pregnant, and dreads the bishop's next visit. When she asks the Virgin for help, Mary delivers the child in secret and takes it to a hermit to be raised—again, a religious man is seen as a natural "mother." The reputation of the abbess and the convent is

88. Caesarius, *Dialogue*, 1:471, 480.
89. Ibid., p. 29.
90. Ibid., p. 38.

preserved, and the child survives to become a monk and faithful servant of Mary.[91]

The story of Beatrice the sacristan, another erring nun, was as popular as that of the pregnant abbess. Beatrice ran away with a lover, leaving her keys on Mary's altar. Fifteen years later she returned, miserable and repentant, to find that "Beatrice" had been doing her work all the time, and achieving a reputation for sanctity as well.[92] In this and several other stories, Mary changes her shape like a character in folklore. She appeared in one story as a soldier, taking the place of a knight who missed a tournament because he stopped to say his prayers at her shrine. When he finally arrived, he was welcomed with the news that he had won all the prizes.[93] One could not lose through faithfulness to Mary.

Several popular stories featured Mary's milk, or her breasts—powerful symbols and sources of power. The twentieth-century fascination with breasts as erotic objects was not characteristic of the twelfth century, when all children, in order to live, were fed by women. Breasts represented health and life and strength; in the case of Mary, who fed Christ, they also represented supernatural healing. Her milk cured sick or dying holy men, especially if the illness affected the lips, tongue, or throat: medieval people believed that any source of power worked most effectively in direct contact with the injured area. When important people like St. Bernard were involved, Mary's milk was a reward for devotion, but with simple monks or clerks it was restorative. I know of no miracles involving Mary's milk in which the beneficiaries were others than monks and priests; to the men who told these stories, the Virgin's milk was a resource for her favorite sons.[94]

91. In the version of this story told in Herolt's *Miracles*, p. 43, "this very boy, proving his fitness for it by his learning and his holy life, was the successor of that bishop." Such stories should be read also in the context of satirical writings in secular literature: see Graciela S. Daichman, *Wayward Nuns in Medieval Literature* (Syracuse, N.Y.: Syracuse University Press, 1986).

92. Herolt, *Miracles*, pp. 43–45.

93. *Golden Legend*, pp. 525–526.

94. *Stella Maris*, pp. 155–156. See also Paule-V. Bétérous, "A propos d'une des légendes mariales les plus répandues: Le 'lait de la Vierge,' " *Bullétin de l'Association Guillaume Budé* 4 (1975), 403–411. Fulbert of Chartres, who wrote hymns and sermons for Mary and established the feast of her Nativity at Chartres, was one of the beneficiaries of this cure, according to William of Malmesbury in

Christian motherhood has been profoundly influenced by the historical construction of the mother of God. Using scraps of evidence in the canonical gospels and the rich material of the apocrypha, early Christians built a towering female presence in theology, art, and worship. Her status was assured by developments in Christology: the God-man saved all men and women through humanity derived from his mother, and in learned writing and preaching, Mariology conformed to Christology. The figure of Mary also had aspects independent of Christology, gradually acquiring certain functions and attributes of the mother-goddesses of the old religions. In the Virgin, Christians discovered and made manifest in art and worship the powers of a sacred female being common to many of the world's religions.

In the West in the early Middle Ages, Mary was perceived as a queen-empress, presiding in a distant heaven with God the Father and God the Son; the healing and cherishing, erotic and reproductive powers of the sacred were left to more immediate saints. Amid the rapid economic, social, and cultural development of the eleventh century, Mary became again an immediate and vital presence in the experience and imagination of her devotees. The Virgin of the Gothic cathedrals, the loving Madonna of painting and sculpture, was represented in many kinds of religious literature, from the treatises and prayers that arose in reformed monastic orders to stories that circulated far outside the cloister. Men like St. Anselm and St. Bernard brought a new intensity to their praise of Mary, converting Mother and Queen into Lover and Bride. The Mary legends, shaped in part by the values and experience of lay people, reflected a similar intensity: their Mary is passionate, beautiful, and exclusive—an exemplary mother to small children, a jealous lover and devoted helpmate of religious men. The major contributions of twelfth-century Christians to the history of motherhood in the West were made through the cult of the Virgin, which stimulated a new recognition of the erotic aspects of mother love and appreciation of its passionate intensity.

Gesta regum anglorum, ed. William Stubbs (London: Rolls Series 90, 1887–89), 2:341.

CHAPTER FIVE

"Mother of Love, Mother of Tears": Holiness and Families in the Later Middle Ages

In the later Middle Ages, Christian teachers, artists, and religious leaders expressed a new appreciation of marriage, family, and motherhood, while certain women rediscovered in their lives the compatibility of holiness and physical maternity. For a thousand years, physical and spiritual motherhood had been perceived and presented as alternatives; the martyrdom of Perpetua and Felicitas was celebrated, their maternity forgotten or ignored.[1] The hierarchy of sanctity (virgins first, then widows, then wives) was arranged according to sexual, not parental status, but physical motherhood was at least a glaring reminder of sexual activity and sometimes also an obstacle to the way of life expected of saints. Mary was the perfect mother, but her virginity was emphasized over her maternity; medieval women were not often exhorted to emulate Mary in relation to their own children. In the monastic ethos that had permeated Christian spirituality since the fourth century, true holiness required the renunciation of physical comfort, sexual passion, and all the joys and burdens of family life.

Between the thirteenth and the fifteenth centuries there were significant shifts in these traditional attitudes. Renewed attention

---

1. In *The Sarum Missal*, ed. J. Wickham Legg (Oxford: Clarendon Press, 1916), p. 256, their names appear under the rubric "sanctarum virginum perpetue et felicitas, martyrum." Much more recently, Felicitas was remembered as a "virgin

was paid to families—to the family of Jesus, and to human families. Attentive portrayals of little children and touching representations of domestic relationships appeared more frequently in Christian art and literature. Believers were encouraged to discover and exploit tender family affections, the better to love God. It is more remarkable that increasing numbers of married women were admitted to the company of saints after the thirteenth century. Most of these women had children, whose upbringing and very existence fostered the development of new ideologies both of sanctity and of motherhood. Maternity was understood to include intense suffering and thus was easily associated with the pains and sorrows of Christ and Mary and with the suffering expected of saints in the late Middle Ages. Over time, the domestic and mystical experience of the new saints stretched the boundaries of existing definitions not only of motherhood and holiness but of human and divine love.

Family relationships interested secular as well as religious audiences in late medieval Europe: the story of one long-suffering wife and mother was adapted by the three most prominent literary figures of the fourteenth century. Long established in the oral tradition in Italy and elsewhere, "Patient Griselda" made her first literary appearance in Boccaccio's *Decameron* in 1353. Petrarch's Latin edition of the story, from the 1370s, was borrowed by Chaucer for his "Clerk's Tale," the version of the story most familiar to English readers. With all its ambiguities, and the various interpretations of its meanings, the tale of Griselda sheds a slanting, eccentric light on the development of certain maternal themes in late medieval culture.

The Marquis Walter, "a fair persone, and strong, and yong of age, and ful of honour and of curteisye,"[2] chose the lovely Griselda for his bride—an extraordinary choice because her father, Janicula, was the poorest of all poor folk in the village. Griselda was not only beautiful; she was accustomed to hard work, obedience, and

---

martyr" on the first page of Mary Gordon's novel *The Company of Women* (New York: Ballantine Books, 1980).

2. Geoffrey Chaucer, "The Clerk's Tale," in *The Riverside Chaucer*, p. 138.

deprivation, and she cheerfully promised never to question Walter's actions or decisions. When their first child was born, Walter tested her promise, telling her (untruthfully) that his people would not accept Janicula's grandchild—the baby had to be killed. Griselda offered no objection, saying that since she and her daughter belonged to Walter, he could do as he liked with them. When the sergeant came for the child, Griselda neither wept nor resisted but commended the baby to its merciful Father in Heaven. (She did mention Christ's sacrificial death, in unspoken contrast to the sacrifice of her child to its father's whim.) Chaucer's Clerk commented that even a nurse would have suffered at such cruelty; a mother might have been expected to weep. Griselda simply begged the sergeant to bury the little body in a place where wild beasts could not get it. Walter secretly sent the baby to his sister, but Griselda believed that her daughter was dead.

Four years later a son was born, and Walter arranged another test of his wife's "patience." Griselda agreed again that Walter could do as he wished, observing that her children brought her sickness before they were born and pain forever after. This time the sergeant would not even promise to bury the baby too deep for the beasts, and the Clerk remarked that if Walter had not known how much Griselda loved her child, he might have been surprised at her calm.

The marquis still was not satisfied. In an elaborate final test, Griselda was sent away from the palace, supposedly to make room for a new bride. Gladly leaving her fine clothes and jewels, she asked only for a smock to cover her nakedness; she would not shame Walter by exposing the womb that bore his children.[3] Later she was called back to the palace to prepare rooms and a wedding feast, and again she complied, although she advised Walter to be kinder to his second wife, who was nobly born and unaccustomed to hardship. The "bride" was finally revealed as the lost daughter, returned with her brother in time to see their mother restored to her rightful place. Discovering her children to be alive, Griselda fainted with joy:

3. Christiane Klapisch-Zuber (*Women, Family, and Ritual*, pp. 213–246) discusses the clothing and unclothing of Griselda in the context of Florentine dowries.

She bothe hire yonge children to hire calleth,
And in hire armes, pitously wepynge,
Embraceth hem, and tendrely kissynge
Ful lyk a mooder, with hire salte teeres
She bathed bothe hire visage and hire
    heeres.[4]

Weeping, Griselda at last behaved "like a mother." She told Walter how grateful she was that their children had not been eaten by dogs and worms, and all four lived happily ever after. The Clerk, however, warning that such tests were excessively severe for ordinary women, advised readers to imitate not Walter but Griselda, by accepting with patience the sorrows sent by God.

The several tellers of this tale invited readers to observe the behavior of a jealous husband and a virtuous wife, behavior sufficiently bizarre to lend itself to diverse interpretations. For some Chaucer scholars, Griselda is best understood as the opposite number of the Wife of Bath within the "Marriage Group" of Canterbury Tales, whose plots revolve around a struggle for mastery between husbands and wives. In Christian dress, the story has been seen as paradigmatic of the relation of the soul to God, whose will, inscrutable to human reason, is to be obeyed without question: the Clerk himself pointed that moral. As myth or folktale, "Patient Griselda" belongs to the large number of stories that explore the relationship, usually the marriage, of a mortal and an immortal—of Cupid and Psyche, or a man and a "fairy wife." Such interpretations may be plausible within their own interests and perspectives, but they do not explain why tears identify Griselda as a true mother, or—more difficult—why a mother exemplifies virtue when she acquiesces in infanticide.[5]

The story is grounded in assumptions about class and gender, specifically the economic power of husbands and their families over wives.

4. Chaucer, "The Clerk's Tale," p. 151.

5. See Mary J. Carruthers, "The Lady, the Swineherd, and Chaucer's Clerk," *Chaucer Review* 17 (1983), 221–234. For versions of the tale and its relationship to folk literature, see D. D. Griffith, *The Origin of the Griselda Story* (Chicago: University of Chicago Libraries, 1931). Few commentators have paid attention to its infanticidal theme; recent exceptions are Boswell, *Kindness of Strangers*, p. 412; and Stiller, *Eve's Orphans*, p. 3.

The origins and meanings of "Patient Griselda" are ancient and complicated; what claims attention here is its popularity in the fourteenth century.[6] Whatever the story says about the relationship of men and women, of nobles and peasants, or of God and the soul, what it does *not* say is equally important, as are the values that are *not* upheld. Griselda is expected not to protect her children from their father but to obey him. The relationship between husband and wife is morally more significant than that of parent and child. Maternal love, although admirable and expected, is not the core of a woman's "virtue," nor is a mother's care for her children an exclusive or even a primary good. Griselda is revealed as extraordinary through her preternatural calm, "like a mother" when she weeps. Motherhood—true motherhood—is inseparable from suffering and pain.

In literary form, "Patient Griselda" is a product of the late Middle Ages, a period characterized in the traditional historiography of northern Europe by decadence and decline in cultural and religious as well as political and economic life.[7] In recent years, historians have modified their image and interpretations of that era, perceiving creative ferment along with chaos and decay. The diverse contributions of the fourteenth and fifteenth centuries in art and architecture, political theory, and theology and religious life are recognized along with the disasters of plague, schism, and war. We still appreciate the distinctness of the period but also observe its continuities with the spiritual and intellectual achievements of the preceding High Middle Ages and with the theological insights and social reconstruction of the succeeding sixteenth century. Historians who investigate the experience of

6. On the uses of Griselda in the late Middle Ages, see Carruthers, "The Lady"; also Joan B. Williamson, "Philippe de Mezière's Book for Married Ladies: A Book from the Entourage of the Court of Charles VI," in *Spirit of the Court*, pp. 393–408.

7. The fourteenth and fifteenth centuries comprise both "the late Middle Ages" in northern Europe and "the Renaissance" in Italy (the Renaissance in the North is usually assigned to the sixteenth century). These two entities have been characterized very differently by historians, but they shared many things, including economic crisis, population decline, artistic creativity, religious ferment, and married saints. This chapter includes material from both North and South.

women and of men outside the ruling class have reevaluated the stereotype of late medieval decline, acknowledging that periods of social, theological, and artistic disorder tend to be productive as well as problematic.[8]

Late medieval culture was shaped by distinct, powerful geographic and economic factors affecting all of Europe. The long warming trend of the climate between the eighth and twelfth centuries came to an end in the thirteenth. Cold winters, short growing seasons, and erratic rainfall produced repeated crop failures, so that long before the Black Death of 1348, starvation and disease reversed the demographic growth that had tripled the population of Europe between the tenth century and the thirteenth.[9] A series of devastating famines began late in the thirteenth century and became more severe and widespread in the fourteenth. Without effective means of distributing food, local shortages resulted in malnutrition and starvation. Hungry people are especially vulnerable to disease, and fertility as well as infant and maternal mortality is much affected by diet. The intense suffering caused by hunger and illness, by the deaths of children and of parents, was a constant presence in the experience of late medieval people. Its sharpness and poignancy were exacerbated by the awareness that the times had been better and were growing worse. Pain and sorrow and the shadow of death were never far away, and the eternal association of birth with death, of suffering with motherhood, was dramatically underlined during these hard years.

The sharp decline in agricultural productivity and population did not, however, reverse all the social changes of the twelfth

8. See, e.g., David Herlihy, "Did Women Have a Renaissance? A Reconsideration," *Medievalia et Humanistica*, n.s. 13 (1985), 1–22. Herlihy responds to Joan Kelly Gadol's important essay, "Did Women Have a Renaissance?" in Bridenthal and Koonz, *Becoming Visible*, pp. 137–164. See also Clarissa W. Atkinson, *Mystic and Pilgrim: The Book and the World of Margery Kempe* (Ithaca: Cornell University Press, 1983), pp. 202–207.

9. The population of Europe increased from about twenty-five to seventy-five million between c. 950 and 1250; see Robert S. Gottfried, *The Black Death* (New York: Free Press, 1980), p. 17. The plague reduced the population by about a third in the middle of the fourteenth century; by the end of the fifteenth, it had come back to about sixty-five million; see Carlo Cipolla, *Before the Industrial Revolution* (New York: Norton, 1976), p. 200.

century. Towns and cities still accommodated people and groups outside the feudal classes of peasants, clerks, and nobles. Students, the urban middle class, and the urban poor were overrepresented among the heretics and other dissidents who plagued clerical and temporal authorities in the fourteenth century. In traditional church history, the "decline" of the institutional Church and of scholastic theology from the triumphs of the thirteenth century was analyzed in terms of overexpansion, corruption, and resultant disorder. With growth and bureaucratization, the legacy of Peter was sacrificed to that of Constantine.[10] The achievements of the great lawyer-popes included such positive elements as the creation and development of canon law, the regularization and elaboration of moral and theological doctrine, and the extension of religious instruction into dioceses and parishes. But such achievements were costly, producing too close an identification of Christ and culture. Spirituality could not be nurtured, controlled, or contained by the ecclesiastical bureaucracy. Charismatic leadership moved outside the Church, which was confronted by the threat of large popular heresies and by a torrent of scathing criticism from friends and enemies alike. Movements of reform produced disillusioned reformers. The disasters of the fourteenth century culminated in the crisis of the popes' removal to Avignon and the scandal of the Schism.

It is no wonder, perhaps, that heterodox movements and eccentric individuals attracted followers in the fourteenth century, or that unorthodox and "extreme" forms of piety and spiritual experience became almost commonplace.[11] Mystics, visionaries, and wandering preachers played a conspicuous part in the religious

10. The analogy was used even before the thirteenth century by Bernard of Clairvaux, among others; see his *Five Books on Consideration* IV.6, in *The Works of Bernard of Clairvaux*, vol. 3, trans. John D. Anderson and Elizabeth Kennan (Kalamazoo, Mich.: Cistercian Publications, 1976).

11. Religious "extremism" and "hysteria" have been much discussed in recent scholarship. See Atkinson, *Mystic and Pilgrim*, chap. 7; Bynum, *Holy Feast*, esp. pp. 161–165, 194–195, 202–203; Kieckhefer, *Unquiet Souls*, esp. the first and last chapters; Ilza Veith, *Hysteria: The History of a Disease* (Chicago: University of Chicago Press, 1965); Hope Weissman, "Margery Kempe in Jerusalem: *Hysteria Compassio* in the late Middle Ages," in *Acts of Interpretation: The Text in Its Contexts, 700–1600*, ed. M. J. Carruthers and E. D. Kirk (Norman, Okla.: Pilgrim Press, 1982), pp. 201–217.

life of the later Middle Ages. Such persons aspired to holiness and even to perfection. They attracted a great deal of attention and in some cases large followings; they were perceived as numinous figures even though, or perhaps because, they did not look or behave like members of the upper clergy.[12] Many of them—an alarming number, according to some observers—were women, and of these a considerable number were wives and mothers, for whose participation in such activities there was no precedent. No proper niche existed for them within prevailing notions either of holiness or of domesticity.

Women as well as men had been inspired by the example of the Franciscans and Dominicans in the thirteenth century. Unlike their monastic predecessors, the mendicants lived intensely in this world while preaching of the next. They worked among the poorest people in the most crowded places: the first Franciscans preached in a marketplace or a field in preference to a cathedral pulpit. Traditional monasticism was based on the assumption that God was best served by those who were separate from and unlike ordinary Christians, but the friars built bridges over the gulf between lay and monastic status and spirituality. They overturned traditional values by placing poverty and service before everything, even virginity, and their Third Orders offered the possibility of committed religious life to men and women with continuing secular and domestic responsibilities. The new "saints" of the fourteenth century followed the friars into the "borderland" between the lay and monastic worlds, and into the embrace of Lady Poverty.[13]

The friars' accommodation to the spirituality of lay people, including married people, occurred in a context of increasing respect for the estate of marriage. Since the Gregorian reform, lead-

---

12. R. W. Southern noted that St. Dominic was successful in part because he realized that would-be reformers marked by arrogance and extravagance were doomed to failure: *Western Society and the Church in the Middle Ages* (London: Penguin Books, 1970), p. 279. Among the Cathars, too, the *perfecti* were noted for their austerity; see Emmanuel LeRoy Ladurie, *Montaillou: The Promised Land of Error* (New York: George Braziller, 1978), pp. 78, 81.

13. Kieckhefer (*Unquiet Souls*, p. 193) speaks of saints from the "border zone. . .the boundary between the laity and the clergy," and of the ways in which this location shaped their spirituality.

ers of the Church had aspired to govern the marital behavior and arrangements even of kings and emperors and had worked hard to impose their views on a recalcitrant ruling class.[14] With the help of legal and theological systematization in the twelfth century and the regularization of Church order and practice in the thirteenth, marriage was defined as one of the seven sacraments. Clerics began to acquire a firm grip on the intimate domestic conduct of lay people, and clerical ideologies of conjugal and parental behavior were established as a permanent presence in the bedrooms and nurseries of Christian homes.[15]

Increased clerical attention to family life may have been inevitable after the twelfth century, when the menace of the Cathar heresy began to force rethinking and revision of ancient attitudes. Cathars believed that marriage and procreation were iniquitous, that the powers of evil endured through sexual reproduction. Their substantial threat to orthodox Christianity stimulated the development of legal, moral, and theological rationales for Christian marriage. With a new force and precision, the clergy regulated who could marry and under what circumstances and preached to husbands and wives about their duties, privileges, and responsibilities. The debates and decisions of theologians and canon lawyers were carried to the people through sermons and catechisms and imposed through the authority of pulpit and confessional. Instructions about marriage were included in the large-scale effort to institute and maintain appropriate religious education after the Fourth Lateran Council in 1215.[16] In the course of the thirteenth

14. Christian kings continued to take concubines and to divorce their wives, but not with the freedom of Charlemagne; see Georges Duby, *The Knight, the Lady, and the Priest* (New York: Pantheon Books, 1983).

15. In "Birth Control in the West in the Thirteenth and Early Fourteenth Centuries," *Past and Present* 94 (1982), 3–26, P. P. A. Billar differs with Noonan (*Contraception*) with regard to the extent of contraceptive practice among medieval Christians. Billar's estimate is considerably higher, but both scholars emphasize the extensive efforts of clergy and canonists to make and enforce rules governing sexual practice. Such efforts continue in modern times: see *Humanae vitae*, the 1968 encyclical of Paul VI; and *Pastoral Letters of the U.S. Catholic Bishops* (1983–88), ed. Hugh J. Nolan (Washington, D.C.: National Conference of Catholic Bishops, 1989), 5:551: "Human sexuality. . .is to be genitally expressed only in a monogamous, heterosexual relationship of lasting fidelity in marriage."

16. See Marc Glasser, "Marriage in Medieval Hagiography," *Studies in Medieval and Renaissance History* 4 (1981), esp. the bibliography on p. 22 n.4.

century, marriage drew increasingly enthusiastic support from prominent (celibate) churchmen: Jacques de Vitry called it an "order" with its own duties and obligations.[17]

Positive regard for marriage did not necessarily imply a new attitude toward sex. Even conjugal passion remained suspect, and men who loved their wives "too ardently" attracted clerical denunciation.[18] All sexual activity outside the marriage bed, and much within it, continued to be considered sinful, and marriage was still portrayed as a safety net for those at risk of fornication, adultery, sodomy, or masturbation. In moral if not in social terms, marriage remained a lesser good—but a good, nonetheless. The relationship of Mary and Joseph, honorably united without sexual involvement, became a model for the "best" Christian marriage. Canon lawyers used the example of Christ's parents to argue that the essential constitutive element of valid marriage was neither the act of intercourse nor the intentions of parents and kin but the consent of bride and groom.[19] In a wider moral and spiritual sense as well, the example of Mary and Joseph legitimated and dignified marriage and married people.

Late medieval Christians were fascinated not only by the parents of Jesus but by all the persons and relationships within his family—by the Holy Child as infant and boy and by his cousins and his grandmother. In art, preaching, and hagiography these shadowy figures took on flesh. Devout people were encouraged to meditate not on Christ's unique salvific work alone but on the sweetness and vulnerability he shared with other infants. Mary and Joseph represented the protective and loving qualities to which all parents might aspire, including spiritual parents who

17. Cited in M. D. Chenu, *Nature, Man, and Society in the Twelfth Century* (Chicago: University of Chicago Press, 1968), pp. 221–222.

18. See Henry A. Kelly, "The Too Ardent Lover of His Wife Classified," in *Love and Marriage in the Age of Chaucer* (Ithaca: Cornell University Press, 1975), pp. 245–261.

19. On the doctrine of consent, see esp. Penny Schine Gold, "The Marriage of Mary and Joseph in the Twelfth-Century Ideology of Marriage," in *Sexual Practices in the Medieval Church*, ed. Vern L. Bullough and James Brundage (Buffalo, N.Y.: Prometheus Books, 1982), pp. 102–117; also Charles Donahue, Jr., "The Canon Law on the Formation of Marriage and Social Practice in the Later Middle Ages," *Journal of Family History* 8 (1983), 144–158; Jack Goody, *The Development of the Family and Marriage in Europe* (Cambridge: Cambridge University Press, 1983), pp. 146–153.

conceived and bore the Christ Child in their hearts. Interest in families and childhood found expression in iconography and mystical experience; it is possible, but difficult to prove, that the cult of the Holy Family inspired and supported family affection in return.[20]

In the fourteenth-century illustrated Franciscan manuscript "Meditations on the Life of Christ," the pregnancy of Elizabeth and infancy of John the Baptist inspired the devout imagination. In one picture the newborn Baptist stands in a fontlike bath at center stage while his mother reclines, attended by the Virgin. The author rhapsodizes over the delightful scene: "Oh, the house, the room, the bed in which live and rest together the mothers of two such sons, Jesus and John!" Domestic arrangements, family relationships, and the behavior of infants intrigued the friar-author, who observed that John was an unusually wise child, preferring Mary even to his own mother: "Contemplate the magnificence of the precious John! No one ever had a nurse or governess like this." The author was knowledgeable about children's needs and behavior and alert to the difficulties involved in caring for them. Meditation on the flight into Egypt prompted the notion that the return might have been more trying than the flight itself, since Jesus had grown "too big to be easily carried and yet too young to travel on His feet."[21] For a reader interested in children, such a realistic consideration might jolt the imagination into a livelier appreciation of an old story.

Christ's birth, unlike John's, was afflicted by poverty—or enhanced by poverty, according to Franciscan values. Joseph, at first

20. In "Holy Dolls: Play and Piety in Florence in the Quattrocento" (in *Women, Family, and Ritual*, pp. 310–329), Klapisch-Zuber suggests: "Florentines may have begun to take a better look at their own flesh-and-blood babies because their practice in the sphere of the sacred had led them to cuddle plaster and papier-mache figures of Jesus" (p. 328). William A. Christian argues that high infant mortality sharpened parents' love of their own children and made them responsive to the "childhood of Christ and Mary and motherliness of Mary and Anne": *Apparitions in Late Medieval and Renaissance Spain* (Princeton, N.J: Princeton University Press, 1981), p. 219.

21. *"Meditations on the Life of Christ": An Illustrated Manuscript of the Fourteenth Century* (Ms. Ital. 115, Paris Bibl. Nat.), ed. Isa Ragusa and Rosalie B. Green (Princeton, N.J.: Princeton University Press, 1961), pp. 24, 25, 80.

"downcast perhaps because he could not prepare what was necessary," did what he could: took hay from the manger, put it at Mary's feet to receive the Child, and sat down with his face politely turned away. The birth itself was instantaneous and painless; in the view of medieval theologians, realistic labor and delivery was incompatible with Mary's intact virginity. But the full humanity of mother and child, and Mary's likeness to other women, were reasserted immediately after the delivery. The author noted and celebrated the physical and emotional realities of motherhood: "Unable to contain herself, the mother stooped to pick Him up, embraced Him tenderly and, guided by the Holy Spirit, placed Him in her lap and began to wash Him with her milk, her breasts filled by heaven."[22] Like a midwife, the Holy Spirit instructs the new mother and fills her breasts. Mary's motherhood is rich with human feeling as well as sacred significance.

The author of the "Meditations" believed that the meaning of the Incarnation is most accessible through our affection for the tender flesh of a child. Christ's circumcision, performed by his mother with a stone knife, was an occasion for sorrow: "The child Jesus cries today because of the pain He felt in his soft and delicate flesh, like that of all other children." That pain foreshadowed the agony of the Crucifixion and brought home its meaning. The bond between savior and saved was best expressed by concrete representation of the most familiar and basic relationship in human experience, that of a mother and her baby: "But when he cries, do you think the mother will not cry? She too wept, and as she wept the Child in her lap placed His tiny hand on His mother's mouth and face as though to comfort her by His gestures, that she should not cry, because He loved her tenderly . . . the mother wiped His eyes and hers, laid her cheek on His, nursed Him, and comforted Him in every way she could."[23] Mary's love for Jesus, intensely physical in expression and passionate in feeling, modeled for all Christians the most direct approach to God.

The "Meditations" were written for a nun, who was instructed

22. Ibid., pp. 32–33. Some theological implications of Mary's virginity *in partu* are addressed in Graef, *Mary*, esp. 1:35, 176; and also in Wood, "Doctors' Dilemma," pp. 710–727.

23. "Meditations," p. 44.

in the proper use of text and pictures. She was advised to follow the angels and shepherds to Bethlehem: "Kneel and adore your Lord God, and then His mother, and reverently greet the saintly old Joseph. Kiss the beautiful little feet of the infant Jesus. . . . Pick Him up and hold Him in your arms. . . . Then return Him to the mother and watch her attentively as she cares for Him . . . and remain to help her if you can."[24]

Readers were expected to find infancy attractive and familiar—not to deny or deprive themselves of intimate affections but to put them to use in loving God. The friar did not forget the ultimate goal of such devotion, however. Writing of the twelve-year-old Jesus' visit to the temple and his parents' natural distress, he noted that "he who would approach God must not stay among relatives, but must leave them."[25] The sweetness of family, a most delightful aspect of human experience, is not sufficient for those in religious life, who must face—as Christ did—the loneliness of separation from loved ones. With all his appreciation of childhood and domesticity, the friar stayed well within the norms of traditional teaching on the religious life.

Concern and affection for the distinctive physical and emotional characteristics of childhood were not limited to devotional writing. In the fourteenth and fifteenth centuries, secular as well as religious works of art were rich with representations of infants and little children. The *putti* of Italian paintings—cherubic figures representing the souls of dead infants—convey delight in the joy and pathos of vulnerable early childhood.[26] Interest in childhood (almost exclusively, however, in male childhood)[27] was one out-

24. Ibid., pp. 38–39.
25. Ibid., pp. 92–93.
26. On the *putti*, see Klapisch-Zuber, "Childhood in Tuscany," in *Women, Family, and Ritual*, pp. 94–116; and Ross, "The Middle-Class Child," pp. 204–205.
27. Except when the Italian humanists wrote explicitly about the education of girls, they were concerned with boys; the "generic child" was male. The traditional neglect of gender in interpretations of humanism and the Reniassance is now being addressed: see Kelly Gadol's reinterpretation in "Did Women Have a Renaissance?"; and (among others) Margaret Leah King, "Book-lined Cells: Women and Humanism in the Early Italian Renaissance," in *Beyond Their Sex: Learned Women of the European Past*, ed. Patricia R. Labalme (New York: New York University Press, 1980), pp. 66–90. Gender is one determinant even of the physical

growth of the humanist passion for education; it was understood as the ground of moral, intellectual, and civic reform. Humanists believed that virtue could be taught and learned, and the Italian Renaissance produced an outburst of attention to the teaching role of the mother, who provided with her milk a child's first lessons, the basis for all future education. For fifteenth-century humanists Augustine's mother Monica was the model for a new, idealized mother-teacher. Her son pointed to the essential imprint of the child's first relationship: "From the time when my mother fed me at the breast my infant heart had been suckled dutifully on his name, the name of your Son, my Saviour. Deep inside my heart his name remained, and nothing could entirely captivate me . . . unless his name were in it."[28]

The discourse of humanists and reformers about breast-feeding, and about the good and bad qualities of mothers and nurses, took place against the background of an established system of commercial wet-nursing. Celibate men exhorted women to feed their own children, while middle-class married men negotiated for their babies' care with the husbands of the nurses.[29] In Leon Battista Alberti's dialogue on the family, men discuss the joys and troubles of fatherhood, which include the responsibility of finding a proper nurse "free, clear, and clean of those vices and defects which infect and corrupt the milk and the blood."[30] Lionardo—unmarried, like Alberti himself—insists that the mother is the best nurse and that nursing strengthens mother-love; all agree on the crucial importance of securing the best available care and nourishment for an infant. Alberti's gentlemen, gathered at the deathbed of a

---

survival of children. Boswell (*Kindness of Strangers*, p. 432) notes that abandonment "enabled parents to correct for gender": that is, in almost every case, to preserve sons at the expense of daughters. According to Klapisch-Zuber ("Childhood in Tuscany," p. 104), two-thirds of the children abandoned in Florence in the early fifteenth century were girls.

28. Augustine, *Confessions* III.4, p. 59. On Monica as a model, see Atkinson, "Your Servant, My Mother."

29. Klapisch-Zuber, "Blood Parents," pp. 132–164; see also Ross, "The Middle-Class Child," pp. 194–196.

30. Leon Battista Alberti, *The Family in Renaissance Florence: A Translation by Renee Neu Watkins of I libri della famiglia by Leon Battista Alberti* (Columbia: University of South Carolina Press, 1969), bk. 1, p. 51.

patriarch, discussed these matters within a wider context in which the children of well-to-do urban parents like themselves were sent to nurses in the country for the first two years of life, and many died. The gulf between moral ideals and social realities in the matter of wet-nursing serves as a reminder that the lively interest in children should not be misread: they were neglected and abused during the Renaissance as before (and after). The appearance of foundling homes in fifteenth-century Florence may signal an increased public responsibility for children but serves also as evidence of continued abandonment.[31]

In northern as in southern Europe, moralists and reformers pointed to the central place of children and families in any hope or plan for the reform of Church or society. Jean Gerson, chancellor of the University of Paris, used a Christmas sermon to remind women that the Virgin nursed her son and that mother's milk was not only the natural food for an infant but the beginning of its Christian education.[32] Gerson was an intellectual who praised the spirituality of simple, unlettered people, a mystic who worried about visionary delusions, and an advocate of the significance of families whose views on the "best" Christian life were entirely traditional. Writing to his sisters, he insisted that marriage and parenthood could not compare to the blessings bestowed on virgins by a heavenly bridegroom.[33] He reminded noble parents, who depended on their children to advance their worldly goals, that a family mansion eventually becomes a tomb. He warned them to avoid endangering their souls by caring too much for their children; for such people, a child's early death might be a valuable lesson.[34] But even that harsh note was engendered by the assumption that is is possible or easy to love one's children "too much."

---

31. Richard C. Trexler discusses infanticide and abandonment in "The Foundlings of Florence, 1395–1455," and "Infanticide in Florence: New Sources and First Results," *History of Childhood Quarterly* 1 (1973), 259–83; 2 (1975), 98–117. See also Boswell, *Kindness of Strangers*, pp. 431–434; and Klapisch-Zuber, "Childhood in Tuscany," pp. 104–105.

32. Jean Gerson, "Pour le jour de Noël," in *Oeuvres complètes*, ed. Palémon Glorieux (Paris: Desclée, 1968), vol. 7, pt. 2, no. 385, p. 953.

33. Gerson, "Sur l'excellence de la virginité," in ibid. pt. 1, no. 337, p. 417.

34. Gerson, "Consolation sur la morte des amis," in ibid., no. 321, p. 322.

Gerson was the chief sponsor of the new cult and image of St. Joseph in the fifteenth century. In ancient and medieval legend and iconography, whose theological sources were Mary's virginity and Christ's divinity, Joseph was portrayed as an aged widower, a feeble old man. Unlike the author of the "Meditations," whose "saintly old Joseph" was too simple and patient to reproach Mary for her pregnancy before the truth was disclosed to him, Gerson emphasized that Jesus and Mary obeyed Joseph as their lord. The divine plan required him to take his family to Egypt, a terrible journey that could not have been accomplished by a man who was "old, ugly, ineffectual, feeble, and unable to work—more a burden than a helpmate to Mary." The marriage of Christ's parents also served to conceal the Virgin Birth from the Devil, who would not have been fooled by an aged, impotent bridegroom. Joseph had to have been capable of fathering a child—anything else would detract from the glory of Mary's virginity. Gerson believed that Joseph married in the prime of life, the age designated as "youth" by medieval writers, beginning (for men) in the twenties and continuing through the fifth decade. Blessed with the divine gift of chastity, Joseph was naturally stronger, more beautiful, and healthier than other men, having been spared the "bitter and furious passion of vile carnal desire."[35] Neither the chancellor's deep respect for marriage nor his interest in parents and children modified his traditional aversion to sexual passion and its expression.

From earliest times, the Virgin and Child had been represented with dignity and beauty and adored by devout Christians as central, sacred symbols of their faith. Joseph was a peripheral figure, and often a figure of fun, until the late Middle Ages. As the married state gained importance in Christian ideology, with enhanced respect for the vital authority of fathers, Mary and Jesus were more frequently portrayed with Joseph, who was no longer presented as subservient or faintly ridiculous. The Holy Family became a kind of earthly trinity, intersecting the Holy Trinity through Jesus. In the earthly family, Joseph shared the power and responsibility of

35. Gerson, "Considerations sur Saint Joseph," in ibid., no. 300, pp. 75–77.

human fathers: artists began to paint him alone with Jesus, teaching and playing with his son.[36] Joseph's vigorous paternity symbolized and legitimated the new family of early modern Europe, and he has served since then as a religious symbol of the "intact family," which requires a father vested with dignity and authority.

If the cult of Joseph was the creation of ecclesiastical men, the cult of Anne appealed to broad popular tastes in late medieval Europe. The Apocrypha supplied material for imaginative reflection on the history, genealogy, and attributes of Christ's grandmother. In the *Golden Legend*, the tale of the Nativity of the Blessed Virgin begins with the lineage of Anne, her three husbands, her three daughters (all named Mary), and their children, the "brethren" of Jesus.[37] The three marriages, with complicated relationships among the offspring, were not entirely consistent with other stories about Anne's marriage to Joachim and their twenty-year wait for a child. On that point, the author of the *Golden Legend* remarked that when God "closes a womb, it is only that He may later reopen it more wondrously," mentioning Sarah and Rachel, "barren" mothers who brought forth nations.[38] Anne's long childlessness made Mary's birth semimiraculous and linked it to crucial biblical events but did not satisfy the medieval taste for establishing ties of kinship among significant figures. The *Golden Legend* expressed no concern about consistency, but later, as the notion of the Immaculate Conception of Mary gained ground, Anne's second and third marriages began to seem inappropriate and to disappear.

Artists depicted the grandmother of Jesus at the head of a large family and the center of a lineage. In little devotional dolls, the

36. Marjory B. Foster, *The Iconography of St. Joseph in Netherlandish Art, 1400–1550* (Ann Arbor: University of Michigan Press, 1979), p. 235; see also John Bossy, *Christianity in the West, 1400–1700* (New York: Oxford University Press, 1985), pp. 10–11.

37. According to legend, Anne first married Joachim and had Mary, the Blessed Virgin. Then she married Cleophas (the brother of her son-in-law Joseph) and had the second Mary, who became the mother of James the Less, Joseph the Just, Simon, and Jude. She married a third husband (Salome) and had the third Mary, who married Zebedee and became the mother of James the Greater and of John, the beloved disciple (and cousin) to whom Jesus entrusted his mother (John's aunt).

38. *Golden Legend*, p. 522.

figure of St. Anne could be opened to find Mary within, and within Mary, the infant Christ. St. Anne became important and accessible as a court of first resort, a loving grandmother who influenced events through her daughter and grandson. According to legend, the young student Martin Luther, terrified by a thunderstorm, vowed to St. Anne that if his life were spared, he would become a monk.[39] In 1406 the Poor Clare Colette Boilet's vision of Anne with her three daughters and seven grandchildren was enthusiastically received and widely reported, inspiring new representations of Christ's Holy Kinship.[40] Such visions and works of art displayed the central figures of Christianity in groupings based on holy women—mothers and grandmothers.

In late medieval Europe the Holy Kinship, centered on Anne, coexisted with the growing cult of the Holy Family with the reconstructed Joseph at its head. Artists and writers portrayed Jesus with Mary and Joseph in domestic roles and relationships that might be emulated by ordinary people. The special obligations and characteristics of fathers, mothers, and children were elaborated and sentimentalized in continuing attempts to link human families with the family of God. For mothers specifically, representations of the Holy Family tended to reinforce the identification of maternity with love, suffering, and sorrow. The fourteenth-century mystical theologian Julian of Norwich went further, identifying mother love with the source of all love—that is, with the loving Christ. Julian believed that God "wanted the second person to become our mother, our brother and our saviour. From that it

39. There is little evidence for this vow outside the *Table Talk*, although the story was repeated early and often: see WA TR 4, no. 4707, p. 440; and 5, no. 5373, p. 99. Its persistence can best be understood in the light of Luther's later rejection of vows and of "idolatrous" prayers to the saints, especially to such "fictional" saints as Anne. See, e.g., *Lectures on Genesis*, LW, vol. 5, p. 238 (WA 44, p. 176); "Sermons on the Gospel of St. John," LW, vol. 24, p. 22 (WA 45, p. 480); "Exhortation to All Clergy Assembled at Augsburg," LW, vol. 34, pp. 9–61 (WA 30, pp. 268–356). Luther apparently told the story of the thunderstorm to illustrate the foolishness of such vows.

40. "Vita B. Coleta," AS March, vol. 1, p. 555. In the Saxon altarpiece (c. 1510) entitled "Altar of the Holy Kinship" (Isabella Stewart Gardner Museum, Boston), Mary and Anne together hold the infant Christ; Maria Salome and Maria Cleophas are seated with their children in the foreground; male family members stand in the rear. The side panels display saints Katherine, Margaret, Barbara, and Dorothy.

follows that as truly as God is our father, so truly God is our mother." Because Jesus behaved like a mother, "all the fair work and all the sweet kindly offices of beloved motherhood belong to the second person."[41] While Joseph provided a renewed husband and father for the Holy Family, Julian understood Christ as a mother for the Holy Trinity—the family within God.

The cult of the Holy Family both reflected and fostered the late medieval emphasis on the humanity of Mary and of Jesus. Artistic naturalism and a taste for the pathetic helped to construct a contemporary Mary who was depicted less often as the Queen of Heaven, more often as the humble young woman nursing her baby or the tortured old woman at the Cross.[42] The appeal of the Pietà and of the Mater Dolorosa arose from Mary's symbolization of the pain and sorrow believed to be characteristic of all maternity. The popularity of the *Planctus Mariae* (literary laments of the Virgin) testifies to a wide fascination with Mary's grief over Christ's brutal death and her own piteous state—widowed, orphaned, deprived of all "family" by the loss of her son. In one Middle English poetic dialogue, Jesus instructs Mary to recognize in her own agony the pain of every mother, to have compassion for all mothers and, through them, for all of suffering humanity.[43] Maternal anguish became the emotional center of Marian piety.

As a theological image of spiritual quickening, the notion of the conception and birth of Christ in the individual soul, or in the body of the Church, goes back to Origen.[44] After the thirteenth century, however, the image was used in new ways with new

41. Julian of Norwich, Revelation 14, in *A Book of Showings*, vol. 2, ed. Edmund Colledge, O.S.A., and James Walsh, S.J. (Toronto: Pontifical Institue of Mediaeval Studies, 1978), chap. 59, pp. 591, 593.

42. Millard Meiss, *Painting in Florence and Siena after the Black Death* (Princeton, N.J.: Princeton University Press, 1951), pp. 145–156.

43. The dialogue "Stond well, moder, vnder rode" is discussed in Sarah Appleton Weber, *Theology and Poetry in the Middle English Lyric* (Columbus: Ohio State University Press, 1968), pp. 126–133.

44. See Hugo Rahner, "Die Gottesgeburt: Die Lehre der Kirchenvater von der Geburt Christi im Herzen der Gläubigen," *Zeitschrift für Katholische Theologie* 59 (1935), 333–418. I am indebted to Rosemary D. Hale for her exploration of this theme.

meanings, and used by women. The Flemish beguine Hadewijch wrote of the humble Christian who might carry Christ "as long as a child grows within its mother."[45] In a long poem she developed the metaphor of spiritual pregnancy, the growth of an infant in the womb and the preparation for birth of both mother and child. For Hadewijch this was an allegory, a way of imagining and speaking about religious truth. In some German Dominican convents of the fourteenth century, the metaphor became an experience of mystical union. Christina Ebner dreamed that she was pregnant with Jesus and gave birth to him. Unable to contain her joy, she "took the child in her arms and carried it to the gathering of sisters in the refectory and said, 'Rejoice with me: I can no longer conceal my joy.'"[46] Adelheid Langmann, among others, delighted in nursing the Christ Child. Mary "gave her the child on her arm while she was in bed. And . . . he suckled her breast and stayed with her until they sounded matins."[47] Such experiences went far beyond allegory and metaphor, and also beyond the instructions of (for example) the Franciscan author of the "Meditations," who advised the reader simply to observe Mary and help her care for the child.

Maternal encounters with the infant Jesus, which increased in number and intensity during the late Middle Ages, offered a significant alternative to traditional bridal mysticism. They also disclosed contemporary assumptions about motherhood as a relationship of extraordinary intensity, both physical and spiritual. In the convents of early medieval Europe the notion of "spiritual motherhood" had characterized the relationship of abbesses to the nuns in their charge: they directed, healed, and corrected their "daughters." In the fourteenth century "spiritual motherhood" was grounded in the physical realities of pregnancy, birth, and lactation, and its fruit was mystical union with the infant God. This new phenomenon of "spiritual motherhood" incorporated an enhanced appreciation of biological and social motherhood, which had acquired its own numinous characteristics. The recog-

45. *Hadewijch: The Complete Works*, ed. Mother Columba Hart, O.S.B. (New York: Paulist Press, 1980), p. 346.
46. Translated in Rosemary D. Hale, "*Imitatio Mariae*: Motherhood Motifs in Devotional Memoirs," *Mystics Quarterly* 16 (1990), 193–203.
47. Ibid.

nition and acknowledgment of the necessity and holiness of suffering, believed to be intrinsic to all motherhood, contributed a sacred dimension to physical motherhood. Furthermore, a significant and growing number of extraordinary women had begun to exemplify its compatibility with holiness.

After the thirteenth century, saints increasingly were drawn from the ranks of lay people and therefore of married people. Holiness could not be restricted to cloisters and convents; men and women "in the world" longed for intimacy with God. For women, however, the Christian tradition offered few precedents and slight rationale for such aspirations. Married women were not expected to do great deeds for Christ; for centuries, the female models of Christian heroism had been virgin martyrs. The legends of St. Margaret, St. Katherine, St. Agnes, and the rest portrayed active, courageous women who stalwartly defended their most precious and sacred possession—their virginity. The twelfth-century Christina of Markyate stood squarely in their footsteps when she resisted the marriage promoted by her parents and the bishop and prayed for "purity and inviolable virginity whereby Thou mayest renew in me the image of Thy Son."[48] For a woman, the image and likeness of God was most readily available through the virginity of Christ. From Bede's celibate queens and holy nuns to the melodramatic Christina, heroic women despised marriage and avoided physical motherhood. Their example continued to inspire holy women—for example, the fourteenth-century Catherine of Siena, who refused to marry and became the "mama" of a spiritual family of male clerics.

The tradition of holy virginity persisted, but new opportunities for sanctity began to be available to married women in the later Middle Ages. Early in the thirteenth century Jacques de Vitry wrote enthusiastic accounts of the beguines of the Low Countries, who dedicated themselves to prayer, poverty, and work for God. The beguines observed the rule of chastity, but their communities included widows and wives (with their husbands' permission) as well as virgins. Sexual status, crucial for Christina of Markyate,

48. *The Life of Christina of Markyate,* ed. and trans. Charles H. Talbot (Oxford: Clarendon Press, 1987), p. 41.

was not an important consideration for the beguines or their ad-
mirers; virginity was no longer an essential sign or criterion of
holiness. De Vitry singled out for attention Marie d'Oignies, a
married woman. He honored the young maidens among the beguines for their renunciation of opportunities for wealthy marriages, but he was more impressed by the choice of poverty in
goods and family relationships than by sexual abstinence.[49] Holy
women in the thirteenth century came to their new vocation from
all kinds of backgrounds: Ivetta of Huy, for example, was a widow
with three sons when she was called to active religious work.
Leaving her children with her father, she devoted the rest of her
life to the care of pilgrims, lepers, and the poor.[50] These women,
and the men who admired them and told their stories, wished to
imitate the apostles in poverty and service. They understood the
renunciation of family obligations and relationships as an aspect
of voluntary poverty, much more significant than their formal
status as virgins, as wives living apart from their husbands, or as
widows with or without children.

In 1211 a four-year-old princess of Hungary was sent to Germany
to grow up in the family of her fiancé, heir to the landgrave of
Thuringia. Ten years later they were married, the bride consenting
"not for pleasure's sake," according to the Golden Legend, "but
in obedience to the will of her father and in order to raise up
children to the service of God."[51] It is unlikely that little Elizabeth's consent represented a real choice, given her social and
political position. Especially for a princess, the will of God was

49. See Brenda M. Bolton, "Mulieres sanctae," in Sanctity and Secularity,
Studies in Church History 10, ed. Derek Baker (Oxford: Basil Blackwell, 1973), pp.
77–96; and Bolton, "Vitae matrum: A Further Aspect of the Frauenfrage," in Baker,
Medieval Women, pp. 253–273.

50. "Vita B. Iutta," AS January, vol. 2, pp. 143–169; see also Bolton, "Vitae
matrum," p. 258.

51. Golden Legend, p. 677. Elizabeth holds a unique place in the Legend as its
only contemporary (medieval) female saint. The other women, mostly virgin-
martyrs, belong to Scripture or antiquity; the other contemporary figures (Bernard,
Francis, Dominic) are men, celibates and founders of religious orders. Sources
for Elizabeth's life and legend include Albert Huyskens, Quellenschriften zur
Geschichte der hl. Elisabeth Landgrafin von Thuringen (Marburg: N.G. El-
weit'sche, 1908).

likely to be identified with the will of a father, and the raising up of children was promoted by ecclesiastical as well as temporal powers. But marriage and motherhood did not stifle Elizabeth's aspirations, and her life and reputation provided a significant alternative to the model of the ancient virgin-martyrs.

Elizabeth became the mother of three children and the mistress of a substantial household. She set a fierce example of charity and austerity, strictly controlling her diet, sleep, and clothing in an ascetic regime that flouted the customary behavior of a married woman of her class. Establishing new patterns, she attempted to fill the hitherto incompatible roles of wife and saint. Elizabeth enjoyed the cooperation of a sympathetic husband who appreciated her virtues and tolerated her charities and her regime; not all her successors were as fortunate. But if her "patience" was not sufficiently tested by her marriage, she found a tormentor in her confessor, Conrad of Marburg, who beat her when she came late to his sermon and separated her from the attendants who were her closest friends. Her cheerful acceptance of his meaningless cruelty may remind us of Griselda, but according to a rhymed life of the saint by a fifteenth-century English Augustinian, she chose to obey Conrad in imitation of Christ's obedience.[52]

Elizabeth's circumstances were transformed when her husband took the cross and died in the Holy Land. As the widow of a Crusader, she was given a second chance at a single-minded pursuit of holiness that was impossible within marriage. A widow could emulate the virgin-martyrs; when her relatives tried to arange a second marriage, she threatened to cut off her nose so that no one would have her. She also sent her children away, even the baby born after its father's death—a separation that was essential to her new life:

> As she desired to turn her spirit wholly to the Lord, and to suffer no hindrance to her devotion, she besought the Lord to infuse into her

52. Osbern Bokenham, *Legendys of Hooly Wummen by Osbern Bokenham*, ed. Mary S. Serjeantson (London: Humphrey Milford, 1938), p. 267. Kieckhefer (*Unquiet Souls*, p. 55) points out that for married saints, "abuse at the hands of a spouse could be a prime occasion for patience." See also Michael Goodich, "*Ancilla Dei*: The Servant as Saint in the Late Middle Ages," in *Women of the Medieval*

a contempt for all passing things, to tear the love of her children from her heart. . . . [When God answered her prayer, she rejoiced:] Henceforth I count all timely goods as dung, I have no more concern for my children than for others, and I make no account of contempt and insults; for I wish it to be seen that I love none save only God!

Attachment to possessions, to children, to social status—all were distractions, all dangerously attractive, all "dung," requiring renunciation. We may understand Elizabeth's prayer in terms of conflict, but it is clear that she herself perceived maternal love as weakness. The energy she might have devoted to her own children she spent on God's children: "Once, in caring for a one-eyed child whose body was covered with scabs, she bore him to the privy in her own arms seven times in one night, and gladly washed his soiled bed-clothing."[53]

According to reputation, Elizabeth was accepted as a mother by the children of the poor. Bokenham said that they ran to her when she visited them and cried when she left "as if she had been their mother."[54] Her iconography displays her dedication to the works of corporal mercy, to the physical needs of suffering people. Scenes of her charities, with graphic representations of the tortured bodies she tended, appear in works of art all over northern and central Europe. The windows of her church in Marburg portray Elizabeth distributing food and washing feet, the work of a woman, a servant, and a mother. Motherhood was comprehended in terms of physical suffering and service, and the mother-saints of the late Middle Ages extended maternal service to all those in need—with the exception, very often, of their own children.

Widowhood was crucial for Elizabeth and for many of the female saints who followed her because the restrictions placed on wives by church and society were much more severe than those placed on mothers. Without special and hard-to-obtain permission from her husband and her bishop, a wife was bound to remain in her husband's company, share his bed, eat at his table, and support

World, ed. Julius Kirshner and Suzanne F. Wemple (Oxford: Basil Blackwell, 1985), pp. 119–136.

53. *Golden Legend*, pp. 683, 685.

54. Bokenham, *Legendys*, p. 272.

his social and economic station through her manners, clothing, and activities. A married woman was expected to bear children "for God" and for her husband's family—in the circumstances of medieval childbearing, an arduous, nearly endless, and life-threatening responsibility. She was required also to see that her children received proper religious upbringing, although not necessarily to conduct that instruction herself.[55] As a woman of the princely class, Elizabeth was not compelled by any standard of maternal virtue to keep her children by her side. She herself was sent away from home at the age of four; noble children were not expected to live with their parents much past babyhood. In hagiography, Elizabeth won special praise for parting from her new baby as well as her older children. The issue was not where the children lived, or their daily care and instruction, but her attachment to them. When holiness was defined as poverty and maternal attachment as a worldly "good," renunciation had to take place on the level of feeling. In relation to their own children, it was more often affection than responsibility that troubled the new saints, at least those of the ruling class.

By turning maternal passion outward toward the sick and the poor, Elizabeth of Hungary transformed mother love from a private, somewhat "selfish" emotion into holy charity. When she died at twenty-four, worn out by austerity, healing miracles began at once to occur at her tomb. She was canonized in only four years, after a widely publicized Process. Her influence was immediate and pervasive, especially in the Germanies but also in distant parts of Europe. Elizabeth's image and reputation established a new model of sanctity for Christian women who were wives and mothers. She was widely known and well loved throughout the

55. Children of the upper class "belonged" to their fathers' families and stayed with them when the father died if the mother remarried: see Klapisch-Zuber, "The 'Cruel Mother': Maternity, Widowhood, and Dowry in Florence in the Fourteenth and Fifteenth Centuries," in Women, Family, and Ritual, 117–131. In the thirteenth century, for a woman of Elizabeth's class, there was little pressure toward saintly or even virtuous child raising, in part because models of holy (physical) motherhood were still rare or nonexistent—except for the mothers of saints. That changed with developing ideologies of maternity and sanctity: Birgitta of Sweden and Frances of Rome were greatly praised for their care and instruction of their children.

Middle Ages, and her fame persists: modern painters and sculptors are still attracted to her life and legend.[56]

In the early thirteenth century many lay people, both women and men, were drawn into intense religious commitment through the influence of St. Francis and the first friars. As a young unmarried girl, Clare of Assisi followed Francis until she was blocked by the implications of religious poverty interpreted through the double lens of gender and class prejudice. Francis required his followers to be as poor as the poorest people, to live with them and share their deprivation. Women of the middle and upper classes, however, were not allowed by church or society to identify with poor women, to live with them or look like them. For women, poverty was associated with sexual immorality and prostitution. Begging was precluded by the perceived sexual stigma; in agreement (for once) with Elizabeth's noble relatives, Conrad of Marburg forbade her to beg. Similarly, Clare was not permitted to follow Francis into the streets and hovels of Italian towns. She became the abbess of an enclosed community and had to struggle even for the relative poverty of a strict monastic rule. For women, the greatest barrier to the apostolic life was the barrier of respectability as defined and enforced by clerical men.

Married as well as single women in Italy wished to follow Francis and, through him, Christ. Angela of Foligno (d. 1309) was in her late thirties, enmeshed in family ties, when she became convinced of her sinfulness. A vision of Francis sent her to confession, and she gradually learned to feel true penitence, motivated by the love of Christ instead of the fear of death and hell. Angela began to give up her worldly possessions and affections, not only fine clothes and delicate food but relationships. Renunciation was nearly impossible while she lived with her husband, but she received a great blessing: "It happened, through the will of God, that at that time my mother, who was a great hindrance to me, died; after that my husband and all my children died within a short time. Because I had set out on the path described above and had

---

56. See, e.g., catalogues compiled for the seven hundredth anniversary of Elizabeth's church in Marburg: *Die heilige Elisabeth in der Kunst-Abbild, Vorbild, Wunschbild,* and *Elisabeth aus der Sicht junger Kunstler* (Marburg, 1983).

asked God that they should die, I therefore had great consolation for their deaths." Elizabeth begged God to take away her love for her children; Angela, to be rid of hers entirely. Her grief was mitigated by the conviction that this answer to her prayer, and solution to her problems, revealed that her will conformed to God's will: "I believed that because God made these things happen to me, my heart would always be in God's heart, and God's heart would always be in mine."[57]

Angela was a venerable, familiar figure in the vivid spiritual landscape of central Italy in the late thirteenth century. She lived to be over sixty, a great age for a holy woman, most of whom died early of malnutrition and disease exacerbated by hard lives and charitable works. Like Catherine of Siena, Angela became the spiritual mother of a group of religious men who followed her, transcribed her visions and her conversation, and participated in her relationships with Christ, Mary, and Francis. Her visions frequently revealed the spiritual state of those to whom Francis referred (in a mystical colloquy) as "those beloved children of yours and mine."[58] That spiritual family, with herself and Francis as mother and father, was much more significant and rewarding than the "carnal" relations who once stood in her way. Following a long tradition of Christian teaching, Angela found physical motherhood a barrier to holiness: it stood in the way of renunciation. Nonetheless, as a married woman and mother who became a holy figure, her life and reputation contributed to the abandonment of the traditional prejudice in favor of virginity for women with aspirations to sanctity.

The life and writings of Birgitta of Sweden (d. 1373), one of the great charismatic mystics of the late Middle Ages, shed a brilliant light on the history of Christian motherhood. Birgitta was the mother of eight children and a prominent figure: after 1350 she

---

57. Angela of Foligno, *Il libro della Beata Angela da Foligno*, ed. Ludger Thier, O.F.M., and Abele Calufetti, O.F.M. (Rome: College of St. Bonaventure, 1985), Memoriale 1, p. 138.

58. Ibid., Instructio 4, p. 502.

lived in Rome and worked publicly and persistently for the return of the pope from Avignon, for peace between England and France, and for ecclesiastical permission to establish the Order of the Most Holy Savior, whose Rule had been revealed to her by Christ. She reported lengthy, colorful accounts of her extraordinary visions and intimate conversations with Jesus and Mary. Her words were quickly translated into Latin and widely circulated. Immediately after Birgitta's death, her supporters set in motion a Process for canonization which involved the collection and publication of extensive biographical and other documentation. In the fifteenth century the saint and her *Revelations* became the focus of a widespread cult and a sharp controversy among learned churchmen—which only increased her fame.

The Birgittine materials constitute a vast, rich source for late medieval theology, spirituality, social and ecclesiastical history, and the history of the family. Unlike the children of other saints, who left sparse and ethereal traces in works by and about their parents, Birgitta's sons and daughters appear frequently in legends about their mother and in her own writings. Their diverse histories, personalities, and complex relationships with their extraordinary mother can be examined in conjunction with Birgitta's mystical theology and her appreciation of human and divine maternity. Her perceptions of the motherhood of Mary and of Christ were rooted in the experience of love, pain, and responsibility.

Birgitta belonged to a noble family with ties to the ruling Swedish dynasty. She was married at thirteen to Ulf Gudmarsson—unwillingly, according to the testimony of their daughter Katarina: "Before she married, living in virginity, she wanted to serve the all-powerful God with her whole heart, to live her whole life in virginity with the status of a virgin, and not to marry, but her family compelled, required, and persuaded her to marry; Birgitta, according to [Katarina], said that at that time she would more willingly have died than married."[59] Whatever she may have felt

---

59. *Acta et processus canonizacionis beate Birgitte*, ed. Isak Collijn, SUSF, ser. 2, Lat. skrifter 1 (Uppsala: Almqvist & Wiksells, 1924–31), p. 305. Other sources for Birgitta and her works are cited in notes below. The modern Latin editions in SUSF ser. 2, include the *Acta et processus*; Bks. I, IV, V, VII of the *Revelaciones*;

at thirteen, such reluctance was a hagiographical fixture, especially in documents promoting the canonization of a married
woman. Written lives of Birgitta report that she used the example
of St. Cecilia to persuade Ulf to wait two years before consummat-
ing their marriage.[60] Then they prayed that whenever they came
together, God would "give them a child who would serve him
continually and never offend him."[61] According to Katarina, they
repeated this prayer every time they made love.

For almost three decades, Birgitta was a devout and conscientious wife, mother, and manager of a large estate. She carefully
supervised the religious education of her children, tended the poor
and sick, and observed strict ascetic practices as far as these were
compatible with married life: when Ulf was away, she slept on
the floor and spent most of the night in prayer.[62] Her teaching
found a wider sphere in the late 1330s when she went to court to
assist with the introduction of the king's foreign bride to the duties
of a Swedish queen. In 1341 she set out with her husband on a
pilgrimage to Santiago in Spain. On their return Ulf became ill;
he retired to the Cistercian monastery of Alvastra, where he died
in 1344.

Like Elizabeth and Angela, Birgitta was set free by widowhood
to live out her vocation according to her perception of divine
commands. She became increasingly clear and self-confident
about her call to serve as seer and interpreter of God's will. Her
sexual status was a troubled issue; she and her advisers kept
insisting that among the criteria for holiness, virginity was less
important than humility and obedience. In a vision (IV.53), Mary
reminded Birgitta that she herself had been maiden, mother, and

the *Extravagantes*; and *Opera minora*, vols. 1 and 2. See also the Old Swedish
Heliga Birgitta's Uppenbarelser, 5 vols., ed. G. E. Klemming, SUSF, ser. 14, (Stockholm: P. A. Norsted & Söner, 1857–84); and the modern Swedish *Himmelska
uppenbarelser*, trans. Tryggve Lunden, (Malmö: Allhems Förlag, 1951–59). References to specific revelations are indicated by book and chapter numbers in the
text; notes cite the sources from which I quote.
60. Cecilia converted her bridegroom to chastity and then to martyrdom:
Golden Legend, pp. 689–695.
61. *Acta et processus*, p. 305.
62. Ibid., p. 78.

"widow" (because her child had no earthly father).[63] Like other married women saints, Birgitta repeated this lesson strongly and frequently—perhaps in order to convince herself and others of its truth.

The goodness of the work of wives and mothers was repeatedly reinforced by references to Mary and to Mary's mother, who taught Birgitta to pray (VI.102): "Blessed be thou, Jesus Christ, the son of God who chose your mother from the wedding of Joachim and Anne. And therefore, through Anne's prayers, have mercy on all those who are married or plan to marry, that they may bring forth fruit to the worship of God."[64] Three statues of Anne were placed in the mother house of the Birgittine order at Vadstena during the fifteenth century, and a chapel in her honor was founded there in 1425 by an English queen of Sweden.[65] Birgitta's *Revelations* display her strong attachment and close identification with Mary, but during the century after the saint's death, her cult and image tended to blend with that of Anne. Like Anne, Birgitta was a mother and grandmother whose work carried forward the history of salvation.

References to Birgitta's four sons and four daughters are scattered through her *Revelations* and the many stories told about the saint. She and Ulf were fortunate: only two of their children died before reaching adulthood. The others lived to develop very different personalities and relationships, noted and remembered by those who watched Birgitta. The eldest, Märta, was married when her mother was pregnant with the youngest. Birgitta disapproved

63. *The Liber celestis of St. Bridget of Sweden* (Middle English version), vol. 1, ed. Roger Ellis (Oxford: Oxford University Press, 1987), p. 300 Several Birgittine revelations concern sexual status and its rewards. The conventional hierarchy was amended by a voice proclaiming, "Virginity deserves a crown; widowhood comes close to God; marriage is not excluded from Heaven, but obedience brings them all into glory": *Den Heliga Birgittas Revelaciones Extravagantes* (SUSF), ed. Lennart Hollman (Uppsala: Almqvist & Wiksells, 1956), chap. 96, p. 218. According to the Rule of St. Savior, the first criterion for the selection of an abbess was humility—a proud virgin was less suitable than a humble widow—but women of illegitimate birth were excluded: *Extravagantes*, chaps. 20–21, pp. 131–132.

64. Birgitta, *Liber celestis*, p. 467.

65. See Aron Andersson, *Vadstena klosterkyrka*, vol. 2 (Stockholm: Almqvist & Wiksells, 1983).

of Ulf's choice of bridegroom and refused at first to attend the wedding. Her anger and grief threatened the fetus, which addressed its mother during Birgitta's frantic prayers, begging her not to let despair kill her unborn child. Unconcerned about her own health and the physical health of the fetus, Birgitta recognized danger to an unbaptized soul and resigned herself to the marriage, which turned out as badly as she had predicted.[66] During the difficult birth of this last child, Birgitta's attendants became aware of a strange woman standing by the bed. After touching each part of the laboring woman's body, the stranger disappeared and the birth proceeded easily. Later, Mary reminded Birgitta of the incident, saying: "When you had difficulty in giving birth, I, Mary, came to your aid, therefore you would be ungrateful if you did not love me above all others. See to it, therefore, that all your children are like my children."[67]

In his life of Birgitta, Birger Gregersson commented on that vision: "Oh happy woman, who deserved to have the Queen of Heaven for a midwife! But happier children, to be chosen through their mother's merits as adopted children of the mother of God." With Mary's assistance and instruction, Birgitta was bound to be an excellent parent. Gregersson compared her to "an eagle, soaring above her flying chicks and calling out to them." He praised her strict discipline and the care she took in appointing tutors and instructors.[68]

Lives of Birgitta frequently refer to her concern for her children's souls and care for their religious training. This, of course, was the great, overriding purpose of marriage and parenthood in traditional medieval teaching, one of the three "goods" of marriage and the only one that truly justified the couple's sexual relationship. Birgitta's *Revelations* (I.43) reveal her traditional view of the intrinsic

66. Margareta Clausdotter, "Chronicon de genere et nepotibus S. Birgittae," in *Scriptores rerum Svecicarum medii aevi*, vol. 3, pt. 2, ed. Claes Annerstedt (Uppsala: Edward Verling, 1871–76), pp. 209–210. Margareta was abbess in Vadstena from 1472 to 1486. I am indebted to Claire L. Sahlin for her translation of this text and for assistance with Birgittine bibliography and interpretation.

67. Birger Gregersson, *Birgerus Gregorii legenda sancte Birgitte*, ed. Isak Collijn, SUSF, ser. 2, vol. 4 (Uppsala: Almqvist & Wiksells, 1946), p. 17; also *Acta et processus*, p. 79.

68. Gregersson, *Legenda*, p. 17.

ugliness of sex: "The mother conceives the child of a little seed that is only foul filth, and so brings forth fruit." Semen might be necessary for "fruit," but in itself it was foul: John the Baptist, Christ told Birgitta (I.20), ate nothing filthy, produced no semen, and thus was entitled to be called "angel and virgin." Only strict, careful training transformed the filth of sex into fruit, and by this definition Birgitta was an excellent mother. She rose at dawn to offer prayers for each child's soul, took her daughters to visit the sick, and wept when her son forgot a saint's day. Mary commended her efforts (IV.53): "You pray God that your children will please God. Truly this is a good prayer. For if she who is a mother pleases my son, and loves him above all other things, and prays for herself and her children, I will help her prayer to be effective."[69]

Parental love, properly directed toward a child's soul, was not supposed to distract the parent from God. Birgitta was told (I.1) to love God "more than father, mother, son or daughter," and she was determined to obey.[70] A contemporary chronicler reported a visit to Birgitta from the Virgin Mary, accompanied by the spirit of the saint's mother, Lady Ingeborg. Mary asked Ingeborg whether she loved her daughter, and Ingeborg replied that like all souls in heaven, she loved her child only if her child loved God.[71] In another vision, Mary spoke to Birgitta of a "pagan" woman who reasoned that she must have been created by a loving God and said (VI.50), "If I had bread in my hand, and all my children cried for bread, and he [God] hungered, I would give him bread before any of them."[72] Even a pagan, using reason alone, perceived the comparative worth of children and of God. When she was about to leave Sweden for Rome, Birgitta worried about leaving her children, who were young, rich, and in danger of worldly temptation. Her anxiety was addressed in a vision of a little demon blowing on a fire: in response to her questions, he said that he was feeding the flames of her maternal love.[73] The vision helped her to correct an anxious love that was excessive and misdirected—even demonic,

69. Birgitta, *Liber celestis*, pp. 76, 36–37, 300.
70. Ibid., p. 7.
71. Clausdotter, "Chronicon," p. 209.
72. Birgitta, *Liber celestis*, p. 438.
73. Birgitta, *Extravagantes*, chap. 95, p. 218.

if it interfered with her love for God. It was assumed that a mother would love her children; her duty was to love God and to make sure that they did too.

Although six of Birgitta's children lived to maturity, some of them died before their mother—not unusual, of course, when a woman lived to be seventy in the fourteenth century. No matter how common, a child's death is never acceptable to ordinary people, but Birgitta was a saint and her "patience" exemplary. When she learned of the death of her daughter Ingeborg, a nun, she thanked God for taking Ingeborg before the world tempted her; perhaps she lacked confidence in her daughter's vocation. Then she wept. When Christ asked why, she said it was not for Ingeborg's death but for her own failures; she had set an example of pride and had not corrected every one of her daughter's faults. Christ reassured her: "Any mother who weeps because her daughter offends God, and who teaches her as well as she can, is a true mother of love and a mother of tears. Her daughter, on account of her mother, is a daughter of God." A "mother of love and a mother of tears" had the dreadful power to determine her child's fate in the next world: "A mother whose daughter knows how to behave (only) according to this world . . . is not a mother, but a stepmother. Your daughter, on account of your love and good will, will cross over to the crown of glory."[74] Even a saint's "patience" (resignation) at the death of her child may give way to fear and guilt about the child's sins. Parents cannot control what happens to their children's bodies, but they are directly responsible for their souls.

Birgitta's son Bengt, while still young, became ill during one of her visits to court and was near death when she returned to Alvastra, where he lived with the monks. Birgitta was afraid that his sickness resulted from his parents' sins, and a demon made matters worse by taunting her about the ineffectiveness of her tears. Christ intervened, announcing that the boy's illness had a natural cause. Promising a quick end to his suffering, he proclaimed that Bengt would "henceforth be known as Benedict, son of tears and prayers." At his death a sweet song was heard and a spirit spoke: "See what the tears have accomplished; now the son of tears has

74. Ibid., chap. 98, pp. 219–220.

gone to his rest." Augustine, of course, was the paradigmatic son of tears: the phrase placed Birgitta in the tradition of Christian motherhood established by St. Monica.[75]

Birgitta's son Karl also followed Augustine—not the bishop and saint but the young sinner whose mother fought for his soul. Karl caused his parents terrible worry and grief.[76] While she was in Rome, Birgitta heard a malicious and false rumor that he had been hanged for his crimes. She remained calm on the surface but was soon reassured by Mary that the scandalmonger was dead, his soul perched in terror over the abyss of hell—the fate of those who tormented God's friends.[77] The story indicates not only that Karl's behavior was scandalous but also that not everyone in Rome loved Birgitta, and that enemies could attack her through her child.

Even on his best behavior, Karl caused his mother embarrassment. When she took her sons to call on the pope, Birger wore ordinary respectable clothing, but Karl dressed up to extravagant excess in furs that looked like live animals, with a silver belt so heavy that the pope called its weight a sufficient penance for sin.[78] Near the end of his life he horrified his mother by becoming involved in a love affair with Joanna, the widowed queen of Naples, whom he had met through Birgitta. He and Birger came to Italy to accompany their mother to the Holy Land, but Karl was ill when they arrived. (He was coughing blood, a symptom of sin to contemporary witnesses and of tuberculosis to modern histori-

---

75. Gregersson, *Legenda*, p. 21; also *Acta et processus*, p. 92. On Birgitta and Monica, see Atkinson, "Your Servant, My Mother," pp. 144–147.

76. Karl may have continued to plague his father past the grave. Shortly after his death, Ulf appeared to Birgitta and reported that five sins kept his soul in purgatory; the first was his encouragement of "that wild boy, whom you know": Birgitta, *Extravagantes*, chap. 56, p. 178. It seems likely that this referred to Karl, for whom he was responsible, and not to the "little Jester" in his entourage, as suggested by Aron Andersson in *St. Bridget of Sweden* (London: Catholic Truth Society, 1980), p. 19.

77. Birgitta, *Extravagantes*, chap. 112, p. 229. It was Birgitta's cook who told her the story. Obviously there were differences of opinion and different degrees of affection for the saint within her own household: when Margery Kempe visited Rome forty years later, Birgitta's maid told her that Birgitta was "kind and meek with everybody": *The Book of Margery Kempe*, ed. and trans. B. A. Windeatt (London: Penguin Books, 1985), p. 132.

78. Clausdotter, "Chronicon," p. 211.

ans.) He died before the pilgrims reached the Holy Land, in the midst of his affair with Joanna. At Karl's death Birgitta neither moved nor cried out but gave thanks and recommended his soul to God. To the queen of Naples and the lords and ladies who staged a great funeral, her patience seemed superhuman.[79]

If Birgitta's public demeanor was impressively calm, her inner life was not: Karl's death provoked agonizing dreams and visions. She was again reassured by Mary (VII.13; IV.54), who had once acted as Birgitta's midwife during the birth of a child into this world and now served in the same capacity during the birth of Karl's soul into the next:

> I did as a woman [does] who stands near another woman when she gives birth, to help the child so it does not die of the flow of blood nor be slain in the narrow place where it comes out, being also watchful that the child's enemies that are in the house slay it not. . . .
>
> I stood near [your] son a little before he gave up the spirit. . . . I helped him also in that narrow place that is in the going-out of the soul from the body so that he should not suffer such great pain in death that would cause him to be unstable or to despair at all, so that he would not forget God at his death. I preserved [his soul] also from his deadly enemies, that is to say, from fiends, so that none of them could touch it.[80]

It took two mothers to keep this sinner out of the Devil's clutches. In a scene unique in the annals of maternal power (VII.13), Karl's soul, naked and trembling, appeared before Christ enthroned in judgment among the angels and saints. Mary stood beside Christ, an angel and a demon on either side of the defendant. The demon protested that Mary had interfered unjustly, that Karl's soul should have come to him when it left the body. Mary an-

---

79. *Acta et processus*, pp. 436, 314. In *Saint Bridget of Sweden* (London: Longmans Green, 1954), 2:236, Johannes Jorgensen refers to Karl's illness in terms of the "hectic passion of the consumptive." Susan Sontag analyzes the attribution of moral implications to tuberculosis in *Illness as Metaphor* (New York: Farrar, Straus & Giroux, 1978); the disease was thought to arise in "too much passion, afflicting the reckless and the sensual" (p. 21).

80. Birgitta, *The Revelations of Saint Birgitta*, ed. W. P. Cumming (London: Oxford University Press, 1929), pp. 117–118.

swered that the soul belonged to her because Karl loved her greatly and rejoiced that she was God's mother. The fiend protested that Karl's wicked deeds still deserved punishment, but the angel responded that Karl's mother, recognizing her son's weakness, had strengthened his case with her own works and prayers. When the demon attempted to recount Karl's sins, he broke down in tears of rage: by making her son confess each one, Birgitta had destroyed the record, and even the "sack" of good deeds left undone had been broken. The angel said: "His mother's tears have robbed you and broken your sack and destroyed your list—so much do her tears please God." The fiend roared: "'My memory is gone from me! I have forgotten even his name.' And the angel answered: 'His name is called in Heaven 'the son of tears.'" Tears were the waters of spiritual birth: the demon cursed the mother's womb "that had such water in it."[81]

The judgment of Karl, with its dramatic presentation of maternal power, makes a strong, explicit statment about a mother's responsibility for her child's salvation. Even though Birgitta was constantly reassured by Mary and by Christ that she was a good mother, she suffered from horrifying visions of the uses of maternal power by bad mothers. Mary showed her a mother, daughter, and granddaughter: the daughter was alive, the mother in hell, the granddaughter in purgatory (VI.52). The mother—her heart cut away, her eyes hanging on strings, her breast full of worms, an adder gnawing at her stomach—said to the living daughter: "Woe is me that I was ever your mother. . . . See how my womb, that you lay in, is eaten with worms! . . . as often as you follow my sins and my teaching, so often I have a new torment." The granddaughter—addressing her mother (the daughter) as "You scorpion!"—reproached her for the teaching and example that had consigned her child to purgatory.[82] The repulsive, degraded state of the physical bodies of these women represents the corruption and spiritual degradation of those who fail their children. Death may strike at any moment, and punishment is eternal: this, rather than worldly success, was what a good mother must teach. In

81. Ibid., pp. 120–121, 123–124.
82. Birgitta, *Liber celestis*, pp. 441–442.

Birgitta's visions, maternal responsibility was heavy, clear, and concrete. On behalf of their own souls and their children's, mothers faced deadly and disgusting dangers, far worse than the dangers of physical childbearing.

Birgitta's daughters received complicated messages about the goodness of marriage and the nature of female holiness. Birgitta objected to Märta's marriage because of the bridegroom. She suspected that only an early death saved Ingeborg from the temptation to leave religious life. Her youngest daughter, Cecilia, ran away from the convent in which her mother had placed her to a marriage arranged by her troublemaking brother Karl. This event, which might have been interpreted as a maternal failure, was rationalized for Birgitta by Christ, who said (IV.71): "It is better for the body to be outside and the soul within, than for the body to be enclosed and the soul wandering about." He took advantage of the opportunity to reiterate that a good wife or chaste widow was the spiritual equal of a virgin.[83]

Birgitta's fourth child, Katarina, lived her life in the shadow of her mother's genius, reflecting and responding to her mother's sanctity, will, and way of life. The Process for Katarina's canonization (never formally achieved, although she is known as St. Katarina of Sweden) includes a story that as an infant, she withdrew from her nurse in horror on account of the woman's "shameful and lascivious life"; she would drink only at the breasts of her mother and other chaste women. When Pope Urban VI praised Katarina by saying "you truly drink your mother's milk," he repeated the theme that governed her entire life.[84]

Katarina was married in her teens to Eggert von Kyren. The young couple, who loved each other very much, imitated the chaste marriage of Mary and Joseph, and of Ulf and Birgitta in their first two years. Their abstinence was discovered by the mischievous Karl, who teased them for sleeping separately in rough beds. (His own wife expressed interest in their example, which may have sharpened his tongue.) While Katarina was visiting her

83. Ibid., p. 316.
84. "Vita S. Catharina," AS March, vol. 3, pp. 503–504, 506. Weinstein and Bell (*Saints and Society*, pp. 24–25) claim that the baby refused her mother's breast when Birgitta had sexual relations, but there is no basis for this in the texts.

mother in Rome, Eggert became ill. She started to return to Sweden, but God warned Birgitta that Eggert would die of his illness and that it would be "more useful" for Katarina to stay with her mother. Katarina obeyed but was unable joyfully and immediately to embrace the new status of virgin-widow to which she had been abruptly called. With Birgitta, she visited their confessor and asked him to beat her until her "hard heart" was changed. From that time on, Katarina expressed no further ambivalence, but served obediently as her mother's daughter.[85]

In one of her encounters with Mary, Birgitta asked for a closer union with Christ—a conventional request, but Mary responded with the unusual suggestion that she turn her attention first to mending her daughter's old, worn tunic. Mary went on to praise Katarina for giving up not only new clothes but her beloved husband, her worldly goods, her brothers and sisters and friends.[86] The passage is unique in its focus on Katarina; elsewhere in Birgitta's *Revelations* the mother is always at the center of the daughter's life. After Birgitta's death, Katarina worked for her canonization, carried her bones back to Sweden, and eventually became the abbess of her mother's foundation at Vadstena.

When Birgitta told Mary that she loved her more than she loved her children, Mary responded by repeating her promise "to be a mother to the children of Ulf and Birgitta"—a reassurance that helped the saint dedicate herself to her vocation.[87] But the co-maternal bond was not entirely one-sided: just as Mary mothered Birgitta's children, so Birgitta conceived and carried Mary's child. During one Christmas at Alvastra, after Birgitta was widowed but before she left Sweden for Rome, she experienced a mystical pregnancy (VI.86): "With a great burst of joy in her heart, she felt as if a living child were moving in her heart."[88] Mary herself, comparing Birgitta's miraculous conception with the Annunciation, adopted Birgitta, pregnant with Christ and impregnated by Christ, as her daughter-in-law (VI.88): "For as a father and mother, growing old and resting, place the burden on their daughter-in-

<hr />

85. "Vita S. Catharina," pp. 505–506.
86. Birgitta, *Extravagantes*, chap. 69, pp. 191–192.
87. Ibid., chap. 63, p. 185.
88. Birgitta, *Liber celestis*, p. 460.

law and tell her what needs to be done in the house, so God and I who are old in the hearts of people, and chilled away from their love, want to make known our will to our friends and to the world through you."[89]

Birgitta's closeness to and identification with Mary culminated in a special revelation of the Nativity (VII.21), promised to the saint in Rome and experienced in Bethlehem during her last great pilgrimage. Birgitta saw a beautiful young woman, her belly swollen in advanced pregnancy, hands raised, facing east, standing as if in prayer. In an instant an infant appeared at her feet, with a radiance more splendid than that of the sun, so bright that it obliterated the light from Joseph's candle. She saw the baby cry and tremble from the cold and the hard floor until Mary held and warmed him. The experienced mother noted that Mary's womb contracted immediately after the birth and that she showed no other physical change or any weakness.[90] The tone of Birgitta's account of her vision of the Nativity is less like that of a daughter-in-law than of another mother or a grandmother, taken into Mary's confidence about the birth of the wonderful child. As Birgitta grew older and more accustomed to heavenly conversation, her relationship with Mary grew stronger, deeper, and more intimate—much as any earthly relationship changes as its participants change, over time.

The imagery of birth is ubiquitous in the *Revelations*, not only in relation to actual births, physical and spiritual, but in metaphors used to illustrate and clarify theological meaning. Christ explained (IV.67) that "just as a woman bears a child, so a good soul, that is God's wife, brings forth good works that are pleasing to God." Comparing sinners to stillborn children and himself to a mother (VI.28), he grieved over the labor expended to no good purpose on lost souls: "Just as a stillborn child does not taste the

89. Birgitta, *Revelationes S. Birgitte*, ed. Barthomeus Ghotan (Lübeck, 1492); this was the first printed edition. See Claire L. Sahlin, " 'A Marvelous Great Exultation of the Heart': Mystical Pregnancy and Marian Devotion in Birgitta of Sweden's Revelations" (unpublished paper, 1990).

90. Birgitta, *Liber celestis*, p. 486. For the ramifications in the history of art of Birgitta's vision of the Nativity, see esp. Henrik Cornell, "The Iconography of the Nativity of Christ," *Uppsala Universitets Årsskrift* 1 (1924), 1–101.

sweetness of the mother's milk, nor the comfort of her words, nor the warmth of her breast, just so thou [sinner] shall not be comforted by my words, nor feel the warmth of my love." Like an unappreciative son who adds gratuitous pain to his mother's inevitable suffering, the sinner adds to Christ's suffering and may as justly be reproached (VI.19), "for I brought him from darkness to light by my Passion, and fed him with milk of my sweetness."[91]

In the course of Birgitta's long life, Mary was at various times her mother, mother-in-law, teacher, and close friend and at all times a mighty representative of God's power and presence. She helped the child Birgitta with her sewing and came to the old woman's death to assure her of forgiveness.[92] Mary shared the responsibility of Birgitta's children and allowed the saint to participate in her own divine motherhood. Hers is the dominant heavenly voice in Birgitta's *Revelations*, although the saving work of mothers (including Mary) is more closely identified with the work of Christ. Like Christ, every mother faced pain and terror and the continuing burden of responsibility for her children's salvation. Julian of Norwich appreciated Christ's motherhood, but Birgitta went further, representing mothers as godlike in their power, sorrow, and responsibility.

The *Revelations* was widely known in most of Europe in the fifteenth century; the first printed edition was produced in Lübeck in 1492. Birgitta's canonization, interrupted by the politics of the Schism, produced massive documentation that was collected and published by her supporters. The Process was begun in 1377, successfully completed in 1391, and reconfirmed in 1414 and 1419, with attendant publicity each time. Birgitta's career, her *Revelations*, and her canonization provoked Jean Gerson to write two treatises on the discernment of spirits, setting forth guidelines for confessors.[93] He urged caution in dealing with visionaries, particularly when they were women. Gerson did not comment directly on Birgitta's *Revelations* or dispute her canonization, but

91. Birgitta, *Liber celestis*, pp. 311, 418, 411.
92. *Acta et processus*, p. 76; *Extravagantes*, chap. 22, pp. 190–191.
93. Jean Gerson, "De distinctione verarum revelationum a falsis," and "De probatione spirituum," in *Oeuvres complètes*, vol. 7, no. 90, pp. 36–56; vol. 9, no. 448, pp. 177–185.

he expressed reservations—especially concerning threats to clerical authority—shared by many leaders of the Church. Neither Gerson's doubts nor those of his colleagues inhibited the growth of Birgitta's cult and reputation or diminished her influence on women who shared her desire to be close to God.

On the way home to Sweden in 1374, Birgitta's bones were carried through Danzig, where they were received by an enthusiastic crowd that included Dorothea of Montau (1347–94), who was, like the Swedish saint, a wife, a mother, and a mystic. Dorothea was inspired to holy tears by a vision of Birgitta's soul joined to God.[94] Trained by her mother to meditate on Christ's Passion, she began in early childhood to experience visions and to undertake severe ascetic practices. At sixteen she was married, and at nineteen she gave birth to the first of nine children. Pregnancy, childbirth, and nursing provided no relief from household chores, and Dorothea relaxed none of her ascetic disciplines, not even her fasting, when she was pregnant or nursing. She found the most painful aspect of childbirth to be exclusion from church for forty days afterwards, but her joy at each rite of purification was dampened by the realization that the care of a new infant would also keep her from church, and that she would have to return to her husband's bed. When an infant cried at home while she was in church, her breasts leaked milk; then she rushed home, through mud and frequently in darkness, to feed the baby. If her husband's needs or some other duty prevented her from returning to church in the morning, she felt a sword pierce her heart—an obvious reference to Mary's pain at the Presentation of Jesus (Luke 2:35).[95]

Dorothea's husband Adalbert was a swordsmith, and her religious activities were restricted by the everyday work of a woman

94. John of Marienwerder, *Vita Dorotheae Montoviensis Magistri Johannis Marienwerder*, ed. Hans Westpfahl (Cologne: Bohlau Verlag, 1964), 7.19.f, p. 355 (hereafter *Vita Dorothea*). See also "Vita B. Dorothea," AS October, vol. 13, pp. 472–584; and John of Marienwerder "Das Leben der Heiligen Dorothea von Johannes Marienwerder," SRP, vol. 2 (Leipzig: Hirzel, 1863).

95. *Vita Dorotheae*, 2.6.h, p. 72; 2.31.a, p. 93; 2.31.c, p. 93; 2.31.i–k, p. 94. The common assumption that medieval women took their babies to church and nursed them there is not supported by Dorothea's story—but in this, too, she may have been unusual.

of the urban artisan class. Unlike Elizabeth or Birgitta, she had to shop for groceries, cook her family's food, and take care of her babies and older children. Like the other mother-saints, however, she struggled to give birth and to nourish each child spiritually as well as physically. She prayed for their souls by day and night, wept over them, and instructed them by word and example. Like St. Augustine, her children imbibed the name of Jesus Christ with their mother's milk. In 1379, on the feast of the Conception of the Virgin, a miraculous insight sent Dorothea home from church just in time to rescue four of her children from a fire.[96] In the next year she gave birth to her last child, Gertrude, and persuaded Adalbert to consent to a chaste marriage. No miracle preserved the eight older children from the plague in 1383, however: Gertrude was the only survivor. In 1385 Dorothea and Adalbert went on a long pilgrimage to Marian shrines in southern Europe. Despite his consent to chastity and his willingness to go on pilgrimage, Adalbert was not an easy husband; he occasionally became cruel and abusive and was intolerant of his wife's asceticism when it disrupted the household.

When Adalbert died in 1390 and Gertrude entered a convent, Dorothea was set free from the responsibilities she had carried for so long. She left Danzig for Marienwerder, where she became an anchoress at the cathedral and a protegée of one of its canons. John of Marienwerder was her confessor and biographer and the earnest promoter of her cult. Like other biographers of holy married women, he insisted on the goodness of marriage when it was approved by the Church and characterized by humble service to the spouse and by the careful raising of children in the fear and love of God. He praised Dorothea's effective work for the spiritual good of her children and claimed that she was rewarded by nine revelations—one for each child—concerning the generation of spiritual gifts.[97] Like other mother-saints, Dorothea experienced a mystical pregnancy more powerful and overwhelming than any physical pregnancy. Her uterus swelled instantaneously, and she

96. Ibid., 2.29.c, p. 91; 2.43.a, p. 109.
97. John of Marienwerder, "Septilium B. Dorotheae," tract. 1, xxv–xxxi, *Analecta Bollandiana* 2 (1883), 454–464.

felt the tremendous pressure, similar to the final stage of labor, of God about to be born in her soul. Feeling God move and leap, she knew God lived within her, and she responded like a mother who recognizes life in her unborn child. John thought this was a natural way for God to communicate with a chosen soul: "How can my bride know me unless she conceives and carries me, and unless I grow in her, and her in me?"[98]

After widowhood set her free to pursue her vocation, Dorothea's spiritual life was marked by growth and glory. Her physical life had been marked from early childhood by an intense preoccupation with pain and deprivation. For her, physical motherhood was itself a road to pain, which she identified with God's will and Christ's suffering. When her first child was born, God placed a sign above her heart—a great wound that lasted twenty years and hurt most intensely when an infant nursed; the wound, associated with the bundle of myrrh between the breasts of the bride, identified her with the "well-beloved" of the Canticle. That was God's act; Dorothea's response, repeated when each of her children was about six months old, was to burn her breasts with a candle so that the infant's nursing caused extreme pain.[99] The obstacles and frustrations to her vocation arising from maternity were to a great extent balanced or compensated for by such suffering. For Dorothea, the boundary between physical and spiritual motherhood was neither sharp nor strict; the pains of physical motherhood, intensified by God's action and her own, were readily associated with the pains of Christ. She identified maternal anguish not with the suffering of the mother, Mary, but with the Passion of God.

In the fourteenth century, more women were included in the company of saints than at any earlier time in the history of Christianity.[100] Such notable figures as Elizabeth of Hungary, Catherine of Siena, and Birgitta of Sweden naturally inspired others; their legends and images circulated widely, offering new possibilities to the imagination of women who were neither noble nor famous.

98. *Vita Dorotheae,* 6.21.f, p. 319. Dorothea's spiritual pregnancy is compared to Birgitta's in John of Marienwerder, "Das Leben," pp. 365, 368.

99. *Vita Dorotheae,* 2.32.c, p. 95.

100. See Weinstein and Bell, *Saints and Society,* p. 220; also Herlihy, "Did Women Have a Renaissance?" and Glasser, "Marriage."

Some connections can be traced, such as the influence of Birgitta on Dorothea; others are suggested by similarities in language, imagery, and behavior. Margery Kempe, for example, knew a good deal about Birgitta and her *Revelations*, was at least aware of the holy tears of Marie d'Oignies and Elizabeth of Hungary, and may have encountered the cult of Dorothea of Montau.[101]

Margery Kempe (1373–c. 1438) belonged to an upper middle-class merchant family of King's Lynn in eastern England. She was the mother of fourteen children, but like other married women, she was hampered more by her husband's wishes, needs, and proper claims than by those of her children. Long after she was called to a vocation of prayers, tears, and intimacy with Christ and Mary, Margery had to stay in her husband's house and bed. At one time during those difficult years, while she slept with her husband (but wore a hair shirt in bed), God announced that she was pregnant. She first expressed anxiety about the baby's care, which she feared would interfere with her religious activities; God promised to make the necessary arrangements. Then she grieved over what her pregnancy revealed, saying, "I am not worthy to hear you speak, and still to make love with my husband, even though it [lovemaking] is great pain and great distress to me." Christ insisted that she *was* worthy of intimacy with him, re-minded her that she was bringing forth "fruit" for God, and said he loved her as much as any maiden.[102] Nonetheless, Margery kept pressing for separation from her husband until she won his agreement and left home. Not even Christ's reassurance truly convinced her that a sexually active woman was the spiritual peer of a virgin.

Christ told Margery that he wished her to love him "as a son should be loved by the mother" and, on another occasion, that "when you weep and mourn for my pain and my Passion, then you are a true mother having compassion on her child."[103] In

---

101. For Kempe, see *The Book of Margery Kempe*, ed. Sanford B. Meech and Hope Emily Allen (London: Oxford University Press, 1940). Allen's notes introduce the connections between Kempe and various Continental women mystics; see also Atkinson, *Mystic and Pilgrim*, pp. 196–199.

102. *Margery Kempe* (Windeatt), p. 84.

103. Ibid., pp. 126–127.

these passages Margery, like other holy mothers, seems to identify maternity with pity and pain. But unlike Birgitta and Dorothea, Margery Kempe used few maternal images and metaphors, and she rarely mentioned her children or her experience of motherhood. One important exception is her description of a desperate illness after her first child was born, when she went mad for "half a year, eight weeks and odd days" and was cured by a vision of a loving, comforting Jesus.[104] The remarks about the feelings of a "true mother," spoken by Christ, seem more relevant to Margery's relationship with him and with Mary than to her own family experience. Motherhood apparently brought her little except trouble and illness, without apparent compensation in terms of theological insight or identification with Christ and Mary.[105] Unlike the *vitae* and the writings of other holy women, her autobiography says almost nothing about care for the spiritual welfare of her children. Her copious tears were all for Jesus, and no spiritual pregnancy transformed her experience of motherhood into mystical union.

Only one of Margery's children made an appearance in her story, a son who was attached to worldly things (his mother said) and fell into the sin of "lechery." Then he became so ill that his appearance was frightening; his face was "full of pimples and pustules, like a leper," and he lost his job. Margery, who had warned him to choose celibacy or marriage, had also asked God to punish him if he disobeyed. When he got sick, the neighbors blamed her for bringing God's wrath down on her own child. Like Birgitta, she was held responsible for her children's troubles and quickly became the object of malicious gossip when something went wrong. In her mind, however, she was vindicated when her son begged her to ask God to forgive him and take away his illness, "for he supposed that by her prayers our Lord sent him that punishment, and therefore he trusted by her prayers to be delivered of it." She did as he asked and "prayed so long, that he was completely freed from his illness and lived many years after, and

104. Ibid., p. 41.
105. Margery is identified with Christ primarily as his lover and beloved, and thus with others who love and are loved by him: Mary, Mary Magdalene, etc. Her own motherhood did not produce or reinforce such identification.

had a wife and child." He reformed his style of life and began to dress and speak soberly instead of indulging in fashion and nonsense. When Margery asked about these changes, he said that he had been drawn to God through his mother's prayers and intended to follow her advice in the future.[106] The people of Lynn, Margery herself, and her son all shared the conviction that she persuaded God both to make him ill and to cure him, physically and socially. As with Birgitta, maternal power in a woman close to God was capable of bringing about both suffering and salvation. Such power might be exerted on behalf of a wayward child, for the salvation of other "sinful wretches," or for the world.[107]

The legend and image of St. Frances of Rome (d. 1440), a near-contemporary of Margery Kempe, illustrate complex developments in the ideologies of motherhood and of female sanctity in the transitional fifteenth century. Frances belonged to a rich, prominent urban family; like other holy persons, she displayed her spiritual distinction very early. The infant Katarina of Sweden rejected the breasts of a "lascivious" nurse, but Frances went further, rejecting all the embraces customarily lavished on infants and refusing even to be touched by any man, including her father. At eleven she was married, unwillingly, to Lorenzo Ponziani. She was gravely ill for a year after the wedding, and even after she recovered, conjugal intercourse so disgusted her that she vomited (sometimes blood) afterward.[108]

In time Frances adapted to the requirements for a Roman matron of the upper class. She bore three children and nursed them herself, winning praise for uncommon maternal virtue. A chronic, painful sore on her breast was healed when the Virgin soothed it with a wonderful liquid (in contrast to the wounds inflicted upon Dorothea of Montau by herself and by God).[109] When Frances's only daughter and younger son died in the same year, she bore their

---

106. *Margery Kempe* (Windeatt), p. 266.
107. Ibid., p. 33.
108. *I processi inediti per Francesca Bussa dei Ponziani*, ed. P. T. Lugano (Vatican: Biblioteca Apostolica, 1945), p. 39. This source contains testimony offered soon after Francesca's death. The *vita* by her confessor, Matteotti, is available in AS March, vol. 2, pp. 92–103.
109. Matteotti, *Vita*, p. 179; *Processi inediti*, pp. 20–21.

deaths with marvelous "patience," and afterward was frequently portrayed in the company of an angelic child, a ghostly reminder of the sorrow of motherhood.[110] Like Elizabeth of Hungary, Frances won special notice for works of love and mercy among the poor and sick of the city. She gathered around herself a group of women who shared her religious and charitable interests; eventually they formed a residential community under Benedictine sponsorship, which she joined after Lorenzo's death in 1438.

Outwardly, Frances conformed to the model of a sober, devout wife and mother, but inside her respectable clothing she wore a hair shirt and an iron girdle that cut into her flesh.[111] Her inner life was marked by passion and violence and by fierce combat with demons who beat and kicked her; on one occasion they pushed her down on top of a corpse. These bloody battles, depicted in frescoes in the house where she lived with her community, conflict in striking ways with her public presence during her lifetime and with her later reputation. Like Angela of Foligno and Dorothea of Montau, Frances maintained an intense, single-minded relationship with God, marked by horrifying instances of self-inflicted abuse. Over time, however, she acquired the reputation of a devoted, self-effacing wife and mother, and her later legend conformed to that aspect of her life. In Alban Butler's *Lives of the Saints*, Frances is credited with saying, "It is most laudable in a married woman to be devoted but she must never forget that she is a housewife. And sometimes she must leave God at the altar and find him in her housekeeping."[112] This is an altogether inappropriate sentiment for the woman revealed in the frescoes, the early *vitae*, and the testimony compiled for the canonization process in the years just after her death.[113]

Chronologically and geographically, Frances was located in a

110. See Guy Boanas and Lyndal Roper, "Feminine Piety in Fifteenth-Century Rome: Santa Francesca Romana," in *Disciplines of Faith*, ed. Jim Obelkevich, Lyndal Roper, and Raphael Samuel (London: Routledge & Kegan Paul, 1987), p. 180.

111. *Processi inediti*, p. 16.

112. Alban Butler, *Lives of the Saints*, vol. 1, ed. Herbert Thurston, S.J., and Donald Attwater (Westminster, Md.: Christian Classics, 1963), p. 530.

113. Bell discusses earlier and later sources for Francesca's history in *Holy Anorexia*, pp. 136–140.

major nursery of the conjugal family of early modern Europe. Fifteenth-century Italian humanists regarded the family as the central institution of society, crucial to virtue, patriotism, and education. Increasingly, the virtue of wives and mothers was evaluated according to their devotion to home and family. The image of Frances as an exemplary Roman matron suited the mood of the times but obscured the cruel conflicts that marked her experience. The infant who would not let herself be touched, the bride who was sickened by lovemaking, and the mother who tortured her body were obliterated in the "perfect" wife and mother of a new age. The complex figure and reputation of Frances of Rome include unassimilated elements of Christian traditions concerning women and holiness: she discovered her vocation in one era, and her reputation was reconstructed for the next.

"Patient Griselda," whose wide appeal in the fourteenth century is puzzling and dismaying in the twentieth, won a kind of victory when she demonstrated that there was no limit to her capacity to accept suffering. Griselda was perceived as an unnatural mother, not because she made no attempt to protect her children but because tears would have been natural, and she did not weep until the ordeal was over. Even more than the brutal Walter, Griselda disrupts our empathy with medieval parents. We recognize in her not an exemplary heroine but a victim of abuse. We may respond by resisting literal interpretations, consigning the story and its protagonist to the realm of allegory, but we note its popularity at a time when famine and war and plague made sudden death commonplace, particularly the untimely deaths of children. However ordinary Griselda's losses and unnatural her behavior, her pain would have been recognized and appreciated in her own time. Mothers were expected to suffer, but the banality of suffering does not diminish its intensity.

The story of Griselda circulated in a society whose established values and institutions were being challenged and in some cases revised. Since the twelfth century, preachers and theologians had been reviewing Christian teaching about marriage and family, affirming the goodness of marriage and the importance of parenthood for the Church and society. In secular as well as religious art and literature, new attention was paid to families and to the sweetness and attractiveness of children. The Holy Family was presented for example and edification: Christians were encouraged to emulate and even to seek holiness through roles and relationships modeled by Jesus and his mother, foster father, and grandmother. With ancient institutions and traditional leaders of the Church under attack, new notions of holiness and new kinds of leaders gained prominence. The mendicant orders reflected and nurtured a "New Piety" that appealed to women as well as men and to married people as well as celibates. As poverty became the preeminent criterion for holiness, virginity lost its central significance, even for women. Marriage and motherhood were no longer insurmountable obstacles to passionate religious commitment.

Nevertheless, the new "saints" (some of whom never achieved canonization) experienced bitter conflict and anxiety about their status and their responsibilities. Their biographers insisted on the acceptability of marriage and the value of parenthood, but Margery Kempe—who had no biographer, only a scribe—expressed a common despair when she said, "Lack of virginity is now great sorrow to me."[114] Married women were uneasy about the traditional relationship of virginity to female holiness, and their vocations were severely restricted by the practical and moral demands of marriage. Almost all the women who achieved fame and prominence outlived their husbands; widowhood set them free to live out the fullness of a special relationship to God.

For women with aspirations to holiness, motherhood was much less inhibiting than marriage. When their children died, or the women sent them away or left them behind, the loss represented an opportunity to experience an intense form of the poverty and pain required of holy persons; indeed, the physical and emotional pains of motherhood could in themselves be a source of divine revelation and an intimate bond with Mary and with Christ. Instead of blocking access to the sacred, motherhood made it available through sorrow and suffering, permitting women to share the tears of Mary and the pains of Christ. The definition of a good

114. *Margery Kempe* (Windeatt), p. 86.

mother as a suffering mother was firmly lodged in the ideologies of sancity and of motherhood.

With the mother-saints came a new recognition and celebration of maternal power and responsibility. When God suffered and wept, God acted like a mother; mothers were identified in return with divine power. Even Griselda, by her passive acceptance of suffering, brought her children "back from the dead"; the women saints did much more. Through prayers and tears and closeness to heaven they could save their children's souls, and they willingly accepted that heavy burden. Through and by means of her identification with Mary, Birgitta fought eagerly for Karl's soul and won an active, dramatic victory over the Devil. In the twentieth century the concept of salvation has been secularized and psychologized, but mothers still are held responsible for their children's well-being—for their moral and emotional, if not spiritual, failure and success.

Through their lives, writings, and reputations the mother-saints of the late Middle Ages made physical maternity again compatible with holiness and spiritual power. Some of them also conceived and gave birth to God, transforming the experience of physical motherhood into mystical union. The incorporation of pain and suffering in the "good mother" and the acceptance of responsibility for a child's salvation are the major legacies of these "mothers of tears."

CHAPTER SIX

Motherhood Reformed: The Parson's Wife and Her Children

In Utopia, wrote Thomas More; "each woman nurses her own offspring unless prevented by either death or disease. When that happens . . . women who can do the service offer themselves with the greatest readiness since everybody praises this kind of pity and since the child who is thus fostered looks on his nurse as his natural mother."[1] This happy, healthy situation reflected the order, harmony, and prosperity of a commonwealth composed of "households, [which] as a rule are made up of those related by blood. . . . Wives wait on their husbands, children on their parents, and generally the younger on their elders."[2] In Utopia, as in More's England, morality and social order were understood to rest upon the conjugal family—on the father's authority, the mother's physical and spiritual service, and the production and socialization of new citizens. Even in the religious battleground of the sixteenth century, the loyal Catholic Thomas More agreed on certain subjects with Martin Luther: on maternal breastfeeding, for example, and on the significance of family and household as basic political, economic, and religious communities. Humanists such as More and his friend Erasmus, who remained in the old Church, partici-

1. *Utopia*, bk. 2, in *The Complete Works of St. Thomas More*, vol. 4, ed. Edward Surtz, S. J., and J. H. Hexter (New Haven, Conn.: Yale University Press, 1965), p. 143.
2. Ibid., pp. 135, 137.

pated with Protestant reformers in the construction and adaptation of ideologies of Christian motherhood for the transformed circumstances of early modern Europe.

Like their Italian predecessors, northern humanists tended to emphasize the virtues and activities of this world over contemplation of the next. And by 1500, "this world" was undergoing transformation in almost every aspect. Histories of Christianity focus on theological and ecclesiastical developments, but even while religious reformers were breaking ancient doctrines and institutions apart and creating new ones, navigators and adventurers were redrawing the map of the world. Religious reform and geographical expansion stimulated and accompanied transformations in politics and society, economic and intellectual life. The world within the household was altered as profoundly as the world outside, with long-lasting repercussions for marriage and parenthood, for the experience of family life, and the place of the household in church and society. The relationship of virtue and holiness to domesticity was turned around: the ideal mother of the sixteenth century was radically different from her medieval predecessor.

From the perspective of the late twentieth century, we can appreciate not only the creativity of the sixteenth century but the impact and duration of its revaluation and reconstruction of home and family. Compared with the exotic terrain of the Middle Ages, the sixteenth century looks remarkably familiar, in part because many of its attitudes and assumptions linger in the background of our own domestic values and arrangements. To study in detail the institution of Christian motherhood in the early modern era would require another volume, but an overview, highlighting certain significant changes, completes the picture of what went before and points up the drastic nature of the transformation. In this chapter I illustrate selected aspects of the domestic revolution of the sixteenth century, both to conclude my study of medieval Christian motherhood and to emphasize the staying-power of developments in family history at the dawn of the modern era.

The shock of recognition that signals the turn to modernity arises in historiography as well as history. Thanks to the invention of printing, the proliferation of books and other materials, and the spread of literacy, the sixteenth century offers a rich and varied archive for the history of the family. Compared with medievalists, historians of early modern Europe can see into more places, find records of more individuals and groups, and discover more direct evidence of domestic affections and allegiances. Especially in the seventeenth century, many men and women developed a new self-consciousness about their own lives, kept diaries, wrote autobiographies and voluminous personal letters, and commissioned portraits of themselves and their children. The sources are still skewed by class and gender but not as markedly as medieval materials. The growing and increasingly literate middle class included women as well as men and many kinds and conditions of persons with varied interests and perspectives. Saints' lives, which are always relevant to the history of Christian ideologies, remain useful, but early modern historians are not restricted to works of hagiography or devotion, or to the writings of celibate men.

Many sixteenth-century texts not only assume and argue for the centrality of marriage and parenthood in human experience but directly address questions that concern historians of the family—questions about the relationship of husbands and wives, about how children ought to be raised, about good and bad mothers. Because the authors of these texts shared our interest in families, we depend less on inference and on arguments from silence than is necessary in the interpretation of medieval materials. The varied documents of the new era, essential for the history of the family in the modern West, shed light backward as well as forward, contributing significant insights into the stories and symbols of Christian motherhood in the Middle Ages.

The reconstruction of family life and of Christian motherhood in early modern Europe occurred within a revolution in church and society produced by sweeping economic and political change. Geographically, the world known to Europeans expanded rapidly and extensively through the discovery, exploration, and exploitation of distant lands and oceans. Between the last quarter of the fifteenth century and the middle of the seventeenth, Europeans traveled around Africa to India, circumnavigated the globe, and planted settlements in the islands and two continents of the Western Hemisphere. The religious reformations, which can be represented on the one hand as culminations of trends and tendencies within medieval Christianity, can be understood also as aspects of the broader turn toward modernity.

The social and economic history of sixteenth-century Europe was shaped in part by slow recovery from the demographic disasters of the late Middle Ages. Outside of the high nobility, late marriage remained customary, especially for men, and a substantial number of women never married.[3] Rural areas suffered loss of population in relation to towns and cities; the urban middle classes gained in prosperity as well as numbers at the expense of peasants and landed nobility. Social and religious change made an earlier and sharper impact in the towns than in the countryside, where traditional values and institutions were retained into the seventeenth century and beyond.

Prices rose more steeply than population in the sixteenth century. The demand for goods in the cities could not be met with existing agricultural and manufacturing technologies and systems of distribution: demand outran supply, and inflation accelerated with the influx of precious metals from the Americas. Inflation favors the economically mobile over those on fixed incomes, and in the sixteenth century it favored elements of the new classes over rural landowners and their dependents. The movement of prices helped to create new wealth and new poverty, and it encouraged reliance on private ownership of the means of production in place of the shared tasks and common lands associated with feudalism. In England, once-common lands were enclosed; in the German cities, household workshops became shops owned by bosses who paid wages according to the sex and status of their workers.[4] New technologies and systems of production, distribu-

3. On demographic trends in early modern Europe, see J. Hajnal, "European Marriage Patterns in Perspective," in *Population in History*, ed. D. V. Glass and D. E. C. Eversley (Chicago: Aldine, 1965), pp. 101–143. See also John T. Noonan, Jr., "Intellectual and Demographic History," and Joseph J. Spengler, "Demographic Factors and Early Modern Economic Development," *Daedalus* 97 (1968), 463–485, 433–446.

4. Joan Kelly Gadol pointed to the relationship between domestic and economic change in early modern Europe in her 1980 essay "Family and Society," in *Women, History, and Theory* (Chicago: University of Chicago Press, 1984), esp. pp.

tion, and labor organization were born in response to economic pressures, stimulating the transition from late feudalism to early capitalism.

The disappearance of feudal structures in early modern Europe was associated with the decline of the old baronial class, whose wealth and power were based on land, and with the rise of national monarchies, notably those of England, France, and Spain. Kings, traditionally first among equals, burst out of feudal restraints in the sixteenth century. Medieval kings had learned to form alliances with urban communes and oligarchies; sixteenth-century rulers continued that practice with great effectiveness, increasing their own wealth and power and the cities' independence at the expense of feudal magnates. More loudly and explicitly than ever before, rulers and political theorists presented royal authority in terms of patriarchy: identifying themselves with the fathers of families, kings claimed the loyalty and obedience owed to domestic rulers. The early modern state, and the kings who represented and personified it, made powerful claims for the affection and service and economic resources of their subjects. The image of the king as husband and father of the nation and of the father as monarch in the home strengthened both sides of the equation: patriarchal rule in state and household was the fundamental political movement of the sixteenth century. James I of England made this plain when he declared: "I am the Husband, and all the whole Isle is my lawfull Wife."[5]

119–125. David Underdown attributes "the preoccupation with scolding [assertive] women during the century 1560–1660. . .[to] the social and economic transformation that was occurring in England during that period—of the decline in the habits of good neighborhood and social harmony that accompanied the spread of capitalism": "The Taming of the Scold," in *Order and Disorder in Early Modern England*, ed. Anthony Fletcher and John Stevenson (Cambridge: Cambridge University Press, 1985), p.126. Economic and domestic changes affecting women in sixteenth-century German cities are analyzed in Lyndal Roper, *The Holy Household* (Oxford: Oxford University Press, 1989); and in Merry E. Wiesner, *Working Women in Renaissance Germany* (New Brunswick, N.J.: Rutgers University Press, 1986).

5. "Speech of 1603," *The Political Works of James I, Reprinted from the Edition of 1616, with an Introduction by Charles H. McIlwain* (Cambridge, Mass.: Harvard University Press, 1918), 2:272. Peter Stallybrass, "Patriarchal Territories: The Body Enclosed," in *Rewriting the Renaissance*, ed. Margaret W. Ferguson, Maureen Quilligan, and Nancy J. Vickers (Chicago: University of Chicago Press, 1986), p. 131, points to certain sixteenth-century political theorists who believed

The establishment of patriarchy in state, economy, and household was one element of a long, gradual transition from the kin-based society of early medieval Europe to a society based primarily on the conjugal family: that is, a married pair and the people intimately related to them by blood and service. Over time, "family" came to refer less significantly to kin and lineage, more significantly to a husband and wife, their children, and the other persons living in their household under their authority.[6] Linda Nicholson, a political philosopher, has analyzed the emergence of the early modern family in relation to political, legal, and economic developments: "The family and the state as we now comprehend them were being created out of the older institution of kinship. Thus kinship systems, which at one time had been the major mechanism for regulating food production and distribution, sexuality, crime and punishment, etc., were replaced by the twin and separate institutions of the family and the state."[7]

Analogous developments can be observed in religion. Among historians of Christianity, John Bossy has been most attentive to the transition from the kin-based religious practices and church organization of medieval Christianity to the parish-and-household-oriented practices and structures of early modern times.[8] The medieval Church offered ecclesiastical support and ritual

---

that "the family is established by the enclosure of private property, and that property is under the absolute control of the father." See also S. D. Amussen, "Gender, Family, and the Social Order, 1560–1725," in Fletcher and Stevenson, *Order and Disorder*, pp. 196–217. For patriarchal theory—the belief that political authority originates in the "natural" authority of fathers—see Gordon J. Schochet, *Patriarchalism in Political Thought* (New York: Basic Books, 1975).

6. In "Ghosts, Kin, and Progeny: Some Features of Family Life in Early Modern France," *Daedalus* 106 (1977), 87–114, Natalie Zemon Davis wrote of "the interests of the immediate family. . .sharply demarcated from others' interests, especially from those of the wider kinship group" (p. 100) and of the development of strategies for the future of the family. See also Herlihy, *Medieval Households*, chap. 4.

7. Linda Nicholson, *Gender and History* (New York: Columbia University Press, 1986), p. 2.

8. Bossy, *Christianity in the West*; see also John Bossy, "Blood and Baptism: Kinship, Community, and Christianity in Western Europe from the Fourteenth to the Seventeenth Centuries," in Baker, *Sanctity and Secularity*, pp. 129–143; Bossy, "The Counter-Reformation and the People of Catholic Europe," *Past and Present* 47 (1970), 51–70; Bossy, "The Social History of Confession in the Age of the Reformation," *Transactions of the Royal Historical Society*, 5th ser., 25 (1975), 21–38.

recognition to human and divine kinship; in both Protestant and Catholic communities after the reformations, religious activities were organized primarily around parishes based on conjugal households. Nicholson and Bossy use different language and select different phenomena to describe and illustrate profound changes in the ways that people lived together, formed and maintained primary attachments and allegiances, and socialized their children. "Religion" and "society" were not separable in early modern Europe; in religious and social aspects alike, systems based on traditional kinship and collectivities gave way to systems based on aggregations of households, and on the married men who ruled and represented them.

The reformations were religious phenomena, but they cannot be understood in terms of theology alone; they supported, complemented, and promoted the other social and political transformations of the sixteenth century. Protestant and Catholic reformers, educated in the languages and literature of biblical and classical learning, shared the humanists' emphasis on the importance of the family for good order and the socialization of the young. The magisterial reformers endorsed the claims and supported the extended authority of kings and princes and of all civil governments. The reality of a fractured church, and the acceptance by midcentury of the principle that the religious affiliation of a people ought to be determined by that of their prince, contributed to the patriarchal authority of rulers, even women rulers. It seemed obvious on the national as well as the domestic scale that the faith of "family members" must be shared and conform to that of the master.[9]

Between the fifteenth and the seventeenth centuries, on every level of society and in several aspects (political, economic, religious), there was increasing pressure to ensure that every person

9. This conviction made possible arguments for divorce in cases of conscience (as among some Anabaptists) and eventually also in cases of extreme incompatibility. As domestic harmony became more crucial, domestic conflict began to be seen as intolerable. See Martin Bucer in *De regno Christi: Opera Latina XV*, ed. François Wendel (Paris: Presses Universitaires de France, 1955), xxii–xlv, pp. 165–231. Milton translated these chapters into English and used Bucer's authority to support his own arguments on divorce; see "The Judgment of Martin Bucer Touching Divorce," in *Complete Prose Works of John Milton*, vol. 2 (New Haven, Conn.: Yale University Press, 1959), pp. 441–479.

belong to a family headed by a father—the "household" of Utopia. The alliances of kinship, which at least in the more prosperous classes had offered a degree of support and certain opportunities for autonomy to women outside the patriarchal household, gave way to the twin edifices of family and state. The closing of convents deprived Protestant women of their only institutional alternative to marriage, while among Roman Catholics after the Council of Trent, women's religious orders came ever more strictly under the "fatherly" authority of bishops. In the course of the century, women's participation in religious, social, and economic activity was increasingly confined to the household, under the rule of its master. Women's reproductive labor served God and men; developing ideologies of motherhood idealized and enforced such service. Outside the family, women began to be perceived as dangerous—threats to society, religion, and good order. The domestic work of wives and mothers was glorified at the expense of all other female participation in church and society.

The earliest articulations of early modern ideologies of marriage, family, and Christian motherhood came from humanists— from the Italians first, and later from their northern colleagues. Their reverence for education, attention to civic virtue, and preference for worldly activity over monastic renunciation helped to promote a new appreciation of marriage and parenthood. The influential Erasmus of Rotterdam (d. 1536) loved to make fun of lazy, vicious monks and nuns; he urged young people, especially young women, to marry and attend to husbands, households, and children. Celibate himself, Erasmus praised the excellence of marriage, warned of the physical and moral dangers of religious life, and lectured parents on their responsibilities.

In a colloquy entitled "The New Mother," Erasmus spoke through the pedantic "Eutrapelus," who calls on "Fabulla," supposedly to congratulate her on the recent birth of her child; he seizes the opportunity to speak at length on psychology, physiology, virtue, and child development. Like many of Erasmus's female protagonists, Fabulla is intelligent and outspoken. When Eutrapelus asks, sarcastically, if she believes that God has "so much leisure that he even attends women in labor," she answers:

"What could he better do, Eutrapelus, than preserve by propagation what he created?" She makes a case for the strength and courage of women compared with soldiers, some of whom manage to avoid actual combat, while "*we* must engage death at close quarters."[10]

Fabulla outthinks and outtalks her guest until the moment when he discovers that her baby has a wet nurse; then he takes over the conversation and begins to win all the arguments—declaiming, insisting, threatening. A woman who will not nurse is only half a mother, he says: "When you see on your breasts those two little swollen fountains, so to speak, flowing with milk of their own accord, believe that Nature is reminding you of your duty." Eutrapelus (and Erasmus) believe that wet-nursing is morally and physically unnatural, and dangerous besides: "I'm convinced that children's characters are injured by the nature of the milk, just as in fruits or plants the moisture of the soil changes the quality of what it nourishes."[11]

Eutrapelus appeals to maternal tenderness: "Isn't it a kind of exposure to hand over the tender infant, still red from its mother, drawing breath from its mother, crying for its mother's care—a sound said to move even wild beasts—to a woman who perhaps has neither good health nor good morals?" Assured that the nurse is healthy and well-behaved, he returns to the argument from natural history, pointing out that "there's no class of living creatures that does not nurse its own young," and asking: "Do you suppose it makes no difference whether a delicate infant drinks in congenial and familiar nourishment and is cherished by the now familiar warmth or is forced to get used to somebody else's?"[12] Eutrapelus obviously shares the ancient assumption about the identity of blood and milk, but unlike earlier Christian teachers (the Desert Fathers, for example), he believes that the health and

10. Desiderius Erasmus, *The Colloquies of Erasmus,* ed. and trans. Craig R. Thompson (Chicago: University of Chicago Press, 1965), pp. 269, 271. Eutrapelus refers to political and economic turmoil—the peasants' revolt, threatened bankruptcy, the Turks, factions in the Church: "Antichrist is awaited; the whole earth is pregnant with I know not what calamity." Fabulla responds, quietly, that all of this may be insignificant to God.

11. Ibid., pp. 282, 283.

12. Ibid., p. 273.

strength of the body determine that of the mind and spirit. Thus it is essential that "the youthful body receive proper care from the minute it's born."[13]

Disruption in the bonding of mother and child may be disastrous, Eutrapelus warns: "Your son may love you less, his natural affection being divided, as it were, between two mothers; and your devotion to him will cool in turn. The result will be that when he's older, he'll be the less willing to obey your commands and you'll care less for him—you'll see the nurse in the way he behaves." Such an estrangement might interfere with the first, vital stages of education: "If, therefore, none of the warmth of natural devotion is lost, you'll instill principles of good conduct into him more easily. The mother is of no small importance in this respect, both because the material she molds is most plastic and because it is responsive to every suggestion."[14]

The idealized Fabulla responds immediately to this basic humanist educational philosophy; her highest aspiration is to raise a virtuous child, and she requires only guidance and instruction to become a perfect mother and teacher. Believing that the "nature" of a human being is formed for good or bad during infancy and early childhood, Erasmus was intent upon persuading women to devote themselves to their crucial task. A mother's work, the mission of her life, is accomplished during her child's earliest years. If the child is a boy, her time is short: "This time too will come some day; if God will, when you must send the boy out from home to learn his letters—and harder lessons, which are the father's responsibility rather than the mother's. Now his tender age should be cherished."[15]

Eutrapelus appeals to Fabulla's intelligence and good will, and to something else—her "natural" maternal sympathies, or what might be called "maternal instinct." Much more than breast-feeding is involved. Even if the nurse is a paragon, *only* a mother can tolerate and love an infant through "the filth, the sitting up late, the bawling, the illnesses, the never sufficiently attentive

13. Ibid., p. 278.
14. Ibid., p. 283.
15. Ibid., p. 273.

watching."[16] Here the ex-monk Erasmus nearly echoed the monastic tradition he despised, but he used the ancient *topos* of the horrors of physical motherhood to convey a message entirely different from (for example) that of Jerome. Motherhood defines and transforms Fabulla; she is not offered an alternative to its hardships. No one else can care for her baby, who thrives only if she devotes herself to him. The child's physical and moral welfare, and his potential intellectual development, are paramount. Physical motherhood, glorified as essential in the civic and Christian formation of the child, is the natural vocation of every woman—even, or especially, of educated and virtuous women.

The first generation of Protestant reformers, building on the teachings of the humanists as well as on the theological rejection of monastic vows, had a consuming interest in matters of marriage and family. Erasmus and Luther differed about the freedom of the will, but both were convinced of the goodness of marriage, the importance of careful child raising, and the value of mother's milk. The reformers had an excellent private reason as well as a theological rationale for their passion for family: their movement demanded personal commitment. Raised in a world that required celibacy of its religious elite, they became a clergy of husbands and fathers. Their domestic lives were self-conscious representations of a revolutionary appreciation of God's plan for human society. They understood marriage, and especially parenthood, as essential vocations, and their lives as well as their teachings produced new chapters in the history of the family.

The most articulate and influential of the first generation was Martin Luther: monk become family man, prototype of the new Protestant parson. His parsonage, shared with Katherine von Bora and their six children, became a model of the Christian home—watched, criticized, emulated, and remembered. Katie herself, once a nun, became a minister's wife and a mother, moving in one lifetime from one version to the next of the holiest life available to a Christian woman. Luther, who defied his own father when he became a monk and later defied his other "father," the pope,

16. Ibid., p. 283.

reified paternity and patriarchy as governing principles of the Protestant reform.[17]

Luther's attitude toward marriage and family developed in conjunction with his emerging theology. As early as 1519 he preached on marriage, which he called a divine institution. At that time he did not move far from his scholastic predecessors in defining woman's nature and calling—she was "created to be a companionable helpmeet to the man in everything, particularly to bear children"—but he displayed much more enthusiasm for the work of parents. Married people, he said: "can do no better work and do nothing more valuable either for God, for Christendom, for all the world, for themselves, and for their children than to bring up their children well . . . bringing up their children properly is their shortest road to Heaven." This privilege and responsibility had its bitter side, for "by the same token, hell is no more easily earned than with respect to one's own children. . . . There is no greater tragedy in Christendom than spoiling children."[18] To the end of his life, Luther harped on the two themes of the divine institution and goodness of marriage and the critical importance of parenthood. His ideas grew more complex as the reformers established and argued positions in relation to allies and enemies, and in some respects he grew more understanding and accepting as he lived with Katie and raised children, but he never deviated from his central themes.

Luther's early attitudes on sex and family were shaped by his interpretation of Scripture, by pastoral experience, and by a developing distrust of works-righteousness. When he wrote his three great treatises of 1520 and his pamphlet on monastic vows in 1522 (by which time he had been banned in the Holy Roman Empire and his books burned), he was clear about the futility and danger to souls of vows of virginity and celibacy. He believed there were

17. In *The Beginning of Ideology* (Cambridge: Cambridge University Press, 1981), Donald R. Kelley makes connections between domestic patriarchy and the masculine imagery and rhetoric of the reformers: "The prime source of authority (and so of tyranny) in the sixteenth century . . . was not prince or pope but rather father" (p. 77). According to Kelley, "Lutheranism in particular was a masculine affair" (p. 76).

18. "A Sermon on the Estate of Marriage," LW, vol. 44, pp. 8, 12–13 (WA 2.169, 172).

not two classes of Christians, inside and outside religious life, but one class only, and that all had "vowed enough in baptism, more than we can ever fulfil."[19] Furthermore, "those who trust in works and vows destroy their own faith in the process."[20]

Luther was especially appalled at vows taken by young people before they awakened to their sexual natures and needs, and he urged women as well as men to acknowledge their sexuality. In 1524 he wrote to three nuns who had asked his advice about leaving their convent:

> The other ground is the flesh. Although women are ashamed to acknowledge this, Scripture and experience teach us that there is only one in several thousands to whom God gives the gift to live chastely in a state of virginity . . . God also wills that it be natural for a man and a woman to live together in matrimony. This is enough, therefore, and no woman need be ashamed of that for which God has created and fashioned her.[21]

Luther believed that chastity was a special grace, granted by God to a few individuals and for limited periods even to them. Lifelong celibacy and consecrated virginity he regarded as dangerous, unhealthy, and nearly impossible, producing "horrible crimes . . . like fornication, adultery, incest, fluxes, dreams, fantasies, pollutions" and hindering "many good things, like the bringing to life of children, the activity of the state, and economic life"—a cogent summary of the complex and intertwined agendas of the sixteenth century.[22]

19. "On the Babylonian Captivity of the Church," LW, vol. 36, pp. 74–75 (WA 6.539).

20. "On Monastic Vows," LW, vol. 44, p. 263 (WA 8.585).

21. *Luther: Letters of Spiritual Counsel*, ed. and trans. Theodore G. Tappet (Philadelphia: Westminster Press, 1955), p. 271 (WA Br 3.327). Sigrid Brauner argues that Luther accepted female sexuality and women's "natural" foolishness as useful within the household—"bad" women were those who refused the roles of wife and mother: "Martin Luther on Witchcraft: A True Reformer?" in *The Politics of Gender in Early Modern Europe*, ed. Jean R. Brink, Allison P. Coudert, and Maryanne C. Horowitz (Kirksville, Mo.: Sixteenth Century Journal Publishers, 1989), p. 38.

22. *Table Talk*, LW, vol. 54, p. 335 (WA TR no. 4368). This collection of Luther's remarks at family meals and other occasions was written down by his friends and

Luther's apparent acceptance of sexuality, and his genuine and fervent disapproval of celibacy, masked real ambivalence; he maintained an Augustinian attitude toward sexual passion without Augustine's faith in the possibility and desirability of repression and sublimation. In his *Lectures on Genesis*, begun in 1535 (ten years after his own marriage), Luther said that while God's command to be fruitful would have been a delightful obligation had there been no Fall, sin had attached to procreation an "unavoidable leprosy of the flesh." He described the shame experienced by husbands and wives in "so hideous and frightful a pleasure that physicians compare it with epilepsy or falling sickness." Predictably, ambivalence about sex was reflected in attitudes toward women. On the positive side, Luther rejected the Aristotelian and scholastic designation of women as misbegotten males: "But let themselves be monsters and sons of monsters—these men who make malicious statements and ridicule a creature of God . . . created by a special counsel of God."[23] In his inimitable style, he excoriated the Bishop of Mainz, who "was irritated by no annoyance more than by the stinking, putrid private parts of women. That godless knave, forgetful of his mother and his sister, dares to blaspheme God's creature through whom he was himself born."[24] Women's domestic roles, especially motherhood, ought to be sufficient protection against such scandalous attacks. This defense of course left women vulnerable outside the family—but Luther wanted all women placed safely inside.

Notwithstanding his defense of wives and mothers against the misogyny of celibate men, Luther's domestic prescriptions were based on biological assumptions that were not particularly advanced. In a notorious "joke" he remarked that "men have broad shoulders and narrow hips, and accordingly they possess intelligence. Women have narrow shoulders and broad hips. Women ought to stay at home; the way they were created indicates this, for they have broad hips and a wide fundament to sit upon."[25] In

---

followers. Its range and informality make it a useful source, although care must be taken in evaluating the significance of selections.

23. *Lectures on Genesis Chapters 1–5*, LW, vol. 1, p. 71 (WA 42.54).

24. *Table Talk*, p. 171 (WA TR no. 2807b).

25. Ibid., p. 8 (WA TR no. 55).

a more serious context, a lecture on the striped and speckled flocks of Genesis 30, an anecdote reveals the physiological notions underlying Luther's theories:

> I remember that when I was a boy at Eisenach, a beautiful and virtuous matron gave birth to a dormouse. This happened because one of the neighbors had hung a little bell on a dormouse in order that the rest might be put to flight when the bell made a sound. This dormouse met the pregnant woman, who, ignorant of the matter, was so terrified by the sudden meeting and sight of the dormouse that the fetus in her womb degenerated into the shape of the little beast. Such examples are all too common.[26]

Biology was not all that kept women at home, for the subjection of wives was a consequence of the Fall. Eve was "very free" in the first creation, but now "the rule remains with the husband, and the wife is compelled to obey him by God's command. He rules the home and the state, wages wars, defends his possessions, tills the soil, builds, plants, etc. The woman, on the other hand, is like a nail driven into the wall. She sits at home.[27] "Woman" and "wife" had become interchangeable. Genesis 3 declared wives subject to husbands, not women to men. But because the reformers believed that all women should marry, subjection became the fate of all women, not of wives only.

His own marriage and fatherhood supplied Luther with insight into pregnancy and birth, although conception remained mysterious. He found it "worthy of wonder that a woman receives semen, that this semen becomes thick and . . . is congealed and then is given shape and nourished until the fetus is ready for breathing air"; God "takes a drop from the blood of the father and creates a human being." The suggestion was that fathers are the true parents of their children, but Luther knew very well that the divine work of procreation, and of sustaining the life of a newborn, was accomplished through women: "When the fetus has been brought into the world by birth, no new nourishment appears, but a new way and method: from the two breasts, as from a fountain, there

---

26. *Lectures on Genesis Chapters 26–30,* LW, vol. 5, p. 381 (WA 43.692).
27. *Genesis 1–5,* p. 202 (WA 42.151).

flows milk by which the baby is nourished."[28] Thus, the mother's milk and father's semen alike are identified with blood: each is an aspect of one life-creating and sustaining fluid.

Like Erasmus, Luther described the breasts of the new mother as "fountains," but he credited God, not "nature," with the spontaneous supply of nourishment for the infant. He assumed that mothers suckled their own children, as was the custom in his circle, unlike that of Erasmus's more sophisticated acquaintance. In a much more earthy and practical style than that of Eutrapelus and Fabulla, the qualities of mother's milk and the proper method of weaning an infant were discussed at Luther's table, along with comparisons of the "best" breasts for lactation and appearance.[29]

The contemplation of motherhood filled Luther with awe at God's loving design. He observed that "the entire female body was created for the purpose of nurturing children. How prettily even little girls carry babies on their bosom!" God made them to be mothers; men were clumsy "at the simplest tasks around the baby!" Like Erasmus, he believed that women were designed for motherhood, but he did not romanticize pregnancy and birth. He lived with Katie through six pregnancies and knew something about them: "From the beginning . . . a woman suffers very painful headaches, dizziness, nausea, an amazing loathing of food and drink, frequent and difficult vomiting, toothache, and a stomach disorder." Birth was even more frightening, for "when the fetus has matured and birth is imminent, there follows the most awful distress, because only with utmost peril and almost at the cost of her life does she give birth." In short, countless dangers of miscarriages, monsters, and various deformities" surround pregnant women, whose husbands ought to attend and care for them.[30]

Despite all these difficulties, conception and birth remained marvelous works of God; only "because of their continued recur-

28. Ibid., pp. 126–127 (WA 42.94–95).

29. *Table Talk*, p. 321 (WA TR no. 4105). For Luther, breast-feeding was one of a mother's routine tasks: "A wife too should regard her duties in the same light, as she suckles the child, rocks and bathes it, and cares for it in other ways"; see "The Estate of Marriage," LW, vol. 45, p. 40 (WA 10².289).

30. *Genesis 1–5*, pp. 202, 200 (WA 42.151, 149). *Genesis 26–30*, p. 381 (WA 43.691).

rence they have come to be regarded as commonplace, and we have verily become deaf to this lovely music of nature."[31] The "lovely music" was equated with God's will and with women's work. Even before he was married, Luther wrote a lengthy treatise, "The Estate of Marriage," recommending to all Christians the "golden and noble works" of parenthood. For women, this was the very purpose of existence: "If you were not a woman you should now wish to be one for the sake of this very work alone, that you might thus gloriously suffer and even die in the performance of God's work and will."[32]

Luther's assumptions about God's will for women and the cause for which they might suffer and die were exactly opposite to those of medieval hagiography—for example, of the *Golden Legend*, with its tales of women who died to preserve their virginity. Rejecting the model of the ancient saints and martyrs, Luther declared that even pastoral counseling of women in childbirth ought to be shaped by a proper understanding of the female vocation:

> This is also how to comfort and encourage a woman in the pangs of childbirth, not by repeating St. Margaret legends and other silly old wives' tales but by speaking thus, "Dear Grete, remember that you are a woman, and that this work of God in you is pleasing to him. Trust joyfully in his will and let him have his way with you. Work with all your might to bring forth the child. Should it mean your death, then depart happily, for you will die in a noble deed and in subservience to God."[33]

As the "noble deed" was no longer the preservation of virginity for Christ, St. Margaret and St. Katherine could serve no longer as exemplary figures. They were replaced by the wives of the Hebrew patriarchs, women who recognized their own true nature and had a passion for offspring: "The saintly women desire nothing else than the natural fruit of their bodies. For by nature woman has been created for the purpose of bearing children. Therefore she has

31. *Genesis 1–5*, p. 126. (WA 42.94).
32. "Estate of Marriage," p. 40 (WA 10².289).
33. Ibid.

breasts; she has arms for the purpose of nourishing, cherishing, and carrying her offspring." Leah, for example, was "a chaste and saintly matron who has an aversion for lust and desires the birth of children." These Hebrew "saints" recognized their duty to the patriarchy: "They already had children before, yet they bore in mind that children are mortal. . . . Therefore if one woman had had even a hundred children, still she would always have desired more, for they had in view the promised descendants to whom the preaching they had heard from their husband pertained." Luther reminded his congregations that among the Hebrews, who properly understood sterility as divine punishment, childless women were "rejected and cursed before God." Rachel wept during her six years without children, and when she "wanted to sleep with her husband, she did so only in order to become a mother and to increase the house of Jacob, who had the promise."[34]

Luther scolded those who enjoyed the pleasures of marriage but avoided procreation, "those who are devoted to idleness and laziness and shun the sweat and toil of marriage. But the purpose of marriage is not to have pleasure and to be idle but to procreate and bring up children, to support a household. . . . Those who have no love for children are swine, stocks, and logs unworthy of being called men or women; for they despise the blessing of God, the Creator and Author of marriage."[35] Luther believed that a major purpose of life was to raise children and held a high view of the role of parents as "apostles, bishops, and priests to their children, for it is they who make them acquainted with the gospel . . . there is no greater or nobler authority on earth than that of parents over their children, for this authority is both spiritual and temporal."[36]

Just as Luther's doctrines of God and of ministry shaped his ideas about the work of parents, his experience of parenthood shaped his theology. When he thought about himself and Katie in their protective care for baby Martin or their correction of little Hans, he better understood God's relation to humanity.[37] The reformers associated parenthood with divine power and righteous-

---

34. *Genesis 26–30*, pp. 355, 356, 362, 358 (WA 43.673, 674, 678, 676).
35. Ibid., p. 363 (WA 43.679).
36. "Estate of Marriage," p. 46 (WA 10².301).
37. *Table Talk*, pp. 127, 159 (WA TR nos. 1237, 1631).

ness to a degree that went beyond the traditional assignment to God of the attributes of fathers. The authority and status of mothers were limited by subordination to their husbands, but fatherhood was nearly merged with divinity. Medieval fathers had held enormous powers over their children, but sixteenth-century fathers acquired also a kind of moral righteousness, an assumption of benevolence and correctness that made disobedience a sin as well as a crime. Paternal tyranny had always been a realistic possibility; when justice and righteousness were added to unrestricted power, the psychological and emotional dimensions of modern patriarchy began to take shape.[38]

Luther himself was a loving father, proud of his family and closely involved with his children. His experience with daughters, as well as his conviction that all Christians should read the Scriptures, persuaded him that schools ought to be established in every town—even schools for girls.[39] Like so many of their contemporaries, Martin and Katie suffered the loss of children, one in infancy and a daughter at thirteen. When Magdalena died, Luther was heartbroken; he held his child and, "weeping bitterly, prayed that God might will to save her."[40] During her last illness he sent for his older son: "She herself longs so much to see her brother that I feel compelled to send a carriage [for him]. They loved each other so much, perhaps his arrival could bring her some relief. I am doing what I can so that later the knowledge of having left something undone does not torture me."[41] He worried when his son did not recover quickly from the loss, fearing that he had "turned soft

38. In *When Fathers Ruled: Family Life in Reformation Europe* (Cambridge, Mass.: Harvard University Press, 1983), Steven Ozment noted with admiration the identification of domestic, civic, and moral virtue in early modern Europe: "The home, then, was no introspective, private sphere, unmindful of society, but the cradle of citizenship, extending its values and example into the world around it. The habits and character developed within families became the virtues that shaped entire lands" (p. 9); "The home was a model of benevolent and just rule for the 'state' to emulate" (p. 177).

39. See "To the Christian Nobility of the German Nation," LW vol. 44, p. 206 (WA 6.461).

40. *Table Talk*, p. 431 (WA TR No. 5496).

41. "Letters," LW, vol. 50, p. 235 (WA Br 10, 147).

through the words of his mother, in addition to mourning over his sister's death."[42]

Luther himself—an adult, and convinced of the righteousness of God—was also vulnerable to "softness": "I'm angry with myself that I'm unable to rejoice from my heart and be thankful to God ... I am joyful in spirit but I am sad according to the flesh. ... It's strange to know that she is surely at peace ... and yet to grieve so much." Yet aware of the novelty as well as the pain of his circumstances, Luther noted that "in the last thousand years God has given to no bishop such great gifts as he has given to me."[43]

As one consequence of his struggle for faith in God's justice and his interpretation of the divine will, Luther married and established a family. His experience instructed him and he instructed others in a passionate commitment to marriage and family: "Marriage should be treated with honor; from it we all originate, because it is a nursery not only for the state but also for the church and the kingdom of Christ until the end of the world."[44] The divine injunction to increase and multiply was taken very seriously: the production and raising of children became a central responsibility of all Christians, but especially of women. Scripture and "nature" alike revealed their duty: "A woman does not have complete mastery over herself. God so created her body that she should be with a man and bear and raise children. The words of Gen., ch. 1, clearly state this, and the members of her body sufficiently show that God himself formed her for this purpose."[45]

The roles of mothers and fathers were complementary: fathers were to guide, guard, direct, and provide for the family and to represent the household in church and state. Mothers were to be devout but to express their spirituality at home through care for the family. In Protestant Europe motherhood became a sign, even a precondition, of a woman's moral and physical health. Obedience

---

42. Ibid., p. 239 (WA Br 10.728–729).
43. *Table Talk*, pp. 430, 432. (WA TR no. 5494, 5498). Luther said of St. Jerome: "I wish he had had a wife, for then he would have written many things differently" (p. 72; WA TR No. 445).
44. *Genesis 1–5*, p. 240 (WA 42.178).
45. *Letters of Spiritual Counsel*, p. 271 (WA Br 3.327).

replaced virginity and poverty as the essential female virtue and road to holiness; a good woman obeyed God and her husband—whose wills, increasingly, were identified—and raised virtuous children. By the middle of the sixteenth century it was difficult, or nearly impossible, for a woman to be a good Christian *except* through marriage and motherhood.

In Strasbourg after the reform, prayers were said in the churches for pregnant women, and the Church Ordinance declared that a woman's "greatest honor on earth is her fertility."[46] The chief architect of the Strasbourg reformation, Martin Bucer, left a Dominican monastery in 1518, persuaded by the voice and arguments of Luther. In time Bucer came to differ with Luther over various theological points, but he always agreed about the importance of marriage, family, and education. In 1550 he wrote on Christ's kingdom for the young Edward VI of England; its coming, he believed, depended on cooperation between the churches and the civil government. In England such cooperation rested on the king's good will, and Bucer reminded Edward of his responsibility for the proper ordering of marriage, "this very sacred relationship, the font of the human race." He suggested that "guardians of matrimony" be appointed in the churches, "godly men" whose task was to ensure that husbands provided for their wives and that wives obeyed their husbands, "for unless this source and nursery of good citizenship, holy marriage, is most carefully preserved . . . what . . . can be hoped for the increase of good citizens and the hoped-for ordering and sanctification of the state?"[47] All civil governments, whether of kings or urban councils, held vital responsibility for marriage and for the good order of the households in which citizens and church members were produced and socialized.

In the cities of continental Europe, particularly in imperial cities whose overlord was far away, urban councils assumed responsibility for reforming the churches and for morality as well as public

---

46. Quoted in Lorna Jane Abray, *The People's Reformation* (Ithaca: Cornell University Press, 1985), p. 218.
47. Bucer, *De regno Christi* xv, xxi, pp. 152, 164–165.

peace and welfare. Lyndal Roper has examined the implications of reformation in Augsburg, especially in the craft workshops of that city, where the "politics of marriage" domesticated the reforming impulse. Roper makes plain the interconnections of religion, politics, and households: "By promising a religion of wedded life and a politics of the control of marriage, the evangelical message recruited substantial portions of the guildfolk for a Reformation which favored them, and which gave powerful articulation to the craft values of order, discipline, and the authority of the master." Traditional medieval notions of holiness were definitively overturned when marriage was identified with godliness and productive work, celibacy with vice and idleness. Single women were required to lodge with a family or leave town; journeymen had to marry before they could become masters. Marriage was associated with age, seniority, and power as well as virtue, so that potential class conflicts were disguised and reoriented according to a sex/gender system that encouraged young, unruly, unmarried men to conform rather than rebel. By enforcing gendered standards of behavior and accountability, the Marriage Court established what Roper has described as "the moral ethic of the urban Reformation." The politics of theology and gender linked the reformers' devotion to marriage and procreation to the early development of the social and economic institutions of modern Europe.[48]

Like the German cities, Calvinist Geneva was managed by an oligarchy composed of business and ecclesiastical leaders. Marriage was established as the exclusive option for successful adults; the Consistory summoned recalcitrant young men and told them that it was time to marry.[49] Calvin himself was encouraged and assisted by his colleagues when he looked for a wife; he lacked confidence about his suitability for marriage, but no respectable man could remain single, and certainly not the town's most prominent minister. With his tense, reserved personality and without children of his own, Calvin never developed the passionate enthu-

48. Roper, *Holy Household*, pp. 15, 1.
49. See Robert M. Kingdon, "Calvin and the Family: The Work of the Consistory in Geneva," *Pacific Theological Review* 17 (1984), 15.

siasm and interest in family characteristic of Luther and other leading reformers.[50] Nonetheless, he acknowledged the scriptural injunction toward procreation and affirmed the centrality of marriage and child raising in Christian society. Like Luther, Calvin noted the heroism required of childbearing women and displayed a sympathetic recognition of the physical and emotional consequences of motherhood: the "tedium of pregnancy, distaste for food, illness, difficulty in giving birth . . . anxiety for the fetus."[51]

The magisterial reformers appreciated the faith and devotion of their wives and of all respectable, reformed married women. They recognized motherhood as vital work, deserving sympathy and protection. But their celebration of women's work inside the household did not address the needs or circumstances of women outside the domestic system, whether or not they were mothers. At the opposite extreme—and as far as possible—from their own homes, reforming councils shut down brothels and drove prostitutes from the cities, depriving many women (and their children, of course) of their livelihood. Traditionally, brothels had been regarded as an accommodation for young unmarried men, but the reformers wanted everyone to marry, and to marry young. Luther blamed parents for "unparental conduct when they see that their child is grown up and is fit for and inclined toward marriage, and yet are unwilling to assist and counsel him thereto . . . they are in duty bound to assist their children to marry, removing them from the perils of unchastity.[52] Acknowledging the sexual energy of the young, the reformers attempted to sweep it into safe channels of domesticity.

---

50. On Calvin's personality and marriage, see William J. Bouwsma, *John Calvin* (New York: Oxford University Press, 1988), esp. pp. 22–23.

51. John Calvin, Commentary on 1 Tim. 2:15, in *Ionnis Calvini Opera* (Brunswick: Schwetschke, 1895), 53:278. Calvin insisted that marriage and motherhood do not constitute a woman's whole duty unless they proceed from faith and love of God. In Sermon 19 on the same text (52:228), he compared the acceptable sacrifice of women who "clean up [their children's] filth and kill their lice" to the useless lives of nuns and whores (closely identified with one another) in whom Eve's sin is *not* redeemed.

52. "That Parents Should Neither Compel nor Hinder the Marriage of Their Children," LW, vol. 44, p. 390 (WA 15.168). On the closing of brothels in the sixteenth century, see Roper, *Holy Household*, chap. 3; also Susan C. Karant-Nunn, "Continuity and Change: Some Effects of the Reformation on the Women

In the sixteenth century, middle- and working-class women were gradually excluded from guilds and from official posts in the towns, narrowing their economic as well as social options. Unmarried women were encouraged to enter domestic service in preference to other business or professions, because such work kept them "safe" in households headed by masters. Some married women with children chose part-time work with lower status and pay in order better to serve their families.[53] The celebration and spiritualization of motherhood within male-headed households had complex and long-lived consequences for mothers and children in the developing economy of early modern Europe.

Among the most articulate proponents of love, marriage, and motherhood were the Puritans of sixteenth- and seventeenth-century England and New England. They promoted literacy for both men and women, and because they developed the habit of examining their lives and feelings along with their consciences, their letters and journals addressed intimate domestic as well as religious affections. Puritan poetry, sermons, and legal documents provide a record of familial emotion and experience more extensive than anything available for medieval Europe. Their appreciation of conjugal passion went far beyond Luther's ambivalence; they assumed the centrality of married love in the economy of salvation.

In *Paradise Lost* the greatest Puritan poet celebrated the love-making of the first parents. Milton marked their innocence and enthusiasm:

> nor turn'd I ween
> Adam from his fair Spouse, nor Eve the Rites
> Mysterious of connubial love refus'd:
> Whatever Hypocrites austerely talk

---

of Zwickau," *Sixteenth-Century Journal* 13 (1982), 24; Wiesner, *Working Women*, pp. 97–109.

53. In *Working Women*, pp. 75–92, Wiesner points out that "women's work" was increasingly "defined as that which required little training or initial capital, could be done in spare time, and was done by men only as a side occupation, carried low status, and was informally organized and badly paid" (p. 92).

> Of purity and place and innocence,
> Defaming as impure what God declares
> Pure, and commands to some, leaves free to all.
> Our Maker bids increase, who bids abstain
> But our Destroyer, foe to God and Man?

Sexual abstinence was the Devil's program; marriage, God's:

> Hail wedded Love, mysterious Law, true source
> Of human offspring.

Milton sang a lullaby over Adam and Eve:

> Sleep on,
> Blest pair; and O yet happiest if ye seek
> No happier state, and know to know no
> more.[54]

Their blessedness, and that of all humanity after them, depended not on love alone, however, but on an ordered relationship. Eve's body and soul belonged to her husband: Adam, not God, was her "Author and Disposer."[55] When Eve became too independent for a good wife, and Adam too obliging for a proper husband, the disruption of domestic order produced cosmic catastrophe.

Milton's assumptions were not unique; such ideas can be found in sermons and household books as well as epic poetry. Preachers reiterated domestic values and virtues, setting forth appropriate relationships between husbands and wives, parents and children, masters and servants. In the section of his *Catechism* devoted to "The Offices of All Degrees," Thomas Becon used didactic dialogues between a father and son to spell out the privileges and responsibilities of every station. Father and son discussed the duties of magistrates ("ordained of God"), ministers, citizens ("who ought to love and reverence the civil magistrates"), husbands, wives, widows, maids, schoolteachers, poor men, and every

54. *Paradise Lost* 4.741–51, 773–75, in *John Milton: Complete Poems and Major Prose*, ed. Merritt Y. Hughes (New York: Odyssey Press, 1957), pp. 295–296.
55. Ibid., 4.635, p. 293.

other imaginable group.[56] Becon offered the example of Monica not to mothers but to wives—because Monica patiently tolerated her husband's brutality, hid his faults from outsiders, and blamed other women for their husbands' abuse.[57] The marital relationship remained at the center of the English Puritans' attention to domestic matters.

Mothers had a vital, if circumscribed role in Becon's chain of duty and command. They were reminded that God gave them breasts for a purpose and a penance, that they offended God and corrupted their children if they failed to nurse. Fathers were supposed to see that their wives, by nursing, followed the example of "ancient godly matrons of the old testament" and of "the mother of Christ, Mary the Virgin." Young children required primarily physical care and protection from "bodily harm . . . by fire, water, overlaying, or otherwise." These were a mother's responsibility; fathers had to attend to the family's support.[58] Parenthood was always presented in the context of the conjugal household, and it was assumed that widows and widowers would remarry as soon as possible. The duty of both mother and father was to see to their offspring's education and behavior and to be sure that the children in turn were properly married in good time so that the cycle could begin again.

Because maternal and infant mortality remained extremely high in early modern times, motherhood and death were still closely associated. When Puritan women prepared for a birth, they prepared also for death, although not always with the certainty of Elizabeth Jocelin, who bought a shroud for herself when she felt the fetus move for the first time.[59] Puritan mothers were not necessarily more aware than their ancestors of the risks of childbirth, but many of them were literate and inclined to record in writing their thoughts and feelings.

56. *The Catechism of Thomas Becon*, ed. John Ayre (Cambridge: Cambridge University Press, 1844), pp. 302–410.

57. Ibid., pp. 343–344.

58. Ibid., p. 348.

59. Elizabeth died in childbirth. See R. V. Schnucker, "The English Puritans and Pregnancy, Delivery, and Breast-Feeding," *History of Childhood Quarterly* 1 (1974), 637. On Puritan women and childbirth in New England, see Laurel Thatcher Ulrich, *Good Wives* (New York: Oxford University Press, 1982), chap. 7.

The flourishing genre of spiritual autobiography was used by women as well as men; mothers tended to write for the benefit and guidance of their children. The New England poet Anne Bradstreet, mother of eight, addressed her "dear children . . . that when I am no more with you, yet I may be daily in your remembrance." Bradstreet's narrative captured the Puritan notion of maternal responsibility: "It pleased God to keep me a long time without a child, which was a great grief to me and cost me many prayers and tears before I obtained one, and after him gave me many more, of whom I now take the care, that as I have brought you into the world, and with great pains, weakness, cares, and fears brought you to this, I now travail in birth again of you till Christ be formed in you."[60]

The literature of English Puritanism, including sermons and catechisms, emphasized woman's role as wife, consort, helpmate, and lover—like Eve before the Fall, a central figure but secondary and complementary to her husband. Among New England Puritans, on the other hand, women were perceived primarily as mothers. Old women—even those without children, even suspected witches—were called "Mother."[61] The title was accorded automatically, and the status assumed: what else could an old woman be, if not a mother?

The reorientation of religion and society around conjugal households in early modern Europe was not restricted to reformed communities, although Protestants produced its initial ideologies of domesticity. An entire literature of argument and justification was inspired by the defense and promotion of clerical marriage and by the closing of convents. In its official, institutional aspect the initial response of the Roman Catholic Church was to adopt a fiercely defensive posture. The third session of the Council of Trent in 1563 affirmed the superiority of virginity to marriage and of clerical celibacy to clerical marriage.[62] The major agenda of

60. *The Works of Anne Bradstreet*, ed. Jeannine Hensley (Cambridge, Mass.: Harvard University Press, 1967), pp. 240, 241.
61. Ulrich, *Good Wives*, p. 158.
62. *Conciliorum oecumenicorum decreta* (Bologna: Istituto per le Scienze Religiose, 1972), p. 755.

Trent was reform, especially of the training, morals, and service of the regular and secular clergy, whose real and reputed absenteeism, concubinage, and ignorance had provoked so much criticism and caused so much scandal during the late medieval centuries. In relation to sex and marriage, the mood and decrees of Trent ran counter to contemporary trends. In other areas, however—particularly in the restructuring of religious life around the parish and the household—Tridentine reforms ran parallel to contemporary changes and contributed to them. By the early seventeenth century, Roman Catholic teachers had also discovered and developed a distinctive ideology of marriage, motherhood, and holy domesticity.

The sixteenth century was an age of renewed energy and dedication for religious orders; new groups were established for women and men. In Spain the conventual reforms and mystical writings of Teresa of Avila were only one outstanding example of a broad phenomenon of female holiness. In the cities, even outside of convent walls, *beatas* attracted enthusiastic followings. Identified with the poor and representing the "community of believers," these women dedicated their lives to service in the new urban centers of sixteenth-century Spain.[63] In other parts of Europe, however, where the Protestant menace was more immediate, the gender-restrictive ethos of Trent prevailed. The tendency of church leaders to respond to criticism by confining women within walls and habits inhibited the contemporary surge of energy for renewal and service. While new and reformed male orders (the Jesuits being only the most notable example) took on the enormous challenge of mission at home and overseas, founders of women's orders were repeatedly frustrated by the bishops' insistence on cloister and veil. The battle between episcopal notions of respectability and women's desire to serve raged in the Tridentine atmosphere of retrenchment and reform.[64]

63. Jodi Bilinkoff, "The Holy Woman and the Urban Community in Sixteenth-Century Avila," in *Women and the Structure of Society*, ed. Barbara Harris and Jo Ann McNamara (Durham, N.C.: Duke University Press, 1984), p. 80.
64. See Ruth P. Liebowitz, "Virgins in the Service of Christ: The Dispute over an Active Apostolate for Women during the Counter-Reformation," in *Women of Spirit*, ed. Rosemary R. Ruether and Eleanor C. McLaughlin (New York: Simon & Schuster, 1979), pp. 132–152. See also John Bossy, "Editor's Postscript," in H. O. Evennett, *The Spirit of the Counter-Reformation* (Cambridge: Cambridge Univer-

Not all of the council's work was reactive. One of its major long-term accomplishments was the establishment of a parish-based Church with an educated, responsible clergy supervised by a reformed episcopate. Inevitably, the parochial emphasis came into conflict with traditional medieval allegiances and associations—with kin and other competing collectivities.[65] The council decreed, for example, that marriages must take place before the couple's parish priest; John Bossy has pointed out that this requirement "transformed marriage from a social process which the Church guaranteed to an ecclesiastical process which it administered."[66] While Protestants removed marriage from the authority of church and clergy and handed it over to sanctified civil governments, Roman Catholics insisted on the sacramental nature of marriage and the necessary role of the priest, strengthening the authority of the parish and weakening that of the kin over the bridal pair. Similarly, the Church began to interfere with traditional baptismal practices, and bishops made rules about the selection and number of godparents; here too, parish competed with kin for the allegiance of new recruits.[67] Roman Catholic parishes, bulwark of the reformed Church, were made up of households based, like Protestant households, upon the conjugal family. Catholics never ceased to insist vigorously upon the value of consecrated virginity and clerical celibacy, but simultaneously the Church developed an increasing dependence upon the conjugal family, supported by a specifically Catholic ideology of marriage and domesticity.

Roman Catholic as well as Protestant domestic teaching was rooted in the work of Catholic humanists such as Erasmus and More. Sixteenth-century preachers and spiritual directors, wishing to address the needs of men and women in the transformed world of early modern Europe, took marriage and family responsibilities very seriously. The influential Francis de Sales, a popular preacher and confessor, wrote *Introduction to the Devout Life* for

---

sity Press, 1968), in which Bossy refers to "Tridentine rigour and sexual vulgarity" in relation to women's orders (p. 144).

65. See Bossy, "Counter-Reformation."

66. Bossy, *Christianity in the West*, p. 25.

67. Ibid., pp. 14–19; see also Bossy, "Blood and Baptism."

lay people in 1609. He reminded Christians that "devotion should be practiced in different ways by the gentleman, the artisan, the servant, the prince, the widow, the young girl, and the wife," pointing out that it would be "ridiculous, unruly, and indefensible" to expect married people to want to be poor, like Capuchins, or to expect an artisan to spend as much time in church as a monk.[68] Class and gender were essential variables in spiritual life. Office and role frequently required good Christian people to participate in activities unsuitable for the life of a religious: De Sales remembered Elizabeth of Hungary, who sometimes played games and danced "without injury to her devotion, which was firmly rooted in her soul."[69] Even a queen, enmeshed in public affairs, could (and must) impress her child with the fear and love of God: St. Louis's faithful attention to his mother's teaching was the bishop's favorite example of the value of a devout life in the world.[70]

De Sales certainly did not share the Puritans' enthusiasm for conjugal sex, but he did believe that marital intercourse could be holy and responsible. He used the modesty and restraint of the elephant to point his moral: "He never changes his mate; he loves tenderly the one he has chosen and is with her only every three years, and then only for five days, so secretly that he is never seen in the act. When he can be seen again on the sixth day he goes straight to a river, in which he washes his entire body all over before he returns to the herd."[71]

De Sales aspired to missionary work among the Huguenots and served as bishop-in-exile of Calvinist Geneva. Although he naturally acknowledged no influence, he did share the Calvinists' appreciation of worldly vocation—an attitude having more to do with the times, perhaps, than with any particular confession. His letters reveal that he consistently urged wealthy, well-born women to avoid giving offense to husbands, parents, or other

68. Francis de Sales, *Introduction à la vie dévote*, in *Oeuvres complètes de S. François de Sales* (Paris: Berche et Tralin, 1875), 3:382. Note that men are classified by work, women by marital status.
69. Ibid., chap. 34, pp. 501–502.
70. Ibid., p. 510.
71. Ibid., 39, p. 513.

family members by spending too much time in church or neglecting their households. "We must, if we can, try not to make our devotion annoying," he said; the behavior of Margery Kempe would have horrified him. He suggested in a letter that the trials and disappointments of upper-class life be used to spiritual advantage:

> I know a lady, one of the greatest souls that I have met, who lived for a long time in such subjection to her husband's moods that in spite of her ardor and devotion she had to wear low-necked dresses and dress up in all kinds of vanities. Except at Easter, she could go to communion only in secret, deceiving everyone, otherwise she would have caused a thousand storms in her household; by this road she advanced to a great height.

He told his correspondent that it was preferable to miss Mass than to annoy her "two superiors"—her father and her husband. Mentioning Paula, and even Angela of Foligno, as models of women who served God, the bishop overlooked or refused to recognize their rejection and defiance of family pressures and responsibilities.[72]

In certain respects, Salesian teaching resembled that of Martin Luther, but it had a distinctive cast. He called marriage "the nursery of Christianity, which fills the earth with faithful people to complete in heaven the number of the elect. Therefore, the preservation of the goodness of marriage is extremely important to the state because it is the root and source of all its streams." He emphasized the third "fruit" of marriage: "the production and lawful raising of children. It is a great honor to you, married people, that God, wanting to multiply the number of souls who can bless and praise Him to all eternity, has made you His partners in such a wonderful work." Parents produced the "bodies into which He infuses, like heavenly drops, the souls as He creates them."[73]

De Sales was extremely respectful of the physical and spiritual burdens of motherhood. He wrote to one of his correspondents: "Look after yourself very carefully while you are pregnant; do not

72. De Sales, *Oeuvres complètes*, letter 815, 6:199–200.
73. De Sales, *Vie dévote*, chap. 38, 3:506–508.

[224]

be in the least anxious about keeping yourself to any sort of spiritual exercise, except in a most gentle way. If you get tired of kneeling, sit down; if you have not sufficient concentration to pray for half an hour, then make it a quarter of an hour or even half of that." Such instruction would have distressed Dorothea of Montau, but de Sales was concerned for the child to come and for the woman's duty to her husband and family. Like Erasmus, he assumed that spiritual health and vigor were influenced by bodily states: "our souls usually catch the qualities and conditions of our bodies." Spiritual heaviness, like physical pain, could be offered to the crucified Christ.[74]

Devout, obedient mothers might be rewarded by holy children, who repaid any amount of suffering. St. Bernard's mother, "well suited to such a son, taking her children in her arms as soon as they were born, offered them to Jesus Christ, and from then on loved them with the respect due to something sacred, entrusted to her by God. This had the happiest results, as all seven of them eventually became very holy."[75] De Sales commented upon the mother-child relationship from several points of view, including that of a grown child who resented maternal overprotection and interference with her spiritual life. He urged an adult daughter to be more sympathetic, to realize that mothers wanted "to carry their children forever, especially only children, between their breasts . . . one can never love [such a mother] enough [and] the only remedy is patience: God is not jealous of time spent with parents."[76]

The best-known disciple of Francis de Sales found her way to religious life and sainthood despite heavy domestic pressures and the "family first" themes of Salesian piety. Jane Frances de Chantal (1572–1641) grew up in a pious family of the noblesse de la robe; her father was president of the Dijon parlement. At twenty she married Baron Guy de Rabutin-Chantal and took over the management of his estates. Like earlier pious married women of

74. De Sales, letter 827, 6:214.
75. De Sales, Vie dévote, chap. 38, 3:510. The memory of St. Bernard and his family was powerful in Dijon, home of Mme. de Chantal.
76. De Sales, letter 660, 6:15. Angela of Foligno called her mother a hindrance in the way of salvation and rejoiced at her death.

the upper class, she practiced charity by caring for poor and sick dependents, especially women in childbirth and nursing mothers. Her son Celse-Benigne was born in 1596, then three daughters in 1598, 1599, and 1601—the year her husband died in a hunting accident. From intense mourning, Madame de Chantal turned to prayer; much later, she recalled feeling not only grief, but joy at the spiritual opportunities of widowhood.[77] She reduced her household, gave away her jewelry, took a vow of chastity, and devoted herself to her children and to prayer. Elizabeth of Hungary was one of her models, and she found a spiritual director who resembled Conrad of Marburg; if he did not abuse her physically, he tormented her psychologically and made her promise not to discuss her spiritual life, or their relationship, with anyone.

When Chantal met Francis de Sales in 1604, the two were immediately drawn to each other, and she was able to cast off her promise to her confessor. She renewed her vow of chastity and took a vow of obedience to de Sales which both regarded as a solemn, lifelong commitment. Later, when her eldest daughter married his young brother, the two families were joined. Francis de Sales occupied the center of Chantal's emotional and spiritual life after 1604: he was her confessor, her closest friend, and her partner in the establishment of a new religious foundation. The Order of the Visitation was designed for the spiritual benefit of its members and for service in the world. The founders intended the nuns to take simple vows and to go out to tend the sick—although that aspect of the plan was soon frustrated by the Archbishop of Lyons. The Visitation was meant to accommodate not only young, unmarried women but widows with children, like Chantal herself.

Between 1604 and 1610—the year Chantal achieved her fondest wish and became a religious (later the abbess) of the Visitation— de Sales encouraged her to regard herself as a novice whose training and necessary discipline were taking place at home. He called the Virgin Mary her abbess and St. Monica her novice mistress—two women whose spirituality had not been hindered by a mother's

77. In *Madame de Chantal* (London: Faber & Faber, 1962), p. 45 n.1, Elisabeth Stopp cites on this point the deposition of the Archbishop of Sens at Chantal's canonization.

essential work.[78] He provided advice and instruction not only on prayer and meditation but also on her children's care and education—especially that of Celse-Benigne, who gave a good deal of trouble then and later. When the boy was eight years old, de Sales wrote: "We must plant in his little soul noble and valiant aspirations towards God's service, and discourage ideas of purely worldly glory." Sexual impurity was the greatest danger for any child: "Take care not only for him but also his sisters, that they sleep alone . . . or else with people in whom you have as much confidence as you do in yourself. This advice is incredibly important; experience commends it to me every day."[79] He recommended St. Jerome's letter on the training of girls as an aid in "root[ing] out vanity of soul from all the girls; it seems almost inborn in the sex."[80] His friendships with Chantal and many other distinguished women were not sufficient to loosen sexual stereotypes.

In 1610 Celse-Benigne was fourteen years old and preparing to leave home; the eldest daughter was married, and the youngest had died. After years of effort, Madame de Chantal had persuaded her father and father-in-law to let her go, accompanied by her second daughter, to enter the first foundation of the Visitation at Annecy. When the family gathered to say goodbye, Celse-Benigne made a terrible scene: throwing himself across the doorway, he cried that his mother would have to walk over him to leave home. Chantal's contemporary biographer, Maupas du Tour, calling her a "true Paula of our times," praised the courage and self-sacrifice required to leave her beloved son in such circumstances.[81] Perhaps

---

78. De Sales, letter 390, 5:441.

79. Ibid. It is unlikely that in the Chantal household children were abused as sexual playthings, as was apparently the case in some noble as well as royal households, if the childhood experience of Louis XIII can be judged at all typical. See David Hunt, *Parents and Children*; also Elizabeth Wirth Marvick, "Nature Versus Nurture: Patterns and Trends in Seventeenth-Century French Child-Rearing," in De Mause, *The History of Childhood*, pp. 259–301.

80. De Sales, letter 390, 5:441.

81. Jane Frances de Chantal, *Oeuvres complètes de Ste. Jeanne-Françoise de Chantal* (Paris: Migne, 1862), 1:102. According to Maupas du Tour, Chantal loved Celse-Benigne "as no mother ever loved her only son"; the story is presented as an object lesson in maternal self-sacrifice.

Celse-Benigne also had heard of Paula's son, the little Toxotius, who reached out his arms to his departing mother. The image clung to Chantal's reputation, and depending on the interpreter's point of view, she was heroic or heartless enough to proceed with her leavetaking over such a protest. Celse-Benigne reproached his mother but not the co-founder of their order, with whom he remained on good terms. Just a few months later, de Sales wrote him an affectionate letter about the dangers of life at court, warning him against vanity and ambition and "bad books . . . [especially] those of that infamous Rabelais."[82]

Chantal continued to worry about her son's debts and duels; these dangers to his soul upset her more than the death in childbirth of her "dear, amiable" elder daughter. On that sad occasion she wrote to her nephew: "The holy and happy death of that dear soul is a great consolation to me, whereas the life of [Celse-Benigne] afflicts me with sadness and upsets me so much that I do not know where to turn except to Providence . . . leaving in [God's] hands the salvation and honor of this half-lost child. Oh! what incomparable grief and affliction, my dear nephew! No other comes close to it."[83] For this Catholic mother, as for Luther, a woman's death in childbirth was a good death, the equivalent of a soldier's sacrifice. She was greatly relieved when Celse-Benigne died honorably in battle and not as she had feared, in a duel.[84]

The situation of mothers like Chantal, who lived intense spiritual lives and even entered religious orders but were permitted and expected to watch over their children, was painful and ambiguous for both parent and child. The mothers were torn between the exclusive commitment to God required of persons in religious life and the powerful commitment to children expected of Christian mothers in the seventeenth century. According to contempo-

82. De Sales, letter 888, 6:266.
83. Jane Frances de Chantal, *Correspondance: Jeanne-Françoise Frémyot de Chantal*, ed. Marie-Patricia Burns (Paris: Cerf, 1986), letter 141, 1:272.
84. Chantal reminded her newly widowed daughter-in-law "of all the occasions in which he risked his eternal salvation" (ibid., letter 1041, 3:273). Responding to friends who wrote letters of sympathy about Celse-Benigne's death, she made distinctions between her inclination to thank God for his "good" death, a response "according to the spirit," and her "natural" suffering (letters 1039–1045, 3:270–278).

rary notions, their children were entitled to a passionate, single-minded maternal devotion, a devotion incompatible with the traditional sacrifice of "carnal" affections by holy men and women. Francis de Sales was at least somewhat aware of this dilemma, and in 1613 he advised Chantal how to behave during a visit from her son: "I am distressed not to be able to watch the caresses he will receive from a mother who is insensible to everything connected with natural love, for I believe that these caresses will be terribly mortified. Ah, no, my dear daughter, do not be so cruel! Let this poor lad Celse-Benigne see how happy you are to have him with you; we must not show outwardly all of a sudden that our natural passions have died within us!"[85]

By early modern times, the "natural passions" of motherhood were not only acceptable but essential and admirable in a pious Roman Catholic woman. The spirituality and good works of a Paula or Birgitta might be exemplary, but saints who left their children, as well as virgin-martyrs, had become problematic models for Christian mothers. Heroic holiness and canonization were not lively options for laywomen in the seventeenth century.[86] Chantal struggled to achieve renunciation in the traditional mode, and she became a nun and a saint—but very much against the current of Salesian piety, which was designed for men and women in the transformed early modern world. Laywomen were expected to put aside their own desires—even desires for spiritual growth— in order to teach and inspire their children, and to find their rewards in that homely work. Outside of clerical and religious life, where celibacy and virginity were obligatory in most cases and deeply respected in all, Roman Catholics—like Protestants— were expected to marry and to raise children for God, for the church, and for the state. The new ideologies of domesticity and of motherhood were not confined within confessional boundaries.

The population of Europe increased slowly in the sixteenth century, and the sex ratio, which had begun to favor women in

85. Francis de Sales, *Selected Letters*, trans. Elisabeth Stopp (London: Faber & Faber, 1960), p. 209.
86. See Weinstein and Bell, *Saints and Society*, pp. 221, 226–238.

the thirteenth century, kept moving in that direction. By 1500 there were more women than men in every age group and therefore many unmarried women, especially in the older cohorts, where widows as well as spinsters filled the ranks. With the closing of convents in Protestant communities, large numbers of single women had to find new means of support and ways of living. The reformers took responsibility for finding husbands for many former nuns, but obviously not for all.

The economic, social, and ideological changes of the sixteenth century made life difficult for unmarried women, both widows and spinsters. Increasingly confined to poorly paid and nonprestigious work in domestic service and in the trades and crafts, single women in the towns as well as the country had difficulty earning a living, especially if they were mothers. Their troubles were exacerbated by contemporary ideology that defined the very existence of "masterless" women as a problem. At the same time, women were for the first time declared to be independently capable of crime and legally liable for their own actions, which were no longer the responsibility of a male protector.[87] On every level—from John Knox's "First Blast of the Trumpet against the Monstrous Regiment of Women [rulers]"[88] to the harassment of independent old women in villages—the organization of economic, social, moral, and religious life around conjugal households made autonomous female activity, and even existence, ever more difficult.

In the sixteenth and seventeenth centuries, male physicians, male midwives, and male authorities on gynecology, obstetrics,

87. See Christina Larner, *Enemies of God: The Witch-hunt in Scotland* (London: Chatto & Windus, 1981). In *Witchcraft and Religion: The Politics of Popular Belief*, ed. Alan MacFarlane (Oxford: Basil Blackwell, 1984), esp. "Witchcraft Past and Present," pp. 79–91, Larner makes connections between the prosecution of older women for witchcraft and of "younger women for infanticide and prostitution. The criminalization of younger women came in the wake of new punitive attitudes to sexual activity" (p. 86).

88. "To promote a woman to bear rule, superiority, dominion, or empire above any realm, nation, or city is repugnant to nature, contumely to God, a thing most contrarious to his revealed will and approved ordinance, and, finally, it is the subversion of good order, of all equity and justice": "The First Blast of the Trumpet against the Monstrous Regiment of Women (1558)," in *The Political Writings of John Knox*, ed. Marvin A. Breslow (Washington, D.C.: Folger Shakespeare Library, 1985), p. 42.

and infant care began to compete with women in the traditional female work of health care for mothers and children.[89] Midwives still worked in villages everywhere and were trained, licensed, and employed by German cities; nevertheless, the long process of denunciation of their competence and contempt for their persons was under way. It became commonplace for midwives to be suspected of every kind of crime and to be blamed for an infant's deformity or a mother's death. Traditionally, they had helped women both with contraception and abortion and with problems of infertility; such activities were now likely to be identified as immoral or criminal and to be prosecuted.[90] There is no evidence that the skill or dedication of midwives deteriorated or that their rate of failure and success altered; what *did* change was attitudes toward birth, toward families, and toward women who held responsibility for the well-being of mothers and children.

The image of the midwife was affected also by the feverish acceleration of trials for witchcraft after the middle of the sixteenth century. Many medieval Christians had believed in witches and feared sorcery and harmful spells, but their Church had discouraged such beliefs and fears as superstition. The Church did not approve or sponsor witch-hunting until late in the fifteenth century, when Innocent VIII published a bull identifying a "present danger" from witches and authorizing two Dominicans to proceed against them. The text produced by Heinrich Kramer and James Sprenger, the infamous *Malleus maleficarum* of 1486, became extremely influential in the sixteenth century; five hundred years later, the bizarre fixations of its authors still provoke a horrified fascination with witches and witch-hunters.

89. In "Women's Medical Practice," Monica Green argues that women's health care was never a female monopoly. Most writers assume that it was: among others, Thomas G. Benedek, "The Changing Relationship between Midwives and Physicians during the Renaissance," *Bulletin of the History of Medicine* 51 (1977), 550–564; and Madeleine Lazard, "Médecins contre matrones au 16e siècle: La difficile naissance de l'obstetrique," in *Popular Traditions and Learned Culture in France: From the Sixteenth to the Twentieth Century*, ed. Marc Bertrand (Saratoga, Calif.: Anma Libri, 1985).

90. See esp. Gunnar Heinsohn and Otto Steiger, "The Elimination of Medieval Birth Control and the Witch Trials of Modern Times," *International Journal of Women's Studies* 5 (1982), 193–214; Nachman Ben-Yehuda, "The European Witch Craze of the 14th to 17th Centuries: A Sociologist's Perspective," *American Jour-*

Kramer and Sprenger identified witchcraft with heresy, and they pronounced authoritatively that most witches were women because of women's inherent wickedness. They also identified the most dangerous work of witches as the evil power they exercised over sex and procreation, "first, by inciting the minds of men to inordinate passion; second, by obstructing their generative force; third, by removing the members accommodated to that act; fourth, by changing men into beasts by their magic art; fifth, by destroying the generative force in women; sixth, by procuring abortion; seventh, by offering children to devils."[91] More than 80 percent of the persons tried and executed for witchcraft were women; most of them were poor and elderly, and a significant number had worked as midwives.[92] The image of the witch as anti-wife and anti-mother—a sexual threat instead of a helpmate, and a frightful danger to reproduction and the Christianization of children—was transformed from a clerical fantasy to a murderous reality.[93]

Connections have been perceived between a low birth rate, the growing needs of the state and the economy for soldiers and workers, and the persecution of "witches" who were charged with interfering with procreation.[94] The significance of such connec-

---

nal of Sociology 86 (1980), 1–31; Anne Llewellyn Barstow, "Charism as Power or as Curse: Healers and Witches" (unpublished paper, 1985).

91. The Malleus maleficarum of Heinrich Kramer and James Sprenger, trans. Montague Summers (New York: Dover, 1971), 1.6, p. 47.

92. Larner asserted in Witchcraft and Religion (p. 84): "The stereotype adult witch is an independent adult woman who does not conform to the male idea of proper female behaviour. She is assertive; she does not require or give love (though she may enchant); she does not nurture men or children, nor care for the weak." Similar points were made by Brauner, "Luther on Witchcraft"; and by Allison P. Coudert, "The Myth of the Improved Status of Protestant Women: The Case of the Witchcraze," in Brink, Coudert, and Horowitz, Politics of Gender, pp. 78–80.

93. See Anne Llewellyn Barstow, "On Studying Witchcraft as Women's History," Journal of Feminist Studies in Religion 4 (1988), 7; also Barstow, "Charism"; and Ben-Yehuda, "European Witch Craze," esp. pp. 16–22.

94. Robert Muchemblad emphasized the repression of many forms of sexual expression in this period and analyzed the relationship between the tyranny of fathers and of the absolute state. See his Popular Culture and Elite Culture in France, 1400–1700 (Baton Rouge: Louisiana State University Press, 1985), esp. chap. 4, "The Constraint of Bodies and the Submission of Souls: New Mechanisms of Power."

tions does not depend on recorded changes in sexual behavior or contraceptive practice, about which few data are available. It *is* certain that a newly anxious attention was focused on conception and birth, areas once understood as women's responsibility, determined by God's inscrutable will. Religious reformers and political theorists spoke and wrote at length of the importance of children and the necessary work of education for the civil society and the kingdom of Christ. Married couples were constantly reminded of the value of their central task of reproduction and socialization.

Furthermore, both Protestant and Catholic reformers insisted on a strict morality intended to confine all sexual activity to married couples. For Roman Catholic clerics, celibacy was not only prescribed, as it had been for four centuries, but rigorously enforced. The new diocesan seminaries indoctrinated students from a young age, and systems of episcopal visitation and discipline were made effective. Clerics and lay people alike were encouraged by trained confessors to examine their consciences in relation to sexual feelings and behavior. Powerful injunctions against fornication, adultery, homosexuality, and masturbation accompanied the new, positive emphasis on marriage and family. In erotic and domestic life, goodness was identified with monogamous marriage and parenthood; it became nearly impossible to be single and virtuous. The Protestant reformers have been credited with producing this situation, but it shaped the lives of Roman Catholics as well.

By the end of the sixteenth century there was a widespread conviction that everyone belonged in a family; even in Roman Catholic religious life the model of male-headed families prevailed. Women and children were not permitted to be "masterless": a woman living on her own, without a husband or father or adult son, was perceived as anomalous at best. If she was old and poor—old enough to be independent, and poor enough to need help and ask for it—she might also be dangerous. Sexual and procreative activities outside of marriage were considered not only problematic but evil and criminal. Prosecutions for bastardy and infanticide kept increasing in the seventeenth century; as it became ever more difficult to raise a child outside of a male-headed family, poor women were more often charged with abandoning and murdering babies.[95] Women's energies, feared as chaotic and disorderly, were directed toward marriage and motherhood, which were identified with God's will and placed under men's authority. The violent, protracted persecution of witches in early modern Europe was a negative, punitive aspect of the domestication of Christianity. There were no witches in Utopia.

The presence of "witches" in sixteenth-century communities betrayed the hopes and violated the intentions of Christian humanists and reformers, who wanted all men and women to live peacefully in the company of blood relations and the "natural" hierarchies of age and sex. True religion, properly understood and interpreted, prescribed ways of living that accorded with nature and with reason. In an ideal society, adult women were wives and mothers—protected, productive, fulfilled. Their sexual, spiritual, and intellectual energies were absorbed in the production and training of Christians for the churches, workers for the marketplace, and citizens for the state. A woman's duty was to give birth to children (as many as possible), to nourish them physically and morally, and to prepare them for the work of church and society, if they were boys, for motherhood if they were girls. She was inclined toward this work by her physical and psychological being; grace, now identified with nature, need no longer triumph over nature to produce a good woman. A mother was inherently disposed to put the welfare of husband and children before her own aspirations, even aspirations to holiness when these threatened distraction from her true vocation. A good mother was potentially a saint; the two roles were perfectly compatible.

That "good mother" is an extremely familiar figure, for early modern ideologies of Christian motherhood put down sturdy roots

95. Midwives were drawn into this "disciplinary" process: they were required to ask an unmarried woman for the name of the child's father before they could help with a birth; see Peter C. Hoffer and N. E. H. Hull, *Murdering Mothers: Infanticide in England and New England, 1558–1803* (New York: New York University Press, 1981), p. 15. Hoffer and Hull examine the accelerating rate of trials and convictions for bastardy and infanticide in the sixteenth and seventeenth centuries (see esp. chap. 2). They attribute infanticide to "indifference for infants" (p. ix), but their own work reveals its connections to the increasing stringency of bastardy laws and the criminalization of women.

and flourished in the modern West. With significant modifications in the wake of the Industrial Revolution, they survived in the middle-class cult of domesticity and True Womanhood in the nineteenth century.[96] With further adjustments for secularization and consumer capitalism, the model could still be discerned in the postwar "Mom" of the 1950s.[97] It lives on in the late twentieth century, if only in the rhetoric of the political and religious right.[98] The mother at home, installed in a patriarchal household and naturally inclined toward service and sacrifice, was created for the West in early modern Europe. Her image is so familiar that we fail to recognize its originality: we are inclined to see her as eternal.

Nonetheless, this book has demonstrated that the Christian mother of early modern times was a new phenomenon in the history of the family and of Christianity. Medieval ideologies of motherhood were rejected, revised, and transformed by humanists and reformers in the sixteenth and seventeenth centuries. Luther had to search the Hebrew Scriptures for images of good women; rejecting medieval models and typologies, he turned to ancient sources for help in building something new. Medieval Christian motherhood, which had its complex beginnings in early Christianity, was thoroughly reconstructed at the dawn of the modern age. Its history demonstrates the interplay and manipulation of cultural and religious symbols involved in the construction of motherhood in any age.

---

96. See Barbara Welter's important formulation in "The Cult of True Womanhood: 1820–1860," *American Quarterly* 18 (1966), 151–162, 173–174.

97. Betty Friedan uncovered the image of this "Mom," its relation to post-war economic pressures, and some of its implications for middle-class women in *The Feminine Mystique* (New York: Dell, 1963).

98. E.g., "Mothering is probably the most important function on earth. This is a full-time, demanding task. It requires a high order of gentleness, commitment, steadiness, capacity to give, and many other qualities. A woman needs a good man by her side so she will not be distracted and depleted, thus making it possible for her to provide rich humanness to her babies and children. Her needs must be met by the man, and above all she must be made secure": psychiatrist Harold M. Voth, quoted in Jerry Falwell, *Listen, America!* (New York: Doubleday, 1980), pp. 129–130. The passage exemplifies not only twentieth-century psychiatry's acceptance of early modern ideologies of Christian motherhood but its identification of the ideal mother with the middle-class, married woman who does not work outside the home.

CHAPTER SEVEN

The Construction
of Motherhood

The birth of a child to that legendary Christian mother Pope Joan was an occasion of scandal and catastrophe. At the height of its popularity at the end of the Middle Ages, the story and image of a pregnant pope inspired anxious, ribald laughter. Motherhood itself, even in proximity to the sacred, was not a joke: Christians adored the mother of their God and frequently portrayed her, crowned and enthroned, next to her divine son. In late medieval Europe, as we have seen, some saints were also mothers. But even as the barricades between physical and spiritual motherhood began to crumble and the prophetic voices of the mother-saints were heard, traditional lines of gender and authority were firmly redrawn and reinforced. Ecclesiastical dignity and public authority still belonged to the male sex; maternal power, acknowledged and feared, was definitively subordinated to God and men. Pope Joan remained a figure of shame, her fate exemplary. The legend and the image, in its outrageous incongruity, still supported the sex-gender system of church and society.

The history of medieval Christian motherhood is richly complicated by the entanglement of images of startling power and beauty with those—like Joan's—of sin and sorrow. In the earliest Christian communities, tightly linked by shared commitment and self-consciously different and separate from surrounding cultures, sex and gender roles tended to blur, and distinctions based on sexual status and social hierarchy to be downplayed. Christians preserved the memory of their founder's associations with women, which transgressed barriers based on physiological condition, marital status, and the demands of custom. Perpetua's dream of becoming male and the miraculous weaning of her baby displayed a transcendence of sex and gender that allowed her to become—not a man, but a witness. The Gospels and the Acts of the Martyrs celebrated behavior and attitudes that violated domestic and cultural norms in the vast world of the Roman Empire. For some of those who departed from patriarchal households to follow Jesus, social and religious distinctions based on reproductive potential were set aside: motherhood was not relevant to salvation.

Christianity did not long remain a radical movement. Ancient codes, reinscribing women in the household, were quickly incorporated into the canon of the New Testament. An increasing emphasis on episcopal authority and ecclesiastical order signaled an end to the strict dichotomy of Christ and culture. As Christian numbers and influence grew and persecution gave way to toleration and then to establishment, customary roles and rules were quickly reassigned. Nonetheless, the legacy of the first three centuries included texts, images, and memories of the early communities. Stories of heroic lives lived outside of patriarchal norms retained a privileged place in the memory and mythology of the churches.

The distinction between "religion" and "society" is a modern conceit. The legacy of ancient Christianity was not confined to matters religious (in modern terms); it included an anthropology as well as a theology, prescriptions for the governance of families and cities as well as of churches, and ramifications in all branches of learning and culture. As its intellectual framework developed within the thought-world of Mediterranean antiquity, Christian creeds and convictions were articulated in the language and categories of late classical thought. In relation to the construction of motherhood, this meant Greek physiology and medicine. Although religion is a powerful force shaping ideologies of motherhood, it is not their sole or even primary determinant: knowledge and opinion about women's bodies and the processes of reproduction are essential too. The attitudes toward women and procreation of learned Christians, including the Church Fathers, were profoundly influenced by Greek observations and interpretations. Long after the end of the patristic age, medieval physiology still consisted of commentaries on Greek texts. Greek science maintained its hegemony in the West until the seventeenth century, when the emergence of modernity necessitated a new construction not only of motherhood but of nature itself.[1]

Traditionally, medicine tends to define women as mothers whether or not they have children—as walking (or wandering) wombs. From Plato onward, male scientists and philosophers perceived and classified women as unlike themselves, therefore as not-men, with "different" reproductive organs and systems. Aristotle defined gender in terms of reproductive potential and identified femaleness itself with reproductive deficiency, the inability to generate. He believed that the male parent supplied form and energy to the fetus, the female only lifeless matter. Not all ancient and medieval thinkers agreed with him—Galen and his followers believed that each parent provided a "seed" for the new child— but Aristotelian biology had a profound effect on theoretical constructions of motherhood in the High Middle Ages, when Christian, Jewish, and Muslim philosophers struggled to integrate Aristotelian "nature" and divine revelation.

We know much more about what Aristotle and his medieval commentators thought about reproduction than about what mothers, and those who cared for women and children, knew and practiced. Surviving fragments of works designed as practical medical guides reveal, however, that medieval people were aware of the requirements of reproductive health: they knew that women needed good food, rest, and peace of mind in order to conceive, give birth to, and suckle healthy children. The *vitae* of saints, on the other hand, reveal that these requirements directly conflicted with regimes adopted by certain women with aspirations to holiness. Women who starved and abused their bodies

---

1. See, e.g., Carolyn Merchant, *The Death of Nature: Women, Ecology, and the Scientific Revolution* (New York: Harper & Row, 1983).

were presented in hagiography as models of spiritual health, and very often as spiritual mothers. A sharp opposition between physical and spiritual health and virtue was built into medieval Christian motherhood.

When Christianity became the established religion of the Roman Empire in the fourth century, men and women flocked to the churches. Joyful acceptance of danger and hardship, no longer the lot of every Christian, became the property of a new elite—those who believed they must choose between this world and the next, between the well-being of the body and that of the spirit, between intimate relationships with other human beings and intimacy with God. Sexual activity and sexual feelings, perceived as unhappy consequences of the Fall, were repressed or denied and the burdens and privileges of family life shunned. Virginity was highly prized, especially for women. Fathers of the Church such as Jerome associated procreation and the love of children with shame and sorrow, although the mother of a virgin or a saint might be rewarded by her child's triumph over the flesh.

The Gospel carried by Christian missionaries who traveled out from the Mediterranean in the early Middle Ages was embedded in the ethos of patristic thought and late antique asceticism. Most of the missionaries were monks, whose perspectives shaped the incorporation of Christianity into the legal and social arrangements of the new Christians of western Europe. Because of the monastic monopoly of education and literacy in the early Middle Ages, the surviving documents of that era—saints' lives, letters, histories, legal codes, and works of art—represent primarily monastic values and perceptions. Christian motherhood, in these texts, is spiritual motherhood: virginity was an essential component of Leoba's vocation as healer, counselor, and exemplar of virtue to her "daughters," the nuns. Her power depended on the conquest of nature, beginning with her own body. The *Life of Leoba* and similar texts were produced, of course, within the ethos of the cloister. The powers and pains of maternity in the world outside are much less well recorded, but there is little evidence that mothers were honored or carefully protected. Dhuoda's book reveals that by the ninth century, in the noble class, children belonged to their fathers.

The early Christian revolution in values, which made sex, gender, and parenthood insignificant in the realm of the spirit, was drastically revised in medieval monastic thought and practice. No longer irrelevant, female sex and physical motherhood became obstacles to be overcome by holy women. Unlike most patriarchal societies, medieval Christianity retained an honorable place for exceptional women, who could be learned, virtuous, and even powerful—if they renounced sexual activity and physical maternity. A choice was available to a small number of women. The vast majority, who did not or could not elect spiritual motherhood, were relegated to the second-best work of physical reproduction, too often equated in reality as well as rhetoric with sorrow, suffering, and death.

The development of ideologies of Christian motherhood in the Middle Ages was significantly shaped by the figure of Christ's mother. To meet the needs of a theology that required a human mother for God, the medieval Mary was constructed in story and symbol by a religious imagination that built a divine mother out of scriptural fragments and the excluded goddesses of pre-Christian religions. The figure of Mary, always a vehicle for special pleading, varied according to prevailing Christologies. The wonder-working Mary of the Apocrypha gave way to the demure Virgin of the monks, modeled on a fourth-century nun. In Carolingian Europe, Mary and Jesus were portrayed by artists and teachers as remote and regal figures, sharing the majesty and distance of the Godhead.

Changes in church and society in the twelfth century transformed Mary, along with her son, into a more humane and immediate presence. In theological commentary as well as poetry and romance, she began to resemble the Lady of the courts—young, beautiful, generous, and loving. Her eternal virginity made it possible for monks and knights alike to adore a mother who belonged to no earthly father; beauty and generosity made her a magnet for erotic and romantic longings. The figure of Mary attracted and held a wide range of powerful feelings about women and mothers; she supplied hope and consolation to the grim realities of the experience of most medieval mothers and children. In stories of the Virgin's miracles, written down in the eleventh century and later, she answered the desperate wishes and needs of her lovers and servants.

From the twelfth century onward, an increased respect for marriage and for the special responsibilities of married people began to narrow the gap between lay and monastic virtues and values. Virginity lost its preeminence in the lives of women saints when the new mendicant orders, more attentive than earlier monks to this world and its needs, identified poverty as the essential element of holiness. A lively interest in the Holy Family and the Christ Child reflected a new enthusiasm for families and for childhood. Mary's humanity was increasingly emphasized; she remained lady and queen but appeared also as a loving young mother, not so different from other young mothers. Strikingly, and more frequently in the fourteenth and fifteenth centuries, she was also represented as the Mother of Sorrows, whose love and pain gave meaning to all suffering and particularly to the inevitable suffering of mothers. Amid the wars, disease, and economic crises of the late Middle Ages, sorrow and suffering became hallmarks of sanctity. This was true for all Christians but especially for women, some of whom went to extraordinary lengths to participate in Christ's Passion and to stand with Mary under the Cross.

In part through the association of motherhood with suffering and of suffering with holiness, it became possible for women who were mothers to be eligible also for sainthood. A holy woman who gave up passionate affection and concern for her children achieved a special kind of poverty through renunciation. Although her sexual status no longer necessarily blocked access to her vocation, her marital status might: parents were allowed to leave their children but not wives their husbands, and most of the married women saints had to wait for widowhood to live out their calling. Nonetheless, for the first time in a thousand years, a woman might actually be assisted and not impeded by physical maternity in her approach to God. Julian of Norwich recognized and asserted the maternal aspect of Christ; certain other mystics experienced and represented the soul's encounter with God as the union of mother and child instead of bride and bridegroom. Maternal power was associated with divine power and perceived as salvific: a holy mother could save her children, and by extension, other sinners. Through the cults of the great mother-saints of the late Middle Ages, the gulf between physical and spiritual motherhood began to be repaired.

Amid the vast changes in religion and society that characterized the sixteenth century, ideologies of Christian motherhood were drastically revised—indeed, transformed—but not toward reclamation of the ancient conviction that physical motherhood was irrelevant to holiness. On the contrary, motherhood became a necessary component of a woman's virtue and an essential element in the good order and prosperity of household, church, and state. For sixteenth-century humanists and reformers, a woman's work was reproduction; her obligation was to her husband and children and her true vocation domestic. Protestants rejected the independent powers of the Virgin and of consecrated virginity; Roman Catholics insisted that laywomen marry and put husband and children first. A good woman was a good mother; her virtue and her labor served the interests of the state, of the economic system, and of reformed churches in all parts of the confessional map of early modern Europe. The confinement of maternal power and of women within the household was enforced by economic, judicial, and moral sanctions. Maternal duty and domestic sanctity were preached by Protestant and Catholic teachers. On the positive side they drew the image of the good mother; on the negative, the old maid, the witch, and the whore—women whose sexuality and reproductive potential did not serve the household and its master. Religious sanctions indoctrinated women into motherhood; poverty, criminalization, and hellfire threatened those who strayed.

The domestic ideology of sixteenth-century Christianity was intrinsically connected to the political, social, and economic institutions of the modern West: all shared the same material base and depended on the same sex-gender system. The very long half-life of the "good mother" of the sixteenth century demonstrates her usefulness; rooted in religious teaching, she survived secularization, adapting to new times and circumstances. With the departure of men into factories and offices during and after the Industrial Revolution, the middle-class mother became ever more powerful within her sphere, which became tinier, more restricted, and more isolated from the world of business and politics.[2] Gradually, she

2. For an analysis of one form of representation of this narrow, intense maternal power, see Joanna B. Gillespie, " 'The Sun in Their Domestic System': The Mother in Early Nineteenth-Century Methodist Sunday School Lore," in *Women*

took over from her husband the responsibility for domestic piety and family morality. Some women learned to turn the ideology of Christian motherhood against itself: by insisting on their responsibility for the weak, and for virtue, they expanded their activities outside the home. Female reformers in the United States in the nineteenth century used motherhood to justify women's participation in the public sphere.[3] The ideology of service and of care for the weak authorized women to work for temperance, against slavery, and even for female suffrage—anywhere women and children were brutalized, the stability of families threatened, or women's energies needed for reform.[4]

Outside the haven of the patriarchal household, however, economic destitution and moral condemnation awaited many mothers and their children. Despite the efforts of reformers who used maternity in the service of social goals, the "sanctity" of motherhood failed to protect those who gave birth and raised children in urban poverty or rural slavery. When women were used to breed slaves and children were sold away from their mothers, the bankruptcy of the ideal was exposed, along with its role in enforcing race and class as well as gender privilege. As a universal category equated with nature, "motherhood" does not survive historical deconstruction.

The ideologies of motherhood are persistent *and* adaptable. We have observed the extraordinary endurance of notions about what good Christian mothers ought to be—notions and prescriptions that survived even secularization. But the only truly eternal char-

---

in New Worlds, vol. 2, ed. Rosemary Skinner Keller, Louise L. Queen, and Hilah F. Thomas (Nashville, Tenn.: Abingdon Press, 1982), pp. 45–59.

3. Welter made this point in "True Womanhood"; see also Dorothy C. Bass, " 'In Christian Firmness and Christian Meekness': Feminism and Pacifism in Antebellum America," in Atkinson, Buchanan, and Miles, *Immaculate and Powerful*, pp.201–225. I am indebted to Elizabeth B. Clark for allowing me to read her Ph.D. dissertation, "The Politics of God and the Woman's Vote" (Princeton University, 1989), in which she argues that the WCTU was a "Mother's movement" (chap. 4, p. 2).

4. The destruction of families, black and white, was a central theme in abolitionist literature, including *Uncle Tom's Cabin*, and the theme of sexual abuse of black women was prominent in women's writing in both North and South; see, e.g., Harriet A. Jacobs, *Incidents in the Life of a Slave Girl Written by Herself*, ed. Jean Fagan Yellin (Cambridge, Mass.: Harvard University Press, 1987).

acteristic of Christian motherhood, as of any historical institution, is change itself. With all their persistence, ideologies of motherhood respond to material as well as social and religious innovation. In the twentieth century in the West, the rapid pace of technological change has had enormous impact on motherhood. At least for the privileged, new contraceptives and developments in gynecology and obstetrics made reproductive choice more feasible and available than ever before. And for certain women, technological and social change created alternatives to the identification of "good woman" and "good mother." A woman might remain unmarried without being harassed by the specter of the "old maid"; she might be sexually active without the stigma of the whore. Married or not, if she was the victim of rape or incest, or too young, too old, too ill, or unwilling to carry and raise a new child, the decision of the Supreme Court in *Roe v. Wade* (1973) allowed her legally to terminate a pregnancy.[5] Inherited ideologies survived and even flourished, but their exclusive influence was weakened by "the pill," by the so-called sexual revolution,[6] and by the women's movement of the 1960s and 1970s.

But motherhood is an institution as well as a vocation, and its ideologies are embedded in established traditions of church and society. These do not change easily or quickly, particularly because their defenders—who tend to insist that motherhood is "natural" (even in an age of high-tech obstetrics)—do not acknowledge its historical character or the inevitability of change. Thus when *Roe v. Wade* made abortion legal, it also threatened deeply held assumptions about sexuality and social roles and helped to bring into being a powerful anti-abortion movement based on

5. More precisely, the court declared that "except in narrow circumstances, the Constitution of the United States does not permit the government to interfere with a woman's right to choose abortion": quoted in Laurence H. Tribe, *Abortion: The Clash of Absolutes* (New York: Norton, 1990), pp. 3–4. The events and decisions leading up to *Roe v. Wade*, and its aftermath, are also described by (among others) Kristin Luker in *Abortion and the Politics of Motherhood* (Berkeley: University of California Press, 1984).

6. According to many participants, this "revolution" apparently served the needs of radical men more than those of women: see, e.g., Sara Evans, *Personal Politics: The Roots of Women's Liberation in the Civil Rights Movement and the New Left* (New York: Vintage Books, 1979), esp. chap. 9.

alliances between new activists and older conservative forces, the New Right and the Old.[7]

After a decade and a half of struggle in the courts and in the streets outside clinics, the Supreme Court (with three justices new since 1973)[8] heard the case of *Webster v. Reproductive Health Services* in the summer of 1989. An abortion clinic challenged a Missouri law which stated in its preamble that human life begins at conception, restricted abortions in public institutions, and required tests for fetal viability under certain circumstances.[9] The court was sharply divided, but the plurality upheld the Missouri law—a decision that threatened to overturn *Roe v. Wade*. In his dissenting opinion, Justice Harry Blackmun stated his concern that the court's decision might

> clear the way once again for government to force upon women the physical labor and specific and direct medical and psychological harms that may accompany carrying a fetus to term. The plurality would clear the way again for the State to conscript a woman's body and to force upon her a "distressful life and future." . . . millions of

7. Luker (*Abortion*, p. 145) described "the new activists [as] predominantly women homemakers without previous experience in political activities. . . . Unlike the predominantly male professionals who had preceded them, the new activists were people whose values made pregnancy central to their lives . . . faced by a Supreme Court decision that seemed to devalue not only the status of the embryo but pregnancy itself." Luker argues that the contemporary abortion debate arouses extreme passion on both sides precisely because each position seems to represent an entire world view: "Different beliefs about the roles of the sexes, about the meaning of parenthood, and about human nature are all called into play when the issue is abortion" (p. 158).

8. For a description of the reconstitution of the Supreme Court between 1973 and 1989, see Tribe, *Abortion*, pp. 11–21.

9. A summary of the Webster case is provided in ibid., pp. 21–26. Tribe points out that questions about when human life begins—whether understood as a "moment of conception" or as the time when the fetus might be viable outside the womb—are technically difficult as well as controversial: "Modern embryology reveals that fertilization is a *process*, not a moment" (p. 123). *Roe v. Wade* used viability as a criterion: "the point at which the fetus is capable of surviving outside the womb, at approximately the beginning of the final third of a fetus's gestation, [when] protection of fetal life also becomes a compelling reason. . .to justify interference with the exercise of the right to choose an abortion" (quoted, p. 12). On the "fetal rights" movement and its implications for motherhood in the 1990s, see Katha Pollitt, " 'Fetal Rights': A New Assault on Feminism," *Nation* 250, no. 11 (1990), 409–418.

women, and their families, have ordered their lives around the right to reproductive choice, and . . . this right has become vital to the full participation of women in the economic and political walks of American life.[10]

Arguing thus for "the assumptions and settled understandings" of contemporary women,[11] Blackmun implicitly asserted the historicity of motherhood—an institution constructed over time and differently enforced and experienced in different times and places. In the late twentieth century, for example, North American women live within the historical particularities of *this* time and place, where the status and welfare of the mother and the status and viability of the fetus are measured and determined by technologies that require reconstructed understandings of sex and gender.

Motherhood never was purely "natural"; it has always been shaped by religious systems, power relationships, and material structures. Its historicity and contingency have become increasingly apparent in our time. Concluding his dissent, Justice Blackmun expressed an appropriate anxiety: "For today, the women of this nation still retain the liberty to control their destinies. But the signs are evident and very ominous, and a chill wind blows."[12] The contemporary controversy demonstrates that public policy and women's lives depend on our understanding and interpretations of the history of motherhood. The laws governing abortion may be read in part as representations of prevailing ideologies of gender and maternity, which, like all ideologies, respond to historical change. Motherhood is an ancient vocation, profoundly shaped in the West by medieval Christianity. It is also a historical construction—embattled, vulnerable, requiring re-creation in each generation. To recognize its historicity is to begin to assume responsibility for the character of its reconstruction.

10. Justice Harry Blackmun, *Webster v. Reproductive Health Services*, 109 Supreme Court 3040 (1989), p. 3077.
11. Ibid., p. 3078.
12. Ibid., p. 3079.

Works Cited

Sources

Abelard, Peter, and Heloise. *The Letters of Abelard and Heloise*. Ed. and trans. Betty Radice. New York: Penguin Books, 1974.

Acta et processus canonizacionis beate Birgitte. Ed. Isak Collijn. SUSF, ser. 2, Lat. skrifter 1. Uppsala: Almqvist & Wiksells, 1924–31.

Acta sanctorum. Paris: Palmé, etc., 1863– .

Acts of the Christian Martyrs. Ed. Herbert Musurillo. Oxford: Clarendon Press, 1972.

Acts of Thomas. In *New Testament Apocrypha*, vol. 1, ed. Wilhelm Schneemelcher. Philadelphia: Westminster Press, 1983.

Aelred of Rievaulx. *The Works of Aelred of Rievaulx, vol. 1: Treatises: The Pastoral Prayer*. Spencer, Mass.: Cistercian Publications, 1971.

Albert the Great. "Quaestiones super de animalibus." In *Alberti Magni Opera Omnia*, vol. 12, ed. Bernhardus Geyer. Aschendorff: Monasterii Westfalorum, 1955.

———. *De animalibus libri XXVI, nach der Cölner Urschrift*. Vol. 1. Münster, 1916.

Alberti, Leon Battista. *The Family in Renaissance Forence: A Translation by Renee Neu Watkins of "I libri della Famiglia" by Leon Battista Alberti*. Columbia: University of South Carolina Press, 1969.

Ambrose. *Sancti Ambrosii opera*, pt. 6. Ed. M. Petschenig. CSEL, vol. 64. Leipzig: G. Freytag, 1919.

Andreas Capellanus. *The Art of Courtly Love by Andreas Capellanus*. Trans. John Jay Parry. New York: Ungar, 1957.

Angela of Foligno. *Il libro della Beata Angela da Foligno*. Ed. Ludger Thier, O.F.M., and Abele Calufetti, O.F.M. Rome: College of St. Bonaventure, 1985.

Anselm of Canterbury. *S. Anselmi opera omnia*. Ed. F.S. Schmitt. Edinburgh: Thomas Nelson, 1946.

Aquinas, St. Thomas. *Summa theologiae*. Vol. 13. Ed. Edmund Hill. London: Blackfriars, 1964.

Aristotle. *The Generation of Animals*. Trans. A. L. Peck. Cambridge, Mass.: Harvard University Press, 1979.

———. *Parts of Animals*. Trans. A. L. Peck. Cambridge, Mass.: Harvard University Press, 1945.

———. *The Politics*. Trans. H. Rackham. Cambridge, Mass.: Harvard University Press, 1959.

Athanasius. "On the Incarnation of the Word." In *Contra gentes and De Incarnatione*, ed. and trans. Robert W. Thomson. Oxford: Clarendon Press, 1971.

Augustine. *Confessions*. Trans. R. S. Pine-Coffin. London: Penguin Books, 1961.

———. *The Passion of Perpetua and Felicity: The Sermons of S. Augustine upon the Feast of Sts. Perpetua and Felicity*. Trans. W. H. Shewring. London: Sheed & Ward, 1931.

Bartholomaeus Anglicus. *On the Properties of Things: John Trevisa's Translation of Bartholomaeus Anglicus, De proprietatibus rerum*. Vol. 1. Ed. M. C. Seymour. Oxford: Clarendon Press, 1975.

Becon, Thomas. *The Catechism of Thomas Becon*. Ed. John Ayre. Cambridge: Cambridge University Press, 1844.

Bede: A History of the English Church and People. Ed. Leo Sherley-Price. London: Penguin Books, 1970.

Bernard of Clairvaux. *Five Books on Consideration*. In *The Works of Bernard of Clairvaux*, trans. John D. Anderson and Elizabeth Kennan. Kalamazoo, Mich.: Cistercian Publications, 1976.

———. *Magnificat: Homilies in Praise of the Blessed Virgin Mary by Bernard of Clairvaux and Amadeus of Lausanne*. Trans. Marie-Bernard Saïd and Grace Perigo. Kalamazoo, Mich.: Cistercian Publications, 1979.

———. *On the Song of Songs III*. Trans. Kilian Walsh, O.C.S.O., and Irene M. Edmonds. Kalamazoo, Mich.: Cistercian Publications, 1979.

———. "Sermo in nativitate Beatae Mariae." In *S. Bernardi opera*, vol. 5, ed. Jean Leclercq and Henri Rochais. Rome: Editiones Cistercienses, 1968.

Birgitta of Sweden. *Den Heliga Birgittas Revelaciones*. Ed. Birger Bergh. SUSF, ser. 2, vol. 7. Uppsala: Almqvist & Wiksells, 1967.

———. *Den Heliga Birgittas Revelaciones Extravagantes*. Ed. Lennart Hollman. SUSF. Uppsala: Almqvist & Wiksells, 1956.

———. *The Liber Celestis of St. Bridget of Sweden*. Vol. 1. Ed. Roger Ellis. Oxford: Oxford University Press, 1987.

————. *Revelationes S. Birgitte.* Ed. Bartholomeus Ghotan. Lübeck, 1492.

————. *The Revelations of Saint Birgitta.* Ed. W. P. Cumming. London: Oxford University Press, 1929.

Blackmun, Harry A. Dissenting opinion. *Webster v. Reproductive Health Services.* 109 Supreme Court 3040 (1989).

Boccaccio, Giovanni. *Concerning Famous Women.* Trans. Guido A. Guarino. New Brunswick, N.J.: Rutgers University Press, 1963.

Bokenham, Osbern. *Legendys of Hooly Wummen by Osbern Bokenham.* Ed. Mary S. Serjeantson. London: Humphrey Milford, 1938.

Bradstreet, Anne. *The Works of Anne Bradstreet.* Ed. Jeannine Hensley. Cambridge, Mass.: Harvard University Press, 1967.

Bucer, Martin. *De regno Christi: Opera latina XV.* Ed. François Wendel. Paris: Presses Universitaires de France, 1955.

The Burgundian Code. Trans. Katherine Fischer Drew. Philadelphia: University of Pennsylvania Press, 1972.

Caesarius of Heisterbach. *Dialogue on Miracles.* Ed. G. G. Coulton and Eileen Power. London: George Routledge, 1929.

Calvin, John. *Ioannis Calvini opera,* vols. 52, 53. Brunswick: Schwetschke, 1895.

"De S. Catharina." AS March, vol. 1, pp. 501–529.

Chantal, Jane Frances de. *Correspondance: Jeanne-Françoise Frémyot de Chantal.* 3 vols. Ed. Marie-Patricia Burns. Paris: Cerf, 1986.

————. *Oeuvres complètes de Ste. Jeanne Françoise de Chantal.* Paris: Migne, 1862.

Chaucer, Geoffrey. *The Riverside Chaucer.* Ed. Larry D. Benson. Boston: Houghton Mifflin, 1987.

Clausdotter, Margareta. "Chronicon de genere et nepotibus S. Birgittae." In *Scriptores rerum Svecicarum medii aevi,* vol. 3, pt. 2, ed. Claes Annerstedt. Uppsala: Edward Verling, 1871–76.

"De B. Coleta." AS March, vol. 3, pp. 531–626.

Conciliorum oecumenicorum decreta. Bologna: Istituto per le Scienze Religiose, 1972.

Damien, Peter. *Opuscula* 17 and 18. In *S. Petri Damiani opera omnia,* vol. 2; PL 145, cols. 379–425.

De Sales, Francis. *Oeuvres complètes de S. François de Sales.* 6 vols. Paris: Berche et Tralin, 1875.

————. *Selected Letters.* Trans. Elisabeth Stopp. London: Faber & Faber, 1960.

The Desert Fathers. Ed. Helen Waddell. Ann Arbor: University of Michigan Press, 1981.

Dhuoda: Manuel pour mon fils. Ed. and trans. Pierre Riché. Paris: Cerf, 1975.

"The Didache." In *The Apostolic Fathers,* vol. 1, ed. Kirsopp Lake. Cambridge, Mass.: Harvard University Press, 1945.

"De B. Dorothea." AS October, vol. 13, pp. 472–584.

Eadmer. "Tractatus de conceptione B. Mariae Virginis." In *S. Anselmi opera omnia*, vol. 2. PL 159, cols. 301–326.

Erasmus, Desiderius. *The Colloquies of Erasmus*. Ed. and trans. Craig R. Thompson. Chicago: University of Chicago Press, 1965.

Etudes sur les miracles de Notre-Dame par personnages. Ed. Marguerite Stadler-Honegger. Geneva: Slatkine Reprints, 1975.

"De S. Francisca." AS March, vol. 2, pp. 89–219.

Gerson, Jean. *Oeuvres complètes*. Vols. 7, 9. Ed. Palémon Glorieux. Paris: Desclée, 1968.

Gregersson, Birger. *Birgerus Gregorii legenda sancte Birgitte*. Ed. Isak Collijn. SUSF, ser. 2, vol. 4. Uppsala: Almqvist & Wiksells, 1946.

Gregory of Nyssa. *Saint Gregory of Nyssa: Ascetical Works*. Trans. Virginia Woods Callahan. Washington, D.C.: Catholic University of America Press, 1966.

Gregory of Tours. *Gregorii Turonensis opera*. Ed. Bruno Krusch. SRM, vol. 1, pt. 2. Hanover: Hahn, 1885.

Gregory the Great. *St. Gregory the Great: Pastoral Care*. Trans. Henry Davis, S. J. Westminster, Md.: Newman Press, 1950.

Guerric of Igny. *Liturgical Sermons*. 2 vols. Trans. Monks of Mount Saint Bernard Abbey. Spencer, Mass.: Cistercian Publications, 1970–71.

Guibert of Nogent. *Self and Society in Medieval France: The Memoirs of Abbot Guibert of Nogent*. Ed. and trans. John F. Benton. New York: Harper & Row, 1970.

Hadewijch: The Complete Works. Ed. Mother Columba Hart, O.S.B. New York: Paulist Press, 1980.

Herolt, Johannes. *Miracles of the Blessed Virgin Mary: Johannes Herolt*. Trans. C. C. S. Bland. London: George Routledge, 1928.

Hildegard of Bingen. *Hildegardis causae et curae*. Ed. Paulus Kaiser. Leipzig: Teubner, 1903.

Hippocrates. *Hippocrates*. Ed. and trans. W. H. S. Jones. Cambridge, Mass.: Harvard University Press, 1967.

———. *Hippocratic Writings*. Ed. G. E. R. Lloyd. London: Penguin Books, 1978.

Holy Bible. Revised Standard Version.

Ignatius of Antioch. "Letter to the Ephesians," and "Letter to the Magnesians." In *The Apostolic Fathers*, vol. 1, ed. Kirsopp Lake. Cambridge, Mass.: Harvard University Press, 1945.

Irenaeus. *Sancti Irenaei adversus haereses*. Vol. 2. Ed. W. Wigan Harvey. Ridgewood, N.J.: Gregg Press, 1965.

The Irish Penitentials. Ed. Ludwig Bieler. Dublin: Dublin Institute for Advanced Studies, 1983.

"De B. Iutta." AS January, vol. 2, pp. 145–169.

Jacobus de Voragine. *The Golden Legend of Jacobus de Voragine*. Ed. Granger Ryan and Helmut Ripperger. New York: Arno Press, 1969.

Jerome. *Sancti Eusebii Hieronymi epistulae*. Vols. 1, 2. Ed. Isidore Hilberg. CSEL, vols. 54, 55. Leipzig: G. Freytag, 1910–12.

———. *St. Jerome: Select Letters*. Trans. F. A. Wright. Cambridge, Mass.: Harvard University Press, 1980.

John of Garland. *The 'Stella Maris' of John of Garland*. Ed. Evelyn Faye Wilson. Cambridge, Mass.: Medieval Academy of America, 1946.

John of Marienwerder. "Das Leben der Heiligen Dorothea von Johannes Marienwerder." SRP, vol. 2. Leipzig: Hirzel, 1863.

———. "Septilium B. Dorotheae." Tract. I. *Analecta Bollandiana* 2 (1883), 454–464.

———. *Vita Dorothea Montoviensis Magistri Johannis Marienwerder*. Ed. Hans Westpfahl. Cologne: Bohlau Verlag, 1964.

Julian of Norwich. *A Book of Showings*. Ed. Edmund Colledge, O.S.A., and James Walsh, S.J. Toronto: Pontifical Institute of Mediaeval Studies, 1978.

Kempe, Margery. *The Book of Margery Kempe*. Ed. Sanford B. Meech and Hope Emily Allen. London: Oxford University Press, 1940.

———. *The Book of Margery Kempe*. Ed. and trans. B. A. Windeatt. London: Penguin Books, 1985.

The Life of Christina of Markyate. Ed. and trans. Charles H. Talbot. Oxford: Clarendon Press, 1987.

Luther, Martin. *Letters of Spiritual Counsel*. Ed. and trans. Theodore G. Tappet. Philadelphia: Westminster Press, 1955.

———. *Luther's Works*. St. Louis: Concordia Publishing Co., 1955–86.

———. *D. Martin Luthers Werke*. Weimar: Hermann Bohlau, 1883– .

———. *D. Martin Luthers Werke: Briefwechsel*. Weimar: Hermann Bohlau, 1967– .

———. *D. Martin Luthers Werke: Tischreden*. Weimar: Hermann Bohlau, 1912–21.

Malleus maleficarum of Heinrich Kramer and James Sprenger. Trans. Montague Summers. New York: Dover, 1971.

Medieval Handbooks of Penance. Ed. John T. McNeill and Helena M. Gamer. New York: Columbia University Press, 1938.

Medieval Woman's Guide to Health: The First English Gynecological Handbook. Ed. Beryl Rowland. Kent, Ohio: Kent State University Press, 1981.

"*Meditations on the Life of Christ*": *An Illustrated Manuscript of the Fourteenth Century* (Ms. Ital. 115 Paris Bibl. Nat). Ed. Isa Ragusa and Rosalie B. Green. Princeton, N.J.: Princeton University Press, 1961.

The Middle English Miracles of the Virgin. Ed. Beverly Boyd. San Marino, Calif.: Huntington Library, 1964.

Milton, John. "The Judgement of Martin Bucer Touching Divorce." In *Complete Prose Works of John Milton*, vol. 2, ed. William Alfred. New Haven, Conn.: Yale University Press, 1980.

———. *Paradise Lost*. In *John Milton: Complete Poems and Major Prose*, ed. Merritt Y. Hughes. New York: Odyssey Press, 1957.

Miracles de Notre-Dame de Chartres. Ed. Pierre Kunstmann. Ottawa: Editions de l'Université d'Ottawa, 1973.

More, Thomas. *Utopia.* In *The Complete Works of St. Thomas More,* vol. 4, ed. Edward Surtz, S. J., and J. H. Hexter. New Haven, Conn.: Yale University Press, 1965.

Odes of Solomon. In *The Old Testament Pseudepigrapha,* vol. 2, ed. James H. Charlesworth. New York: Doubleday, 1985.

Pastoral Letters of the U.S. Catholic Bishops. Vol. 5. Ed. Hugh J. Nolan. Washington, D.C.: National Conference of Catholic Bishops, 1989.

Patrologia cursus completus: Series latina. Ed. J. P. Migne et al. Paris: Migne, 1841–1864.

Paul the Deacon. *History of the Lombards.* Ed. and trans. William Dudley Foulke. Philadelphia: University of Pennsylvania Press, 1974.

Plato. *The Republic.* In *Plato,* vol. 5, trans. Paul Shorey. Cambridge, Mass.: Harvard University Press, 1982.

——. *The Timaeus.* In *Plato,* vol. 7, trans. R. G. Bury. Cambridge, Mass.: Harvard University Press, 1961.

Pliny: Natural History. Vol. 8. Trans. W. H. S. Jones. Cambridge, Mass.: Harvard University Press, 1963.

Plutarch. *Plutarch's Lives.* Vol. 10. Ed. Bernadotte Perrin. Cambridge, Mass.: Harvard University Press, 1959.

I processi inediti per Francesca Bussa dei Ponziani. Ed. P. T. Lugano. Vatican: Biblioteca Apostolica, 1945.

Rudolf, "The Life of Saint Leoba by Rudolf, Monk of Fulda." In *Anglo-Saxon Missionaries in Germany,* ed. and trans. Charles H. Talbot. London: Sheed & Ward, 1954.

Soranus of Ephesus. *Soranus' Gynecology.* Ed. Oswei Temkin. Baltimore, Md.: Johns Hopkins University Press, 1956.

Trotula of Salerno. *Diseases of Women by Trotula of Salerno.* Trans. Elizabeth Mason-Hohl. New York: Ward Ritchie Press, 1940.

"Vita Sanctae Geretrudis." Ed. Bruno Krusch. SRM, vol. 2. Hanover: Hahn, 1888.

Studies

Amundsen, Darrel W., and Carol Jean Diers. "The Age of Menarche in Medieval Europe"; "The Age of Menopause in Medieval Europe." *Human Biology* 45 (1973), 363–369, 605–612.

Amussen, S. D. "Gender, Family, and the Social Order, 1560–1725." In *Order and Disorder in Early Modern England,* ed. Anthony Fletcher and John Stevenson. Cambridge: Cambridge University Press, 1985.

Andersson, Aron. *St. Bridget of Sweden.* London: Catholic Truth Society, 1980.

——. *Vadstena klosterkyrka.* Vol. 2. Stockholm: Almqvist & Wiksells, 1983.

Ariès, Philippe. *Centuries of Childhood: A Social History of Family Life.* Trans. Robert Baldick. New York: Knopf, 1962.

Arnold, Klaus. *Kind und Gesellschaft in Mittelalter und Renaissance: Beitrage und Texte zur Geschichte der Kindheit.* Cambridge, Mass.: Harvard University Press, 1985.

Atkinson, Clarissa W. *Mystic and Pilgrim: The Book and the World of Margery Kempe.* Ithaca: Cornell University Press, 1983.

———. " 'Precious Balsam in a Fragile Glass': The Ideology of Virginity in the Later Middle Ages." *Journal of Family History* 8 (1983), 131–143.

———. " 'Your Servant, My Mother': The Figure of St. Monica in the Ideology of Christian Motherhood." In *Immaculate and Powerful: The Female in Sacred Image and Social Reality,* ed. Clarissa W. Atkinson, Constance H. Buchanan, and Margaret R. Miles. Boston: Beacon Press, 1985.

Barstow, Anne Llewellyn. "On Studying Witchcraft as Women's History." *Journal of Feminist Studies in Religion* 4 (1988), 7–19.

———. "Charism as Power or as Curse: Healers and Witches." Unpublished paper, 1985.

Bass, Dorothy C. " 'In Christian Firmness and Christian Meekness': Feminism and Pacifism in Antebellum America." In *Immaculate and Powerful: The Female in Sacred Image and Social Reality,* ed. Clarissa W. Atkinson, Constance H. Buchanan, and Margaret R. Miles. Boston: Beacon Press, 1985.

Bearsley, Patrick J., S. M. "Mary the Perfect Disciple: A Paradigm for Mariology." *Theological Studies* 41 (1980), 461–504.

Bell, Rudolph M. *Holy Anorexia.* Chicago: University of Chicago Press, 1985.

Benedek, Thomas G. "The Changing Relationship between Midwives and Physicians during the Renaisance." *Bulletin of the History of Medicine* 51 (1977), 550–564.

Benton, John F. "Clio and Venus: An Historical View of Medieval Love." In *The Meaning of Courtly Love,* ed. Francis X. Newman. Albany: State University of New York Press, 1968.

———. "Trotula, Women's Problems, and the Professionalization of Medicine in the Middle Ages." *Bulletin of the History of Medicine* 59 (1985), 30–53.

Ben-Yehuda, Nachman. "The European Witch Craze of the 14th to 17th Centuries: A Sociologist's Perspective." *American Journal of Sociology* 86 (1980), 1–31.

Berger, Pamela. *The Goddess Obscured.* Boston: Beacon Press, 1985.

Berkvam, Doris Desclais. *Enfance et maternité dans la littérature française des XIIe et XIIIe siècles.* Paris: Librairie Honoré Champion, 1981.

Bétérous, Paule-V. "A propos d'une des légendes mariales les plus répandues: Le 'lait de la Vierge.' " *Bullétin de l'Association Guillaume Budé* 4 (1975), 403–411.

Bilinkoff, Jodi. "The Holy Woman and the Urban Community in Sixteenth-Century Avila." In *Women and the Structure of Society,* ed.

Barbara Harris and Jo Ann McNamara. Durham, N.C.: Duke University Press, 1984.

Billar, P. P. A. "Birth Control in the West in the Thirteenth and Early Fourteenth Centuries." *Past and Present* 94 (1982), 3–26.

Boanas, Guy, and Lyndal Roper. "Feminine Piety in Fifteenth-Century Rome: Santa Francesca Romana." In *Disciplines of Faith*, ed. Jim Obelkevich, Lyndal Roper, and Raphael Samuel. London: Routledge & Kegan Paul, 1987.

Bolton, Brenda M. "Mulieres sanctae." In *Sanctity and Secularity*, Studies in Church History 10, ed. Derek Baker. Oxford: Basil Blackwell, 1973.

———. "*Vitae matrum*: A Further Aspect of the *Frauenfrage*." In *Medieval Women*, ed. Derek Baker. Oxford: Basil Blackwell, 1978.

Bossy, John. "Blood and Baptism: Kinship, Community, and Christianity in Western Europe from the Fourteenth to the Seventeenth Centuries." In *Sanctity and Secularity*, Studies in Church History 10, ed. Derek Baker. Oxford: Basil Blackwell, 1973.

———. *Christianity in the West, 1400–1700.* New York: Oxford University Press, 1985.

———. "The Counter-Reformation and the People of Catholic Europe." *Past and Present* 47 (1970), 51–70.

———. "Editor's Postscript." In H. O. Evennett, *The Spirit of the Counter-Reformation*. Cambridge: Cambridge University Press, 1968.

———. "The Social History of Confession in the Age of the Reformation." *Transactions of the Royal Historical Society*, 5th ser., 25 (1975), 21–38.

Boswell, John E. *The Kindness of Strangers: The Abandonment of Children in Western Europe from Late Antiquity to the Renaissance.* New York: Pantheon Books, 1988.

Bouwsma, William J. *John Calvin.* New York: Oxford University Press, 1988.

Boylan, Michael. "The Galenic and Hippocratic Challenge to Aristotle's Conception Theory." *Journal of the History of Biology* 17 (1984), 83–112.

Brauner, Sigrid. "Martin Luther on Witchcraft: A True Reformer?" In *The Politics of Gender in Early Modern Europe*, ed. Jean R. Brink, Allison P. Coudert, and Maryanne C. Horowitz. Kirksville, Mo.: Sixteenth Century Journal Publishers, 1989.

Brown, Peter. *The Body and Society: Men, Women, and Sexual Renunciation in Early Christianity.* New York: Columbia University Press, 1988.

Brown, Raymond E., Karl P. Donfried, Joseph A. Fitzmyer, and John Neumann, eds. *Mary in the New Testament.* Philadelphia: Fortress Press, 1978.

Brumberg, Joan Jacobs. *Fasting Girls: The Emergence of Anorexia Nervosa as a Modern Disease*. Cambridge, Mass.: Harvard University Press, 1988.

Bullough, Vern L. "Medieval Medical and Scientific Views of Women." *Viator* 4 (1973), 485–501.

——. *Sexual Variance in Society and History*. New York: Wiley, 1976.

Bullough, Vern L., and Cameron Campbell. "Female Longevity and Diet in the Middles Ages." *Speculum* 55 (1980), 317–325.

Bynum, Caroline Walker. "Fast, Feast, and Flesh: The Religious Significance of Food to Medieval Women." *Representations* 11 (1985), 1–25.

——. *Holy Feast and Holy Fast: The Religious Significance of Food to Medieval Women*. Berkeley: University of California Press, 1987.

——. *Jesus as Mother: Studies in the Spirituality of the High Middle Ages*. Berkeley: University of California Press, 1983.

Cadden, Joan. "It Takes All Kinds: Sexuality and Gender Differences in Hildegarde of Bingen's 'Book of Compound Medicine.' " *Traditio* 40 (1984), 149–174.

Carruthers, Mary J. "The Lady, the Swineherd, and Chaucer's Clerk." *Chaucer Review* 17 (1983), 221–234.

Chodorow, Nancy. *The Reproduction of Mothering: Psychoanalysis and the Sociology of Gender*. Berkeley: University of California Press, 1978.

Christian, William A. *Apparitions in Late Medieval and Renaissance Spain*. Princeton, N.J.: Princeton University Press, 1981.

Cipolla, Carlo. *Before the Industrial Revolution*. New York: Norton, 1976.

Clark, Elizabeth A. "Friendship between the Sexes: Classical Theory and Christian Practice." In *Jerome, Chrysostom, and Friends*. New York: Edwin Mellen Press, 1979.

Clark, Elizabeth Battelle. "The Politics of God and the Women's Vote." Ph.D. diss., Princeton University, 1989.

Coleman, Emily. "L'infanticide dans le Haut Moyen Age." *Annales E.S.C.* 29 (1974), 315–335.

Cornell, Henrik. "The Iconography of the Nativity of Christ." *Uppsala Universitets Årsskrift* 1 (1924), 1–101.

Corrington, Gail Paterson. "The Milk of Salvation: Redemption by the Mother in Late Antiquity and Early Christianity." *Harvard Theological Review* 82 (1989), 393–420.

Coudert, Allison P. "The Myth of the Improved Status of Protestant Women: The Case of the Witchcraze." In *The Politics of Gender in Early Modern Europe*, ed. Jean R. Brink, Allison P. Coudert, and Maryanne C. Horowitz. Kirksville, Mo.: Sixteenth Century Journal Publishers, 1989.

Daichman, Graciela S. *Wayward Nuns in Medieval Literature*. Syracuse, N.Y.: Syracuse University Press, 1986.

Davies, Stevan L. *The Revolt of the Widows: The Social World of the Apocryphal Acts*. Carbondale: Southern Illinois University Press, 1980.

Davis, Natalie Zemon. "Ghosts, Kin, and Progeny: Some Features of Family Life in Early Modern France." *Daedalus* 106 (1977), 87–114.

Dodds, E. R. *Pagan and Christian in an Age of Anxiety.* Cambridge: Cambridge University Press, 1985.

Donahue, Charles, Jr. "The Canon Law on the Formation of Marriage and Social Practice in the Later Middle Ages." *Journal of Family History* 8 (1983), 144–158.

D'Onofrio, Cesare. *La Papessa Giovanna: Roma e papato tre storia e leggenda.* Rome: Romana Societa Editrice, 1979.

Douglas, Mary. *Purity and Danger: An Analysis of Concepts of Pollution and Taboo.* New York: Praeger, 1966.

Dronke, Peter. *Women Writers of the Middle Ages.* Cambridge: Cambridge University Press, 1984.

Duby, Georges. "Au XIIe siècle: Les 'Jeunes' dans la société aristocratique." *Annales E.S.C.* 19 (1964), 835–846.

———. *The Knight, the Lady, and the Priest.* New York: Pantheon Books, 1983.

El Saadawi, Nawal. *The Hidden Face of Eve: Women in the Arab World.* Ed. and trans. Sherif Hetata. Boston: Beacon Press, 1982.

Falwell, Jerry. *Listen, America!* New York: Doubleday, 1980.

Forsyth, Ilene. *The Throne of Wisdom: Wood Sculptures of the Madonna in Romanesque France.* Princeton, N.J.: Princeton University Press, 1972.

Foster, Marjory B. *The Iconography of St. Joseph in Netherlandish Art, 1400–1550.* Ann Arbor: University of Michigan Press, 1979).

Friedan, Betty. *The Feminine Mystique.* New York: Dell, 1963.

Frisch, Rose E. "Food Intake, Fatness, and Reproductive Ability." In *Anorexia Nervosa,* ed. R. A. Vigersky. New York: Raven Press, 1977.

———. "Population, Nutrition, and Fecundity." In *Malthus Past and Present,* ed. J. Dupâquier, A. Fauve-Chamoux, and E. Grebenik. London: Academic Press, 1983.

———. "What's Below the Surface?" *New England Journal of Medicine* 305 (1981), 1019–1020.

Gillespie, Joanna B. " 'The Sun in Their Domestic System': The Mother in Early Nineteenth-Century Methodist Sunday School Lore." In *Women in New Worlds,* vol. 2, ed. Rosemary Skinner Keller, Louise L. Queen, and Hilah F. Thomas. Nashville, Tenn.: Abingdon Press, 1982.

Glasser, Marc. "Marriage in Medieval Hagiography." *Studies in Medieval and Renaissance History* 4 (1981), 1–34.

Gold, Penny Schine. *The Lady and the Virgin: Image, Attitude, and Experience in Twelfth-Century France.* Chicago: University of Chicago Press, 1985.

———. "The Marriage of Mary and Joseph in the Twelfth-Century Ideology of Marriage." In *Sexual Practices in the Medieval Church,* ed. Vern

L. Bullough and James Brundage. Buffalo, N.Y.: Prometheus Books, 1982.

Goldin, Frederick. "The Array of Perspectives in the Early Courtly Love Lyric." In *In Pursuit of Perfection*, ed. Joan M. Ferrante and George D. Economou. Port Washington, N.Y.: Kennikat Press, 1975.

Goodich, Michael. "*Ancilla Dei*: The Servant as Saint in the Late Middle Ages." In *Women of the Medieval World*, ed. Julius Kirshner and Suzanne F. Wemple. Oxford: Basil Blackwell, 1985.

Goody, Jack. *The Development of the Family and Marriage in Europe*. Cambridge: Cambridge University Press, 1983.

Gottfried, Robert S. *The Black Death*. New York: Free Press, 1980.

Graef, Hilda C. *Mary: A History of Doctrine and Devotion*. 2 vols. New York: Sheed & Ward, 1963.

Green, Monica. "Women's Medical Practice and Health Care in Medieval Europe." *Signs* 14 (1989), 434–473.

Griffith, D. D. *The Origin of the Griselda Story*. Chicago: University of Chicago Libraries, 1931.

Gripkey, Mary Vincentine. *The Blessed Virgin Mary as Mediatrix in the Latin and Old French Legend prior to the Fourteenth Century*. Washington, D.C.: Catholic University of America, 1938.

Hajnal, J. "European Marriage Patterns in Perspective." In *Population in History*, ed. D. V. Glass and D. E. C. Eversley. Chicago: Aldine, 1965.

Hale, Rosemary D. "*Imitatio Mariae*: Motherhood Motifs in Devotional Memoirs." *Mystics Quarterly* 16 (1990), 193–203.

Heinsohn, Gunnar, and Otto Steiger. "The Elimination of Medieval Birth Control and the Witch Trials of Modern Times." *International Journal of Women's Studies* 5 (1982), 193–214.

Herlihy, David. "Did Women Have a Renaissance? A Reconsideration." *Medievalia et Humanistica*, n.s. 13 (1985), 1–22.

——. "The Generation in Medieval History." *Viator* 5 (1974), 347–364.

——. "Life Expectancies for Women in Medieval Society." In *The Role of Women in the Middle Ages*, ed. Rosemarie Thee Morewedge. Albany: State University of New York Press, 1975.

——. *Medieval Households*. Cambridge, Mass.: Harvard University Press, 1985.

Hewson, M. Anthony. *Giles of Rome and the Medieval Theory of Conception*. London: Athlone Press, 1975.

Hoffer, Peter C., and N. E. H. Hull. *Murdering Mothers: Infanticide in England and New England, 1558–1803*. New York: New York University Press, 1981.

Horowitz, Maryanne Cline. "Aristotle and Women." *Journal of the History of Biology* 9 (1976), 183–213.

Hunt, David. *Parents and Children in History: The Psychology of Family Life in Early Modern France*. New York: Basic Books, 1970.

Jordan, Constance. "Boccaccio's In-Famous Women: Gender and Civic Virtue in the *De mulieribus claris*." In *Ambiguous Realities: Women in the Middle Ages and Renaissance*, ed. Carole Levin and Jeanie Watson. Detroit, Mich.: Wayne State University Press, 1987.

Jorgensen, Johannes. *Saint Bridget of Sweden*. 2 vols. London: Longmans Green, 1954.

Karant-Nunn, Susan C. "Continuity and Change: Some Effects of the Reformation on the Women of Zwickau." *Sixteenth-Century Journal* 13 (1982), 17–42.

Keller, Evelyn Fox. *Reflections on Gender and Science*. New Haven, Conn.: Yale University Press, 1985.

Kelley, Donald R. *The Beginning of Ideology*. Cambridge: Cambridge University Press, 1981.

Kelly, Henry A. *Love and Marriage in the Age of Chaucer*. Ithaca: Cornell University Press, 1975.

Kelly Gadol, Joan. "Did Women Have a Renaissance?" In *Becoming Visible: Women in European History*, ed. Renata Bridenthal and Claudia Koonz. Boston: Houghton Mifflin, 1977.

———. *Women, History, and Theory*. Chicago: University of Chicago Press, 1984.

Kieckhefer, Richard. *Unquiet Souls: Fourteenth-Century Saints and Their Religious Milieu*. Chicago: University of Chicago Press, 1984.

King, Margaret Leah. "Book-lined Cells: Woman and Humanism in the Early Italian Renaissance". In *Beyond Their Sex: Learned Women of the European Past*, ed. Patricia R. Labalme. New York: New York University Press, 1980.

Kingdon, Robert M. "Calvin and the Family: The Work of the Consistory in Geneva." *Pacific Theological Review* 17 (1984), 5–18.

Klapisch-Zuber, Christiane. *Women, Family, and Ritual in Renaissance Italy*. Chicago: University of Chicago Press, 1985.

Kristeva, Julia. "Stabat Mater." In *The Female Body in Western Culture*, ed. Susan Rubin Suleiman. Cambridge, Mass.: Harvard University Press, 1986.

Larner, Christina. *Enemies of God: The Witch-hunt in Scotland*. London: Chatto & Windus, 1981.

———. *Witchcraft and Religion: The Politics of Popular Belief*. Ed. Alan MacFarlane. Oxford: Basil Blackwell, 1984.

Lazard, Madeleine. "Médicins contre matrones au 16e siècle: La difficile naissance de l'obstetrique. In *Popular Traditions and Learned Culture in France: From the Sixteenth to the Twentieth Century*, ed. Marc Bertrand. Saratoga, Calif.: Anma Libri, 1985.

Liebowitz, Ruth P. "Virgins in the Service of Christ: The Dispute over an Active Apostolate for Women during the Counter-Reformation." In

Women of Spirit, ed. Rosemary R. Ruether and Eleanor C. McLaughlin. New York: Simon & Schuster, 1979.

Little, Lester. *Religious Poverty and the Profit Economy in Medieval Europe.* Ithaca: Cornell University Press, 1978.

Lloyd, G. E. R. *Science, Folklore, and Ideology.* Cambridge: Cambridge University Press, 1983.

Luker, Kristin. *Abortion and the Politics of Motherhood.* Berkeley: University of California Press, 1984.

MacDonald, Dennis R. *The Legend and the Apostle: The Battle for Paul in Story and Canon.* Philadelphia: Westminster Press, 1983.

McLaughlin, Mary M. "Survivors and Surrogates: Children and Parents from the Ninth to the Thirteenth Centuries." In *The History of Childhood,* ed. Lloyd B. De Mause. New York: Harper & Row, 1974.

McNamara, Jo Ann. "Cornelia's Daughters: Paula and Eustochium." *Women's Studies* 11 (1984), 9–27.

Manselli, Raoul. "Vie Familiale et éthique sexuelle dans les pénitentiels." In *Famille et parenté dans l'Occident médiéval,* ed. Georges Duby and Jacques Le Goff. Rome: Ecole Française de Rome, 1977.

Marchello-Nizia, Christianne. "Amour courtois, société masculin, et figures du pouvoir." *Annales E.S.C.* 36 (1981), 969–982.

Marvick, Elizabeth Wirth. "Nature versus Nurture: Patterns and Trends in Seventeenth-Century French Child-Rearing." In *The History of Childhood,* ed. Lloyd B. De Mause. New York: Harper & Row, 1974.

Meiss, Millard. *Painting in Florence and Siena after the Black Death.* Princeton, N.J.: Princeton University Press, 1951.

Merchant, Carolyn. *The Death of Nature: Women, Ecology, and the Scientific Revolution.* New York: Harper & Row, 1983.

Miles, Margaret R. *Fullness of Life: Historical Foundations for a New Asceticism.* Philadelphia: Westminster Press, 1981.

Monter, E. William. "The Pedestal and the Stake: Courtly Love and Witchcraft." In *Becoming Visible: Women in European History,* ed. Renata Bridenthal and Claudia Koonz. Boston: Houghton Mifflin, 1977.

Muchemblad, Robert. *Popular Culture and Elite Culture in France, 1400–1700.* Baton Rouge: Lousiana State University Press, 1985.

Newman, Barbara. *Sister of Wisdom: St. Hildegard's Theology of the Feminine.* Berkeley: University of California Press, 1987.

Nicholson, Linda. *Gender and History.* New York: Columbia University Press, 1986.

Noonan, John T., Jr. *Contraception: A History of Its Treatment by the Catholic Theologians and Canonists.* Cambridge, Mass.: Harvard University Press, 1966.

———. "Intellectual and Demographic History." *Daedalus* 97 (1968), 463–485.

O'Brien, Mary. *The Politics of Reproduction.* Boston: Routledge & Kegan Paul, 1981.

Okin, Susan Moller. *Justice, Gender, and the Family*. New York: Basic Books, 1989.

Ozment, Steven. *When Fathers Ruled: Family Life in Reformation Europe*. Cambridge, Mass.: Harvard University Press, 1983.

Partner, Nancy F. "The Family Romance of Guibert of Nogent." Unpublished paper, 1987.

Plaskow, Judith. *Standing Again at Sinai: Judaism from a Feminist Perspective*. New York: Harper & Row, 1990.

Pollitt, Katha. " 'Fetal Rights': A New Assault on Feminism." *Nation* 250, no. 11 (1990), 409–418.

Pope Joan: A Romantic Biography by Emmanuel Royidis. Trans. Lawrence Durrell. London: André Deutsch, 1960.

Preus, Anthony. "Galen's Criticism of Aristotle's Conception Theory." *Journal of the History of Biology* 10 (1977), 65–85.

Rahner, Hugo. "Die Gottesgeburt: Die Lehre der Kirchenväter von der Geburt Christi im Herzen der Gläubigen." *Zeitschrfit für Katholische Theologie* 59 (1935), 333–418.

Rich, Adrienne. *Of Woman Born: Motherhood as Experience and Institution*. New York: Norton, 1976.

Roper, Lyndal. *The Holy Household*. Oxford: Oxford University Press, 1989.

Ross, James Bruce. "The Middle-Class Child in Urban Italy." In *The History of Childhood*, ed. Lloyd B. De Mause. New York: Harper & Row, 1974.

Ruddick, Sara. *Maternal Thinking: Toward a Politics of Peace*. Boston: Beacon Press, 1989.

Ruether, Rosemary R. *Mary: The Feminine Face of the Church*. Philadelphia: Westminster Press, 1977.

Sahlin, Claire L. " 'A Marvelous Great Exultation of the Heart': Mystical Pregnancy and Marian Devotion in Birgitta of Sweden's Revelations." Unpublished paper, 1990.

Saliba, John A., S.J. "The Virgin-Birth Debate in Anthropological Literature: A Critical Assessment." *Theological Studies* 36 (1975), 428–454.

Schnucker, R. V. "The English Puritans and Pregnancy, Delivery, and Breast-Feeding." *History of Childhood Quarterly* 1(1974), pp. 637–658.

Schochet, Gordon J. *Patriarchalism in Political Thought*. New York: Basic Books, 1975.

Scholz, Bernhard W. "Hildegard von Bingen on the Nature of Women." *American Benedictine Review* 31 (1980), 361–383.

Schüssler Fiorenza, Elisabeth. *In Memory of Her: A Feminist Theological Reconstruction of Christian Origins*. New York: Crossroad, 1983.

Secor, John R. "The *Planctus Mariae* in Provençal Literature: A Subtle Blend of Courtly and Religious Tradition." In *Spirit of the Court*, ed. G. S. Burgess and R. A. Taylor. Cambridge: D. S. Brewer, 1985.

Southern, R. W. "The English Origin of the Miracles of the Virgin." *Medieval and Renaissance Studies* 4 (1959), 176–216.

———. *St. Anselm and His Biographer.* Cambridge: Cambridge University Press, 1963.

———. *Western Society and the Church in the Middle Ages.* London: Penguin Books, 1970.

Spengler, Joseph J. "Demographic Factors and Early Modern Economic Development." *Daedalus* 97 (1968), 433–446.

Stallybrass, Peter. "Patriarchal Territories: The Body Enclosed." In *Rewriting the Renaissance,* ed. Margaret W. Ferguson, Maureen Quilligan, and Nancy J. Vickers. Chicago: University of Chicago Press, 1986.

Stiller, Nikki. *Eve's Orphans: Mothers and Daughters in Medieval English Literature.* Westport, Conn.: Greenwood Press, 1980.

Stock, Brian. *The Implications of Literacy: Written Language and Models of Interpretation in the Eleventh and Twelfth Centuries.* Princeton, N.J.: Princeton University Press, 1983.

Stopp, Elisabeth. *Madame de Chantal.* London: Faber & Faber, 1962.

Thérèl, Marie-Louise. "Les visages de Marie." *Bullétin de la Société Française d'Etudes Mariales* 33 (1975–76), 5–20.

Thompson, Sally. "The Problem of the Cistercian Nuns in the Twelfth and Early Thirteenth Centuries." In *Medieval Women,* ed. Derek Baker. Oxford: Basil Blackwell, 1978.

Trexler, Richard C. "The Foundlings of Florence, 1395–1455." *History of Childhood Quarterly* 1 (1973), 259–283.

———. "Infanticide in Florence: New Sources and First Results." *History of Childhood Quarterly* 2 (1975), 98–116.

Tribe, Laurence H. *Abortion: The Clash of Absolutes.* New York: Norton, 1990.

Turner, Victor. *The Ritual Process.* Chicago: Aldine, 1969.

Tuttle, Edward F. "The *Trotula* and Old Dame Trot: A Note on the Lady of Salerno." *Bulletin of the History of Medicine* 50 (1976), 61–72.

Ulrich, Laurel Thatcher. *Good Wives.* New York: Oxford University Press, 1982.

Underdown, David. "The Taming of the Scold." In *Order and Disorder in Early Modern England,* ed. Anthony Fletcher and John Stevenson. Cambridge: Cambridge University Press, 1985.

Veith, Ilza. *Hysteria: The History of a Disease.* Chicago: University of Chicago Press, 1965.

Warner, Marina. *Alone of All Her Sex: The Myth and the Cult of the Virgin Mary.* New York: Vintage Books, 1983.

Weber, Sarah Appleton. *Theology and Poetry in the Middle English Lyric.* Columbus: Ohio State University Press, 1968.

Weinstein, Donald, and Rudolph M. Bell. *Saints and Society.* Chicago: University of Chicago Press, 1982.

Weissman, Hope P. "Margery Kempe in Jerusalem: *Hysteria Compassio* in the Late Middle Ages." In *Acts of Interpretation: The Text in Its Contexts, 700–1600*, ed. M. J. Carruthers and E. D. Kirk. Norman, Okla.: Pilgrim Press, 1982.

Welter, Barbara. "The Cult of True Womanhood: 1820–1880." *American Quarterly* 18 (1966), 151–162, 173–174.

Wemple, Suzanne F. *Women in Frankish Society: Marriage and the Cloister, 500 to 900*. Philadelphia: University of Pennsylvania Press, 1985.

White, Lynn. *Medieval Technology and Social Change*. Oxford: Oxford University Press, 1982.

Wiesner, Merry E. *Working Women in Renaissance Germany*. New Brunswick, N.J.:Rutgers University Press, 1986.

Williamson, Joan B. "Philippe de Mezière's Book for Married Ladies: A Book from the Entourage of the Court of Charles VI." In *Spirit of the Court*, ed. G. S. Burgess and R. A. Taylor, Cambridge: D. S. Brewer, 1985.

Wood, Charles T. "The Doctors' Dilemma: Sin, Salvation, and the Menstrual Cycle in Medieval Thought." *Speculum* 56 (1981), 710–727.

Index

political systems (*cont.*)
Middle Ages, 148; patriarchal, 9, 97,
198–201
pollution, 85, 90, 93; and childbirth,
79,184; and menstruation, 39–40,
89; and virginity, 106, 206
polytheism, 101, 107
Ponziani, Lorenzo (husband of Frances
of Rome), 189–90
Pope Joan, 1–6, 21, 139, 236
poverty: beguines' dedication to, 164–
65; and holiness, 168–70, 192, 214,
221, 241; mendicants' dedication
to, 151, 154, 192, 241
pregnancy, 3, 6, 23, 27, 63, 82; birth
defects, 39n, 47, 91, 231; and
breast-feeding, 58–59; dangers and
difficulties of, 52, 54, 57, 83, 209;
the embryo, 41, 47–49, 51; fertility,
40, 46, 86, 107; the fetus, 50–51,
53, 55, 58, 88; and menstruation,
41, 49; miscarriages, 39, 52, 54, 57–
58, 84, 87, 209; moral theology on,
78–80; mystical, 181, 185–86, 193;
and nutrition and activity, 45, 48,
84, 116, 149; in penitentials, 85–86,
89; spiritual, 163, 188
*I processi inediti per Francesca Bussa
dei Ponziani,* 189–90
Proclus of Constantinople: "Oratio I,
De laudibus Sanetae Mariae," 114
procreation, 62; and the Fall, 9–10,
72–73, 77, 207; and holiness, 44–
46, 63; and sexual difference, 29–
32, 35, 37, 238; and sexual
intercourse, 13, 17, 28–29, 50, 80,
174–75; theology of, 34, 162, 209–
11; and witchcraft, 232–33. *See also
under* marriage
property, 197; and monastic ideology,
68–69, 77; patterns of inheritance,
90–91, 130; and sex ratio, 83, 84n
prostitution, 92, 169, 216; and
reformations, 242
Puritans, 217–20, 223

rape, 73, 81–82, 244
reformations: Catholic, 8, 220–22,
233, 242; Gregorian, 116–19, 151;
Protestant, 195, 200–201, 204–15,
221–22, 229, 233, 242
religious orders: gender restrictions
of, 169, 221; and reformed

motherhood, 226–29. *See also*
convents; mendicants; monasticism
Renaissance, 3, 148, 157
reproduction. *See* procreation
Rich, Adrienne, ix, 7n
Riché, Pierre, 97
Roe v. Wade, 244–45
romance literature, 129; Mary and the
cult of the Lady in, 130–31, 240
Roman Curia, 116–17
Roman Empire, 9, 11–12, 15, 77, 85,
237, 239
Roman Republic, 12
Roper, Lyndal, 215
Rowland, Beryl, 38
Rudolf, "The Life of Saint Leoba,"
92–94, 96, 99, 239

saints: artistic and literary
representation of, 86–87, 90, 164–
69, 190, 192; asceticism of female,
44–46, 63, 166–67, 172, 185;
canonization of, 117, 164, 168, 186;
canonization of married women,
145, 171–72, 180–81, 225, 229, 240;
cults, 106, 160–61, 171, 173, 184;
"desert," 65, 70–71; laywomen's
relation to, 63, 184, 186–87, 229;
Mary's relation to local, 115, 117–
18, 143; and milk, 60, 94; mother-,
46, 77, 144, 157, 166, 170–81, 183–
86, 188–93, 224–29, 234, 241; and
reformations, 210–11; and Third
Orders, 151
salvation: and Christ's humanity,
102,
118, 143; Mary's association with,
105, 109, 143; mothers as agents of,
76, 126–27, 173–80, 183, 185, 188–
89, 193, 220, 223, 225, 241
Sarah, 10
Satan, 93–94, 110, 135, 137, 159, 178,
193
scholasticism, 36–37, 51, 62, 207
Schüssler Fiorenza, Elisabeth, 14n, 15,
18n
semen: menstrual blood as, 41, 59;
and milk, 59, 209; role in
conception of, 28, 47–51, 175
sex ratios, 36, 81–84, 130, 229–30
sexual difference: and castration, 30;
humoral medicine on, 32–33, 38–
39, 51, 62; and life expectancy, 35–
36, 42, 81; and pollution, 79;

Library of Congress Cataloging-in-Publication Data

Atkinson, Clarissa W.
    The oldest vocation : Christian motherhood in the Middle Ages /
    Clarissa W. Atkinson.
        p.   cm.
    Includes bibliographical references and index.
    ISBN 0-8014-2071-7 (alk. paper)
    1. Mothers—Europe—History. 2. Motherhood—Religious aspects—
Christianity.   3. Mothers—Europe—Religious life—History.
4. Europe—Social conditions—To 1492.   I. Title.
HQ759.A84   1991
306.874'3—dc20   91-16078